The Three Gorges area is renowned for its orange production. [Lu Jin]

A Note on Spelling Yangtze

For many years the Wade-Giles transliteration system (formalised by 1892)
for Romanisation of Chinese spelled the great river's name Yang-tze K'iang,
which was subsequently shortened to Yangtze.
Other translations and spellings have also been used through the ages.
However, within this guide the river is referred to in its correct form of Pinyin
(China's officially accepted form of Romanisation), which is *Yangzi*.

Also, in deference to the guide's many contributors, readers may find
American spellings employed in addition to the main text's English.

A Note on Dates

In this guide, the traditional BC (Before Christ) and AD (Anno Domini) have been
replaced with BCE (Before Common Era) and CE (Common Era), whereby "common"
refers to the most frequently used timeline reference, the Gregorian Calendar.

Three Gorges
of the
Yangtze River
Chongqing to Wuhan

RAYNOR SHAW

WITH

PAUL MOONEY & BILL HURST

ODYSSEY BOOKS & GUIDES

Odyssey Books & Guides is a division of Airphoto International Ltd.
903 Seaview Commercial Building, 21–24 Connaught Road West, Sheung Wan, Hong Kong
Tel: (852) 2856-3896; Fax: (852) 2565-8004
E-mail: sales@odysseypublications.com; www.odysseypublications.com

Distribution in the USA by W.W. Norton & Company, Inc., 500 Fifth Avenue, New York, NY 10110, USA
Tel: 800-233-4830; Fax: 800-458-6515; www.wwnorton.com

Distribution in the UK and Europe by Cordee Books and Maps, 3a De Montfort St., Leicester, LE1 7HD, UK
Tel: 0116-254-3579; Fax: 0116-247-1176; www.cordee.co.uk

Three Gorges of the Yangtze River, First Edition

ISBN-13: 978-962-217-774-1
ISBN-10: 962-217-774-3
Library of Congress Catalog Card Number has been requested.
Copyright © 2007 Airphoto International Ltd.

Grateful acknowledgment is made to the following authors and publishers:
Alfred A Knopf, Inc and Brook Hersey for *A Single Pebble* by John Hersey © 1989, 1984, 1956 First Vintage Books; Houghton Mifflin Co, Aitken, Stone & Wylie Ltd and Michael Russell Ltd for *Sailing Through China* by Paul Theroux © 1984, 1983; Jonathan Cape Ltd for *Birdless Summer* by Han Suyin © 1968; Eland Publishing for *Travels with Myself and Another* by Martha Gellhorn © 2002

Managing Editor: Neil Art
Contributors include: Kevin Bishop, Judy Bonavia, Elizabeth Childs-Johnson, Richard Hayman, Peter Hessler, Madeleine Lynn, May Holdsworth, Martin Ruzek, Audrey Topping, a hearty thanks to all.

Design: Au Yeung Chui Kwai
Maps: Moon Street Cartography, De.Style Studio, Traveler's Company
Map Consultant: Professor Bai Yiliang

Production and printing by Twin Age Ltd, Hong Kong
E-mail: twinage@netvigator.com
Manufactured in Hong Kong

Reading the safety information on these websites is advisable before travelling overseas:
US Department of State: www.travel.state.gov/travel warnings.html
UK Foreign and Commonwealth Office: www.fco.gov.uk/travel
Canadian Department of Foreign Affairs & International Trade: www.voyage.gc.ca/dest/sos/warnings-en.asp
Australian Department of Foreign Affairs & Trade: www.dfat.gov.au/travel/

(Front cover) *The Three Gorges Project dam is now as much a dominant feature of the Yangzi as the Three Gorges themselves.* [Huang Zhengping]; (Back cover) *Sailing the Yangzi (see page 76).* [Lu Jin]

(Page 1) *A blanket of mist makes for a moody mountain scene.* [Huang Zhengping]

CONTENTS

SPECIAL TOPICS

LITERARY EXCERPTS

MAPS AND DIAGRAMS

(Left) *Before completion of the Three Gorges Project, many artefacts were unearthed prior to the rise of the reservoir. Several of these and many other relics from across China are on display at Jingzhou Museum (see page 174), such as this lacquerware wine flask from Fenghuangshan's Tomb No. 168. The flask dates from the Western Han Dynasty. A story of predation unfolds upon it, depicted in seven deep-red vignettes, of a leopard stalking, chasing and catching a deer.* [Jingzhou City (Shashi) and Museum]

(Right) *The Three Gorges Dam sluices can discharge 102,500 cubic-metres (3,620,000 cubic-feet) per second at their maximum capacity (excluding discharge through the generating units). Each of the dam's 23 deep outlets measure seven metres-wide by nine metres-high (23 feet by 29.5 feet). The 22 main outlets (pictured) each have an eight-metre (26.25 feet) clear width. Additional discharge outlets perform other functions. The discharge section, located in the central section of the dam and at the centre of the river, links two hydropower stations.* [Huang Zhengping]

INTRODUCTION

Flowing for 6,380 kilometres (3,964 miles) from the Tibetan Plateau to the East China Sea, the Yangzi River is the longest river in China, and the third longest river in the world after the Nile and the Amazon. This extensive waterway has played a pivotal role in the history of China, and in the development of the country's modern economy. Today, with the construction of the Three Gorges Dam and the proposed North Water Transfer scheme, the Yangzi is destined to become even more vital to the future of the country.

In addition to the river's length, its other statistics are equally impressive. Draining an area of approximately 1.8 million square kilometres (695 thousand square miles), or almost 20 per cent of the country, the Yangzi Basin holds 36 per cent of the water resources of China; it is home to more than 30 per cent of China's 1.3 billion population, and unofficially perhaps as much as 45 per cent; and it supports 40 per cent of the country's national economic and industrial output.

Industries include automobile and machinery manufacturing, chemical industries, power generation, metallurgical plants, building materials supply, and, more recently, technological development zones. In addition, there are approximately 100 million hectares (247 million acres) of fertile agricultural land in the Yangzi Basin (about 60 per cent of the basin area, or about 11 per cent of the total land area of China), particularly in the Sichuan Basin and in the Middle and Lower Yangzi valleys, producing foodstuffs for the burgeoning population.

The river is navigable for about half its length—the 3,060 kilometres (1,901 miles) from Shanghai to Yibin. Chongqing, 2,735 kilometres (1,699 miles) from the sea, is an important port that, prior to construction of the Three Gorges Dam, could receive vessels up to 3,000 tons only during the wet season (dry season water levels prohibited the passage of large vessels). With the dam completed the water level at Chongqing will be raised by 45 metres (148 feet) allowing year round navigation. Vessels of up to 2,722 metric tonnes (3,000 tons) currently ply to Yichang, and some 9,072-tonne (10,000-ton) tankers are able to berth at Wuhan, 1,100 kilometres (684 miles) from the sea. Larger vessels, that can pass below under the low bridge at Nanjing and ascend the ship locks of the Three Gorges Dam, will be able to reach Chongqing, reducing transportation costs to the growing economy of southwestern China.

River traffic includes the transport of coal, oil, and manufactured goods, as well as passengers. In 2005, 721 million tonnes (795 million tons) of cargo were carried on the Yangzi, confirming its status as one of the world's busiest waterways.

Human History along the Yangzi

Historically, the Yangzi River has witnessed the rise and fall of kingdoms and dynasties for almost 23 centuries, although scattered evidence of human occupation in the Yangzi basin dates back to the Early Pleistocene (about 2 million years ago). During the Spring and Autumn Period (770–476 BCE), at the time that the Yellow River had a rich cultural development, large populations of Ba and Shu people occupied the western part of the basin, with Chu people in the central area, and Wu and Yue in the east. The milder climate and more settled political situation, than in the Yellow River basin to the north, favoured agricultural development in the Yangzi basin. Thus, China's first large-scale irrigation system was built in the Sichuan Basin near Chengdu, at the end of the Warring States Period (475–221 BCE). Initiated by Qin Shi Huangdi, it considerably increased agricultural output. Marked economic expansion along the Yangzi began during the Han Dynasty (206 BCE–220 CE).

During that period, the river has been instrumental in feeding millions (providing potable water, irrigation for crops, and a transport corridor), and in drowning thousands (as a result of the frequent flooding). Thus, the floods of 1911 killed about 100,000 people, while 145,000 were killed in 1931, 142,000 in 1935, and 30,000 in 1954. However, despite being a main artery for inland navigation and an avenue for trade for 2,000 years the river has, until recently, divided the country into north and south. Thus, the Yangzi has formed a political boundary on several occasions, the national capital has been relocated from Beijing to Nanjing numerous times, and several famous battles have been fought along the banks of the river.

Clearly, the river both provides a lifeline, and acts as a barrier, to economic development. The first bridge across the Yangzi was opened in 1957, the Russian-designed Wuhan Yangzi River Bridge. The Nanjing Yangzi River Bridge was the first Chinese-designed bridge to span the Yangzi and opened as recently as 1968. Compared with the shorter Mississippi River (5,970-kilometres or 3,710-miles long), in 1989 the Yangzi had only six bridges across it (at Nanjing, Wuhan, Yidu (near Yichang), Chongqing, Yibin and Dukou) while 28 bridges spanned the Mississippi, between Baton Rouge and Minnesota. However, by September 2003 there were 25 bridges across the Yangzi, either built or under construction, including four at Wuhan and six (of a total of 11 planned) at Chongqing.

The Name of the River

Originally, the river was known purely as the Jiang, a word that is now synonymous with the word 'river'. Thus, it is probably true to say that the Yangzi is the 'Father of all rivers' in China. Today within China, the river is usually called the *Chang Jiang* (the Long River, or Eternal River), or alternatively the *Da Jiang* (the Great

River). An historical, more poetical, Chinese name is the *Yangzi Jiang* (Son of the Sea River), although the river is occasionally referred to as the "Golden Waterway". A final complication is that the Tibetan word for the river is the *Vbri-chu*.

Perhaps not surprisingly, because the river crosses the nine Provinces of Qinghai, Yunnan, Sichuan, Chongqing, Hubei, Hunan, Jiangxi, Anhui, and Jiangsu, each section has a distinctive regional name.

In the source region, the river is little more than a series of converging rivulets that drain seasonally from melting glaciers in the Tanggula Mountains in southwestern Qinghai Province. There, the small river is called the *Tuotuo*, the Tibetan word for 'soft and clear' (or 'murmuring'), or *Dangqu* in Chinese. The river becomes a more recognizable entity as it crosses the Tibetan Plateau, where it is known as the *Tongtian* (Tung Ting) *Ho*, meaning 'River to Heaven' (or 'Way to Heaven'). Between the edge of the Tibetan Plateau and the head of navigation at Yibin, near the western edge of the Sichuan Basin, the river is referred to as the *Jinsha Jiang* (Jing Sha Jiang), or 'River of Golden Sand(s)'.

In Sichuan Province the river becomes the *Chuan Jiang*, meaning 'Four Rivers' (or 'Four Streams'), which refers to the four main tributaries that converge in the Sichuan Basin, the Minjiang, Tuojiang, Jialing and Wujiang. Locally, the Three Gorges section is called the *Xia Jiang*, or 'Gorges River'. The middle reaches of the river in the Jiangxi Province region, upstream and west of Nanjing, are known locally as the *Xi Jiang*, or the 'West River'. Downstream from the ancient city of Yangzhou are the tidal lower reaches, where the turbid waters of the river mix with the saline waters of the East China Sea. Here, the river understandably is called the *Yangzi* received its designation meaning 'Son of the Sea'. Perhaps not surprisingly given the concentration of foreign influence in the area around Shanghai, this is the name that has been adopted internationally. Finally, near Shanghai, where the Grand Canal enters the river, it is known as the *Yong Zhuo*.

THE FOUR GREAT STEPS OF CHINA

Chinese geographers liken the topography of China to Four Great Steps that descend in elevation from west to east. The Yangzi is the only river to traverse all these four facets of the continent. Most of the prominent rivers of the region, the Bramaputra, Salween, Mekong, Yangzi, and Yellow rivers, have their sources on the First Great Step, the Tibetan Plateau that has an average elevation of about 4,000 metres (13,120 feet) above sea level (asl). The Second Great Step extends from the eastern margin of the Tibetan Plateau to the northeast-southwest trending line of

Glacial meltwaters in western Qinghai Province, on the border of Tibet, feeds the Tuotuo River, once considered to be the source of the Yangzi. Intrepid members of the China Exploration and Research Society recently followed the Yangzi to a different source (see page 23). At 5,000 metres (16,400 feet), sheep find meagre grazing at the snout of this glacier. [Wong How Man]

the Da Hinggan-Taihang-Wushan Mountains, a belt of ridges and valleys on the eastern margin of the Sichuan Basin through which the Three Gorges have been incised. Average elevation of the ranges decline from about 1,000 metres (3,281 feet) asl in the west to 700 metres (2,297 feet) asl in the east, with individual peaks reaching over 2,000 metres (6,562 feet) asl. Eastwards is the Third Great Step, a belt that comprises the largest plains in China. These include the Middle and Lower Yangzi plains, which are dotted with hills generally below 500 metres (1,640 feet) high. The Fourth, and final, Great Step is the offshore continental shelf, which is generally less than 200 metres (656.2 feet) deep.

THE ORIGIN OF THE YANGZI RIVER

The key to the landscape of China, and particularly to the river system of the country, was the uplift of the massive Tibetan Plateau. Covering about 2.5 million square kilometres, and an average elevation of 4,000 metres (13,120 feet) asl, this plateau both created the monsoon climate and gave rise to the main rivers of the region. Prior to the formation of the Himalayan Mountain range, and the associated Tibetan Plateau, neither the Yangzi River nor the Chinese monsoon system existed.

The origin of the Himalayas can be traced back to about 200 million years ago, when the Indian Plate began to migrate, almost imperceptibly, northwards. This slow movement gradually narrowed the Tethys Sea, which once covered the area of what is now China. Closing of the Tethys resulted in the buckling of the seafloor sediments against the Asian Plate, which lay to the north. Thus began the slow rise of the Himalayas and the Tibetan Plateau. However, it was not until much later, during what is termed the Himalayan Orogeny (the mountain-building period between about 10 to 20 million years ago), that there was any noticeable increase in elevation over the area.

By the Late Pliocene geological period (about 3.4 to 1.6 million years ago) the plateau had risen to about 1,000 metres (3,281 feet) asl, and a weak high pressure air system had developed over the present site of Lhasa (at about 30 degrees north). At the end of the Tertiary Period (1.64 million years ago) the plateau was violently uplifted to about 3,000 metres (9,843 feet) asl. This resulted in the strengthening of the incipient high high-pressure air system, which was pushed north to the southern rim of the Tarim Basin at about 40 degrees north. During the Late Pleistocene to Early Holocene (0.8 to 0.01 million years ago) the area experienced a renewed, more violent and massive final uplift to about 4,000 metres (13,120 feet) asl. At this stage the monsoon system was established in its current form, with the Siberian-Mongolian high high-pressure air system located at about 55 degrees north, and the vast deserts of northwestern China fully developed.

Characterised by significant seasonal changes in wind direction, and by a marked seasonality of rainfall, the monsoon system dominates the climate of China. In addition, the rise of the plateau created a pronounced climatic continentality (isolation from the ameliorating influences of the ocean).

Water in the Yangzi River is mostly derived from tributaries entering in the upper (46 per cent) and middle (47 per cent) reaches. Ten of the 700 main tributaries to the Yangzi have flows greater than 1,000 cubic metres (1,308 cubic yards) a second. In fact the flows of the Min Jiang, Jialing Jiang, Yuan Jiang, Xiang Jiang, Han Jiang, Gan Jiang, Ou Jiang and Nanxiang tributaries all surpass that of the Yellow River. Notably, the Min Jiang, with a drainage basin only 20 per cent that of the Yellow River, has an annual flow twice that of the Yellow River.

THE MYTHOLOGICAL ORIGIN OF THE THREE GORGES

Below Yibin, at an elbow bend near the town of Xinshizen, the Yangzi emerges from the uplands to enter the Sichuan Basin. The Sichuan Basin is an extensive, almost circular lowland that is surrounded on all sides by high mountains. Logically, the Yangzi River should have been expected to flow into the Sichuan Basin and create a large lake with no outlet to the sea. Instead, and quite remarkably, the Yangzi follows an eastward course that cuts a series of impressive gorges through the upstanding barrier of the northeastward-trending Wushan Mountain Range.

The Three Gorges of the Yangzi are a geological peculiarity that provide a remarkable scenic attraction. Although the next chapter (see page 20), dealing with the geological development of the Yangzi River, presents a more prosaic scientific explanation of the Three Gorges' origin, folktales offer an appealing alternative to account for, what has long been recognised as, a significant anomaly of nature.

Chinese legend holds that, about 3,000 years ago, 12 terrible dragons created a devastating hurricane over the area of what is now the Three Gorges. This hurricane wreaked havoc on animals, people and homes. Arriving atop coloured clouds, the Goddess Yao Ji intervened. Pointing her finger, she created a thunder flash that instantly killed the dragons, turned their bodies into the Wushan Mountains, and quelled the storm. Yao Ji then settled in the mountains, residing as Goddess Peak (in the Wu Gorge) to keep eternal watch over the people.

Subsequently, while establishing the layout of his kingdom, Emperor Yu had the task of deciding the direction of flow of the rivers in China. Issuing commands from the top of a mountain near Fengjie, Yu the Great's plan was obstructed by an obstinate range of mountains. Wizard Wu Tze came to his assistance. With a powerful breath the wizard parted the mountains to open up Wind Box Gorge, the shortest of the Three Gorges (about 6.5-kilometres or 4-miles long). The Wizard then carved out the remaining gorges with an axe, thus allowing the river to follow an eastward course, bringing prosperity to the eastern plains.

RECENT AND PROPOSED DEVELOPMENTS

Today, human engineering on a mammoth scale is rapidly transforming the Yangzi River. The rate and magnitude of the changes are unprecedented. Natural features and regional water flows that have been established over aeons, are now being altered and reversed. The Gezhou Dam at Yichang and the massive Three Gorges Dam have, in their turn, stemmed the flow of the river, ponding a great artificial lake that extends upstream for 600 kilometres (373 miles) to Chongqing.

Although the Three Gorges Dam will provide vast amounts of electrical power, improved navigation for the many vessels that ply the river, and potentially life-saving flood control measures, the social and environmental consequences are far reaching. Critics note that floods originate from three areas of the Yangzi, from the main river west of Yichang, from the Dongting Lake drainage system, and from the Han Jiang. Clearly, the dam will have little or no impact on the floods that originate below the dam, and sceptics believe that the dam will make the floods from upstream worse. Only time will tell if the Three Gorges Dam will ever fully realise its forecast benefits; few dams have. Nonetheless, eight further dams are planned for the upper Yangzi, two of which are already being constructed near the Great Bend.

Other substantial changes to the flow of the river are soon to be implemented. Largely as a result of human activity, the waters of the Yellow River to the north are drying up. Consequently, plans have been made to divert water, from three sections of the Yangzi River, northwards to the Yellow River Basin, mainly to serve Beijing, which is suffering the consequences of a decreasing Yellow River discharge.

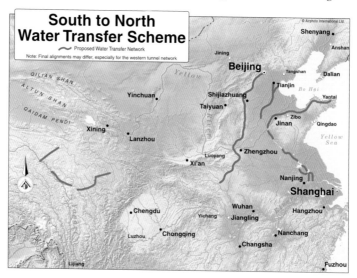

(Right) *A Qing Dynasty Jingjiang Iron Ox fails to ward off the flood dragon, which according to legend should be afraid of the Ox's earthly base element (see page 147). [Huang Zhengping]*

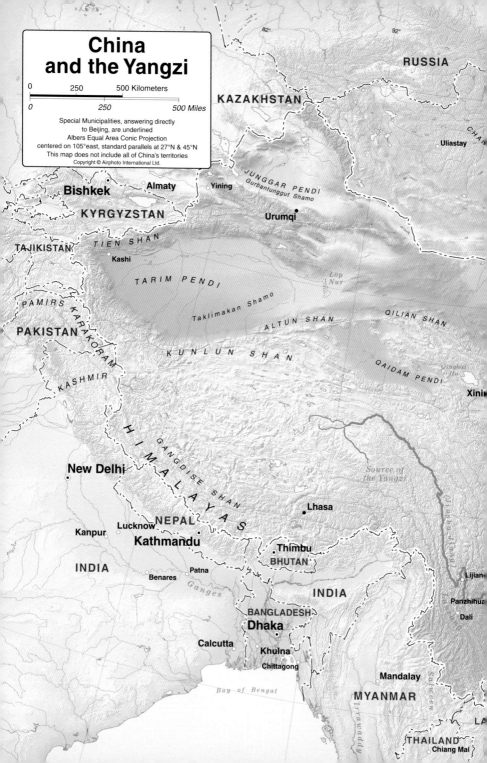

THE RIVER FROM A GEOLOGICAL PERSPECTIVE

THE PECULIAR COURSE OF THE YANGZI

The Yangzi River is remarkable in that, given the rugged topography of western China, it should not be a 'Long River' at all, but should have flowed out to sea via the Mekong or Red rivers, or have been ponded in the Sichuan Basin. However, over the last few million years, the river has changed its course several times, and overcome numerous barriers, to establish a propitious course from west to east across the width of China.

Rising in the Tanggula Mountains, the Yangzi River initially flows northeastwards, before turning eastwards across the Tibetan Plateau. Near the margin of the plateau, the river swings south-eastwards to follow the 'grain' of the folded rocks

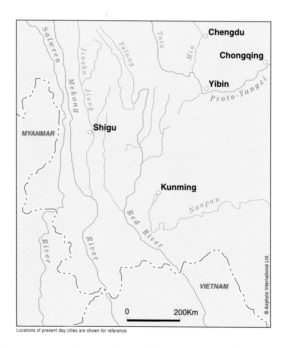

Locations of present day cities are shown for reference

THE COURSE OF THE JINSHA JIANG, TRIBUTARY TO THE MEKONG RIVER, ABOUT 20 MILLION YEARS AGO

THE COURSE OF THE JINSHA JIANG, TRIBUTARY TO THE RED RIVER,
ABOUT 7 MILLION YEARS AGO

THE COURSE OF THE PRESENT DAY JINSHA JIANG (YANGZI RIVER)

that form a sweeping arc of sub-parallel mountain ranges, separated by narrow gorges between 600–1,200 metres (1,969–3,937 feet) deep. Within these gorges are the parallel courses of the Salween, the Mekong and the Yangzi rivers, which here are fast flowing, un-navigable, and tightly confined between the heavily forested valley sides.

About 1,600 kilometres (995 miles) from the source, near the small town of Shigu in northwestern Yunnan Province, the river undertakes the first of several extraordinary changes of direction. Beyond Shigu, the logical extension of the Yangzi is to the southeast through Vietnam, connecting it to the Mekong River. However, encountering Cloud Mountain (*Yun Ling*), the river turns abruptly from a south-southeastward to a north-northeastwards course, at what is termed the First Bend of the Yangzi River. Thus, the Yangzi begins its journey towards China.

About 120 kilometres (75 miles) after the Yangzi leaves Tiger Leaping Gorge, a 3,000 metre (9,843 feet) deep, 30 metre (98 feet) wide cleft through the Jade Dragon Snow Range, the river turns abruptly southwards at the Great Bend to align with the Red River (which flows southwards via Hanoi and Haiphong to the Gulf of Tonkin). However, the Yangzi soon makes a third major turn, this time to the east-northeast. Another sudden change of direction occurs where the Yangzi meets the Yalung River, veering southwards before finally swinging to the northeast.

These dramatic changes of direction were initiated approximately 200 million years ago, when the landmass of India began to move slowly northwards. About 20 million years ago, India collided with Asia. This collision generated immense earth pressures that folded, faulted, and pushed up the rocks to form mountains up to ten kilometres (six miles) high. Collision pressures also created a grid pattern of faults that separated blocks of terrain, the blocks being squeezed and rotated laterally. This northeasterly and northwesterly aligned fault network determined the zigzag course of the Yangzi in this region, confining it within a series of narrow valleys.

Tributary streams were similarly affected by these movements. Several large, southeastward flowing, north bank tributaries enter the Yangzi River, but no large tributaries enter from the south. Following each disruption of the Yangzi's course, the river successively abstracted the headwaters of first the Mekong River, then the Red River, then the Yalung River. These 'river captures' progressively increased the discharge of the Yangzi, enhancing its erosive ability, and consolidating its dominance. Rivers on the south bank are now beheaded remnants of once continuous rivers, which still flow southwards, but with considerably reduced catchments.

THE NEW SOURCE OF THE YANGZI

By Martin Ruzek *(Abridged by Raynor Shaw)*

Remarkably, the sources of the three great rivers of Asia, the Yangzi, Mekong and Yellow rivers, are located within a few hundred kilometres of each other on the Qinghai-Tibet plateau. However, although the official source of the Yangzi is the Geladandong Glacier in the rugged Tanggula Shan, which defines the Qinghai-Tibet border, it has recently been determined that this is not the farthest headwater of the river.

Finding the Source

Officially, the Yangzi originates below the glacier-covered peak of Geladandong (6,535 m)(N33°24' E99°05'), which offers a majestic backdrop for the monument marking the traditional source. Glacial meltwater flows both northward, as the Tuotuo He, and northeastward, as the Gar Qu. The latter stream joins the Dam Qu that, lower down at its confluence with the Tuotuo He, becomes the Tongtian River (named the Jinsha further downstream). The total distance from Geladandong to the Tuotuo He-Dam Qu confluence is 343.8 kilometres, which includes 10.6 kilometres of glacier between the mountain peak and the glacier snout.

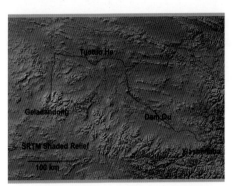

However, expeditions by the China Exploration and Research Society (CERS) in 1985 and 1995 demonstrated that the Ria Sha Neng, in the upper Kaxigong Basin, is a more distant source of the Yangzi, a conclusion that is given credence by local folklore.

Subsequently, based on a detailed examination of satellite data, CERS mounted a third expedition to the region in June 2005. They travelled to southern Qinghai to investigate a possible new source of the Yangzi, which is located in the upper reaches of the Dam Qu at the southern edge of the upper Kaxigong basin, an area dominated by Xiasheriaba Shan (5,374 metres) (N32°36'20" E94°30'37"). On the 15th June 2005, the expedition observed that highest point of open water melting on the flanks of Xiasheriaba Shan was at 5,170 metres at N32°36'14" E94°30'44". From this point water flows northeastward as the Duo Zao Neng to meet the Ria Sha Neng at N32°40'59" E94°32'24". The latter originates at

[Background maps from this and the following page were derived from NGA/NASA Shuttle Radar Topography Mission data, February, 2000]

Technology enabled the CERS team to identify and find the new source, Xiasheriaba Shan. Progress was tracked using visible and infrared satellite photos co-ordinated with daily downloads of GPS information onto a laptop running imaging and GIS (geographical information system) software to plot location. [Martin Ruzek]

N32°44'47" E94°34'19", as documented by the 1985 and 1995 CERS expeditions. From the confluence, the stream flows northwestward as the Dam Qu, turning northward to meet the Gar Qu, and then northeast to join the Tuotuo He.

The expedition calculated that the total distance from Xiasheriaba Shan to the Tuotuo He-Dam Qu confluence is 350.3

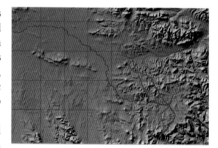

SRTM Shaded Relief
Expedition Track (red) and Dam Qu (blue)

10 km

kilometres. Confirmation of this new source increased the length of the Yangzi by more than two kilometres. Thus, water originating from Xiasheriaba Shan, as the Dua Zao Neng (the 2005 source), travels 2.4 kilometres farther than the waters of the Ria Sha Neng (the 1985/95 source), and 6.5 kilometres farther than water originating from the Geladandong (the traditional source).

Martin Ruzek is a member of the CERS team that found the new source.

CREATION OF THE THREE GORGES

Near the town of Xinshizen, the Yangzi River emerges from the uplands into the Sichuan Basin, which is surrounded on all sides by high mountains. Logically, the Yangzi should have entered the Sichuan Basin and created a large lake, establishing a basin of internal drainage. Remarkably however, the river continues on an eastward course, cutting a series of gorges through the upstanding barrier of the northeastward-trending Wushan Mountain Range. The existence of the famous Three Gorges is another peculiarity of the Yangzi River.

The Wushan Mountains were formed by folding that occurred during the great earth movements of the Yanshanian Orogeny (between about 130 to 190 million years ago). The Three Gorges developed either during, or after, that event.

There are three possible processes that could explain the discordant course of the Yangzi River. The first process is 'river capture', which would require two rivers to develop independently on each side of the newly formed Wushan Mountain range. Flowing in opposite directions, both rivers then eroded their valleys, but the headwaters of the longer and more powerful eastern stream cut back across the summit to capture the headwaters of the weaker western river. Eventually the flow of the western river was completely reversed and became the headwaters of the new,

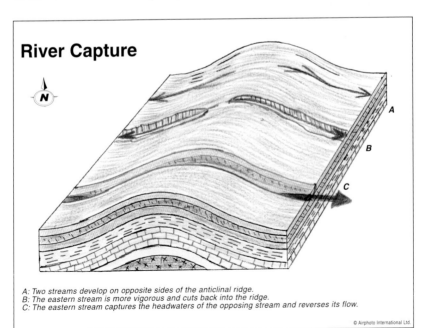

River Capture

N

A
B
C

A: Two streams develop on opposite sides of the anticlinal ridge.
B: The eastern stream is more vigorous and cuts back into the ridge.
C: The eastern stream captures the headwaters of the opposing stream and reverses its flow.

© Airphoto International Ltd.

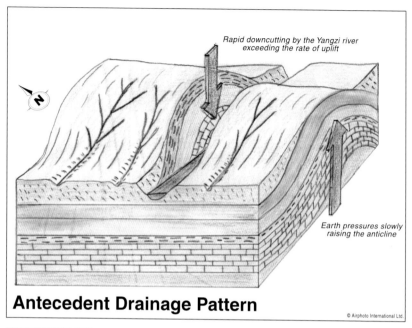

Rapid downcutting by the Yangzi river
exceeding the rate of uplift

Earth pressures slowly
raising the anticline

Antecedent Drainage Pattern

© Airphoto International Ltd.

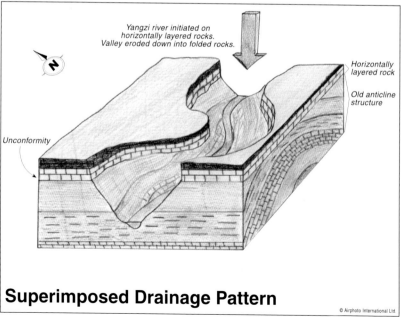

Yangzi river initiated on
horizontally layered rocks.
Valley eroded down into folded rocks.

Horizontally
layered rock

Old anticline
structure

Unconformity

Superimposed Drainage Pattern

© Airphoto International Ltd.

and longer, Yangzi River. The second process is 'antecedence', which assumes that the river course was well-established on the landscape before the fold mountain range was formed. Uplands can rise relatively rapidly, diverting or disrupting an existing drainage system, or they may rise relatively slowly, so that the rate of river downcutting keeps pace with the rate of uplift of the mountains, thus forming a gorge. The third mechanism, termed 'superimposition', postulates that a river system is established on a sequence of horizontally bedded rocks, which themselves overlie an older sequence of folded rocks (in this case, the Wushan Mountains). Eventually, the river erodes a channel down into the folded rocks below, and regional erosion removes the surrounding cover rocks. Consequently, the river system is discordantly superimposed upon the range of fold mountains. Although interpretations differ, there is general agreement that the Yangzi Gorges were formed by superimposition, the original river having established a course on a former surface.

NATURAL HAZARDS ALONG THE YANGZI RIVER

Historically, the mighty Yangzi has presented many dangers to the people who live by, and work on, the river. These dangers have included the rapids of the Three Gorges, and the annual floods that caused extensive damage to crops, property, and life. Adjacent to the river channel is the hazard posed by landslides from the steep valley sides, and from below ground the potential threat of damaging earthquakes.

RAPIDS

The major hazards to navigation through the gorges were the shoals and rapids that occurred within the channel. Records indicate that, prior to 1800, about 33 per cent of all boats and 25 per cent of all goods passing through the Yangzi Gorges were destroyed. During the Nationalist Period, 72 rapids were recorded in the 560 kilometres (348 miles) of channel between Yichang and Chongqing. The majority of these were in the first 240 kilometres (149 miles) above Yichang. In particular, the Xiling Gorge was noted for its dangerous rapids and shoals. Over the years, most of the obstacles were removed, either by dredging or by blasting.

FLOODS

Throughout history, devastating summer floods have been a feature of the Yangzi River, particularly in the lower reaches. More than 1,000 massive floods have been recorded since 206 BCE, with five serious floods this century (in 1931, 1935, 1949, 1954, and 1998). The most disastrous flood was in July 1931 when a series of seven cyclonic storms crossed the area in rapid succession. These storms generated six flood surges that passed down the river destroying 23 dams and associated dykes, inundating 88,000 square kilometres (33,980 square miles) of land, killing an estimated 140,000 people, leaving 40 million people homeless, and crippling the economy. A water level of 16.3 metres (53.5 feet) was recorded at Wuhan, which was two metres (6.5 feet) above the bund. Wuhan and Nanjing remained underwater for weeks. Water levels rose higher during the 1954 flood. In the 1998 flood, about 7,000 people died.

Faced with these devastating floods, the construction of protective dykes began about 1,500 years ago. Today, a primary objective of the new Three Gorges Dam is to control the river levels. Pre-Dam river levels fluctuated by about 20 metres (66 feet), with rises up to 50 metres (164 feet) or more in the narrow gorges. For example, at Old Zigui (in the Xiling Gorge) the level varied seasonally by 21 metres (69 feet), but during the flood of 1871 an 84-metre (276-feet) rise was recorded. Winter water depths were about two metres at Wuhan, rising to 15 metres (49 feet) in the flood season. Rates of rise are also impressive, with a maximum daily rate of rise of 10 metres (33 feet) recorded at Wanxian (at the entrance to the Qutang Gorge).

Discharge volumes are similarly impressive. Each year, the river discharges about 930,000 million cubic metres (840,000 million cubic feet) of water, almost 70 per cent of which flows in the six months from May to October during the summer monsoon rains. The flood season begins in March/April and lasts for about six to eight months. Typically, about 60 per cent of the flood waters originate from the main river west of Yichang, up to 30 per cent arise from the Dongting Lake drainage system, and about 10 per cent from the Han Jiang. Early season floods usually occur in the Dongting Lake drainage system, with later flood waves from the main stream of the Yangzi west of Yichang, and subsequently from the Han Jiang River. In years when flood waters from the three sources combined, the flooding was prolonged and severe.

The average flow of the Yangzi River is about 30,000 cubic metres (1.059 million cubic feet) per second, but at Yichang in 1954, during the worst flood for a century, a flow of 76,000 cubic metres (2.684 million cubic feet) per second was measured. Discharge at Wuhan was 100,000 cubic metres (3.530 million cubic feet) per second during the 1931 flood, and 83,000 cubic metres (2.930 million cubic feet) per second during the 1954 flood.

LANDSLIDES AND ROCKFALLS

Large, potentially damaging, landslides are common in the more mountainous sections of the Yangzi valley above Yichang. Engineering geological surveys in the reservoir area of the Three Gorges Dam identified over 400 landslides and rockfalls. Of these, 24 are located west of Fengjie in the more open Sichuan Basin, and 11 are located to the east of Fengjie in the broad valley sections of the Yangzi Gorges. Thirty-five were classified as large scale.

By way of illustration, the Xintan landslide in Zigui County blocked the Yangzi River on two significant occasions in 1030 and 1542, obstructing navigation for 21 and 82 years respectively. On the 12 June 1985 the Xintan landslide reactivated, completely destroying the 1,000-year-old town. The 2,000,000-cubic-metres (70,630,000-cubic-feet) mass of sliding rock entered the river, created a devastating 35-metre-high (114.8-feet-high) wave surge, and temporarily blocked the navigation channel. The Jipazi landslide in Yunyang County failed on 17 July 1982, blocking the navigation channel and costing 100 million Yuan in channel dredging and landslide control works. Other notable large landslides occurred at Gaojiazui, near Guling Town (18-million cubic metres or 636 million cubic feet of rock above an inclined sliding plane); Baota, near Yunyang Town (100-million cubic metres or 35,315,000 cubic feet); Baihuanping, near Fengjie (129-million cubic metres or 4,556-million cubic feet); Liujiawuchang, near Wushan (18-million cubic metres or 636-million cubic feet); and New Badong (15-million cubic metres or 530-million cubic feet).

Large-scale rockfalls are concentrated in the steeper sections of the Three Gorges, where they originate from the vertical rock walls. Very few rockfalls occur in the broad valley areas. Most of the rockfalls are in the carbonate rocks (limestone).

EARTHQUAKES

Seismological (earthquake) research was carried out as part of the Three Gorges Project. The study concluded that the seismic potential in the region was of medium to strong, but that at the dam site it is weak. Earthquakes with a magnitude of greater than 4 were not recorded within a radius of 50 kilometres (31 miles) from the dam site, and earthquakes with a magnitude of greater than 6 were not recorded within a distance of 200 kilometres (124 miles).

The survey also concluded that the probability of Reservoir Induced Earthquakes (RIE), that is adjustments of the earth's crust in response to loading by the water in the reservoir, was low in the granite rocks surrounding the dam site. However, there is a higher probability in the four reservoir sections underlain by weathered limestone rocks, namely Niuganmafei Gorge and the Jiuwanxi, between Nanmuyan and Peishi, between Daxiaodong and Daninghe, the outlet of the Wu Gorge, and the branches of the Longchuanhe and Wujiang.

Interestingly, a seismic monitoring network set up to detect seismic activity prior to, and post, reservoir filling recorded about 2,000 small earthquakes (of magnitude 2 or less) between June 2003 (when dam filling to 135 metres (443 feet) asl began) and September 2003.

THE SICHUAN BASIN (INCLUDING THE THREE GORGES)

The 260,000-square-kilometre (100,400-square-mile) Sichuan Basin, or Red Basin, is one of the largest topographical basins in China, formed during the Indo-Sinian Orogeny at the end of the Cretaceous Period (about 65 million years ago). Fold mountains enclose the depression on all sides. Defining the western boundary are the 3,000- to 4,000-metre-high (9,843- to 13,120-feet-high) Longmen, Qionglai, Daliang and Emei mountains, marginal mountains of the Tibetan Plateau. In the north are the Micang and Daba mountains, while the Wushan Mountains occur to the east, and the Yunnan-Guizhou Plateau rises to the south.

Geologically, the basin is underlain by nearly horizontal, Jurassic and Cretaceous age (144 to 65 million years ago), red sandstones and purple shales laid down on folded limestones containing coal seams. From the Late Cretaceous (about 99 million years ago) to the Middle Pliocene (about 3.4 to 1.6 million years ago) the basin was an arm of the sea and saline water is still extracted from deep wells in Zigong, Sichuan. Mineral resources of the region consist of coal (both anthracite and bituminous coal), salt, oil, natural gas and iron ore. Today, the Sichuan Basin is a fertile depression, with an average elevation of about 700 metres (2,297 feet) asl, supporting a population of about 100 million people.

The floor of the basin slopes gently from about 900 metres (2,953 feet) asl in the north to around 450 metres (1,476 feet) asl in the south. The Yangzi River flows against the high ground to the south of the basin, occupying a narrow valley that is only about 300 metres (984 feet) wide at Chongqing and extends from Yibin, the head of navigation, in the west to Baidicheng, Fengjie County in the east. Summer and winter water levels vary up to 21 metres (69 feet) in this section. More than 50 tributaries with a length exceeding 100 kilometres (62 miles) enter the Yangzi in the Sichuan Basin, increasing the discharge before the river enters the Three Gorges. Six of these rivers, the Jialing Jiang (at Chongqing), Min Jiang, Tuo Jiang, the Qu Jiang,

This geometrical pattern of concrete slabs was laid in 2003 to protect slopes below New Badong from erosion by the new reservoir. [Raynor Shaw]

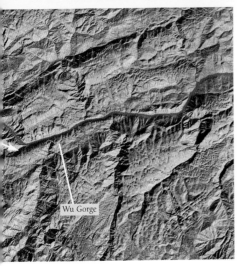

Wu Gorge

The Yangzi River cuts through the Wushan Mountains, creating a series of gorges that alternately follow the structural grain of the folded rocks, and then make sharp turns to cross the folds. This is clearly illustrated in the linear Wu Gorge (above, looking downstream). Note also the steeply-inclined beds of rock on the left hand side of the channel. [Lu Jin] (See also page 125)

In the satellite photograph (left), after traversing a ridge (far left), the river turns almost at right angles to follow a marked structural lineation before leaving it again towards the top right. (The arrow shows the direction of view of the above photograph.) Interestingly, Shengnu Brook tributary enters the Yangzi following this lineation (right of the arrow). [Geocarto and Airphoto International]

Fu Jiang, and Wu Jiang, exceed 500 kilometres (311 miles) in length. These rivers, which are fast flowing and unnavigable except for small river craft, have cut deeply into the soft red sandstones to create deep valleys that have made travel across the basin difficult. However, valley erosion has exposed the harder limestones and the coal seams in many areas, which were mined locally along adits (inclined tunnels).

The famous Three Gorges of the Yangzi extend through the Wushan Mountains, between Chongqing Municipality and Hubei provinces, for a distance of 192 kilometres (119 miles) from Baidicheng in Fengjie County, Chongqing Municipality, to the Nanjin Pass at Yichang in Hubei Province (see satellite image on page 149). In descending order downstream are the Qutang, Wu and Xiling gorges. Surrounded by towering mountains and enclosed by precipitous cliffs, each gorge has its own distinctive and characteristic scenery, features that are largely determined by variations in the geology. Most of the popular names given to sections of the gorges, or features within the gorges, are geological phenomena.

Careful observers will note that in many cases the bedded (layered) sedimentary rocks exposed along the river cliffs are steeply dipping (see opposite page), indicating folding or tilting from their originally horizontal attitude. Steeply inclined bedding is clearly visible, for example, in the Wu Gorge. The exposed rocks also vary in their colour, the thickness of the beds (or bands), and the spacing of joints within the beds. Joint patterns and block detachment also create other features, such as blind arches where closely jointed rocks have collapsed to expose an unjointed (massive) slab of rock framed on the sides and top by a rock canopy.

A ramp or wedge-shaped slope commonly occurs at the foot of the cliffs, or at higher levels where a shelf or platform exists. This feature, which may or may not be vegetated, is termed a scree slope. Screes are accumulations of loose rock debris comprising blocks that have weathered from the vertical rock faces and fallen to the base of the cliff to form a distinctive, linear deposit. Where the cliffs plunge directly into the river, screes will be present below the waters. Their surface gradient varies depending upon the size of the rock fragments, which determines their characteristic equilibrium slope (or angle of rest). The size of the rock fragments depends upon the rock type and the joint pattern and joint spacing in the rocks. Well-developed scree slopes can be observed, for example, on the south bank of the river at Kuimen (at the entrance to the Qutang Gorge), and along much of the Qutang Gorge.

THE QUTANG GORGE

The shortest and most spectacular of the three gorges, Qutang Gorge extends for eight kilometres (five miles) from Baidicheng in the west to Daxizhen in the east. Enclosed by peaks that rise to over 1,000 metres (3,280 feet) above the river, the gorge is noted for its precipitous walls and overhanging precipices. Consequently, sailing through the gorge is commonly likened to passing along an underground cave.

Qutang Gorge is eroded through the anticline (originally flat-lying rocks folded into an arch) of the Qiyue Mountains, forming vertical cliffs of Mesozoic (deposited between 248 to 65 million years ago) limestone and sandstones, associated with metamorphic (rocks altered by the heat and pressure of folding) gneisses and schists, and intruded by granite. Prior to the Three Gorges Dam, the gorge would

(Above left) *These almost vertical beds of red sandstones, located between the Qutang and Wu gorges, were originally deposited as horizontal layers, and then tilted by later earth movements. The slight curvature of the beds indicates that the rocks visible in this cliff section are part of a larger sequence of long-wavelength, open folds. Weathering and erosion have picked out the bedding planes (separations between the beds), and the joints within the beds, to give the rocks a blocky appearance.* (Above right) *Vertical fluting of greyish-white limestone in the Qutang gorge. Limestone is soluble in acidulated water. Consequently, over time, the action of rainwater (dilute carbonic acid) flowing across exposed rock surfaces develops intricate and distinctive solution patterns. Pebbles lodged in the angular flutes were likely placed there during floods.* (Below) *These thinly-bedded sedimentary rocks, exposed on the walls of the Wu Gorge, display tight, wavy flexures (conjugate folds) resulting from intense, large-scale earth movements that also metamorphosed (baked and altered) the original rocks.* [Bill Hurst]

An impressive display of tight, intricate folding and minor faulting (fracturing and displacement) of thinly-bedded rocks in the Wu Gorge. The boat in the foreground indicates the scale of the features. Note the sandbank to the right, which would (before filling the reservoir) have been periodically submerged

and reshaped during floods. Given favourable conditions for preservation, this bedded (layered) deposit could, in several million years, form part of a sequence of fluvial (river-deposited) sandstones similar to the sedimentary rocks that now form the walls of the gorges. [Bill Hurst]

Qutang Gorge's dramatic entrance, Kuimen (Dragon's Gate), as it appeared in 1979. Kuimen is no less dramatic now (see page 90), despite the rise of the giant reservoir. [Bill Hurst]

channel flows of up to 60,000 cubic metres (2.1 million cubic feet) per second during the wet season. In this section, the river could rise by ten to 20 metres (33 to 66 feet) in one day, and 50 metre (164 feet) annual variations were recorded.

Qutang Gorge begins at Kuimen (*men* meaning gate), also known as the Kui Gorge or Qutang Pass, where the river is only 100 metres (328 feet) wide. Prior to 1954, when it was blasted away, a huge rock at the entrance to the gorge was responsible for wrecking innumerable boats over the years. Standing sentinel on the north bank is Red Armour Rock, a magnificent peak stained by ferric oxide (iron) weathered out of the rocks, which is perhaps why it is also referred to as Peach Mountain. In contrast, White Salt Mountain (*Baiyan Shan*) on the south bank results from dissolved calcium carbonate precipitating on the surface.

THE WU GORGE

Upon emerging from the Qutang Gorge and reaching the confluence with the Daning River, a north bank tributary, the Yangzi River enters the secluded beauty of the Wu Gorge (or Great Gorge). Extending from the mouth of the Daning River to Guandukou in the east, the 45-kilometre-long (28-mile-long) Wu Gorge is the second-longest of the Three Gorges.

Wu Gorge is eroded through the anticline (originally flat-lying rocks folded into an arch) of the northeast to southwest aligned Wushan Mountain range. Following a zig-zag course, the river approaches blind walls before turning abruptly to flow relentlessly onwards through deep and beautiful clefts between strangely-shaped peaks. The most spectacular are the famous Twelve Peaks of the Wushan Mountains, which include Goddess Peak (*Shennu Feng*) and the 2,400-metre-high (7,874-feet-high) Rising Cloud Peak. Two distinct sections of the gorge are distinguished. Golden Helmet and Silver Armour Gorge is named after the distinctive yellow-brown limestone peak that rises like a golden helmet, and the closely-bedded, folded, scaly, greyish white rock that looks like armour.

THE XILING GORGE

After flowing past the town of Zigui, located in the broad valley of Xiang Xi (Xiang Stream), a north bank tributary, the Yangzi enters the Xiling Gorge, which extends for 66 kilometres (41 miles) to the Nanjin Pass near Yichang. The Xiling Gorge comprises two distinct sections, west and east, separated by the 31-kilometre-wide (19-mile-wide) Miaonan Valley.

Historically, the Xiling Gorge achieved notoriety for its feared torrential rapids and dangerous shoals that took a great toll in vessels and lives. Since 1949, more than 100 of these obstructions to navigation were cleared by dredging and blasting, and numerous signal stations erected. Especially notorious were the Xintan, Xietan and Kongling shoals, along with the Qingtan and Yaochahe shoals. The Xintan Shoal consisted of rock debris from two big landslides that occurred during the Eastern Han (25–220 CE) and Eastern Jin (317–220) periods. The Kongling Shoal, near Miaohe, was a 200-metre-long (656-feet-long) rock that has since been removed.

Most of the Xiling Gorge is eroded through soluble limestone. Consequently, 174 limestone caves have been recorded between Nantuo and the Nanjin Pass. These caves occur in five distinct elevation groups, which correspond to different levels of the river, and the associated water table, as it cut down over time. Caves developed at between 40 to 55 metres (130 to 180 feet) asl, 80 to 90 metres (263 to 295 feet) asl, 120 to 140 metres (394 to 459 feet) asl, 240 metres (787 feet) asl, and 280 to 290 metres (919 to 951 feet) asl. The 80 to 90 metre level had only sparse cave development, but the caves at the 120 to 140 metre level are characterized by large entrances and rich sinter (precipitated calcium carbonate) deposits.

THE JIANGHAN PLAIN

The Jianghan (East China) Plain, which extends from Yichang, via Wuhan and Najing, to the Yangzi Delta, is characterized by low-lying topography with scattered hills that rise abruptly from the surrounding plains. These plains are the remnants of former basins, underlain by limestones, micaceous sandstones, quartzites and conglomerates, which were filled with sediments transported downstream, notably from the red sandstones of the Sichuan Basin. Economic minerals in this area include high-grade iron ores, coking coal, cement, and oil.

Topographically, the Jianghan Plain can be subdivided into the Upper, Middle and Lower Yangzi plains. The Upper Plain extends from Yichang downstream to near the town of Huangshi, about 120 kilometres (75 miles) below Wuhan, where the Yangzi River cuts a channel only 800 metres (2,625 feet) wide between spurs of the Dabei Mountains to the north and Wanfu Mountains to the south. The largest tributaries enter the Yangzi in this section. From the north the Han River enters at Hankou (Mouth of the Han), which along with the towns of Hanyang and Wuchang make up the metropolis of Wuhan. The Yuan Jiang and the Siang Jiang enter from the south via Dongting Lake.

The Middle Plains extend from Huangshi downstream to near the river port of Anqing where the river is again constricted as it crosses the Dabai Mountians. The Lower Yangzi Plain ends downstream near Ma'anshan, midway between Wuhu and Nanjing. Below Ma'anshan the landscape assumes a more deltaic character, being generally flatter and wetter.

Crossing the Jianghan Plain, the Yangzi is a placid, mature river with a gradient of only 0.03 metres per kilometre. During the winter, water depths at Wuhan are as little as two metres, so the river traveller will observe high brown mud banks flanking the channel. Historically, large areas of the Middle Basin have been prone to devastating floods. During the summer the river could rise by 15 metres (49 feet), transforming the landscape.

Consequently, several thousand kilometres of dykes and culverts have been constructed in the region, all designed to receive the annual flood waters and to mitigate their adverse effects. Much of the site of the city of Sashi is from one to three metres below river level. There are also more than 1,200 large and small lakes scattered over the plain, including Poyang, Dongting, Chao and Tai lakes, and intricate networks of tributaries. An officially stated prime objective of the new Three Gorges Dam is to prevent disastrous flooding in this area, making these old measures redundant.

Colloquially termed 'the land of fish and rice', it is a fertile agricultural district that produces 70 per cent of the country's rice and is among the most densely populated areas of China, supporting 30 per cent of the country's population. More than 4,000 square kilometres (1,550 square miles) of fertile agricultural land have been reclaimed around the shallow margins of Dongting and Poyang lakes.

A rare sight even for 1979: The crew of this sailing junk prepare to settle for the night outside Wuhan with a spectacular view of the great China Plain [Bill Hurst]

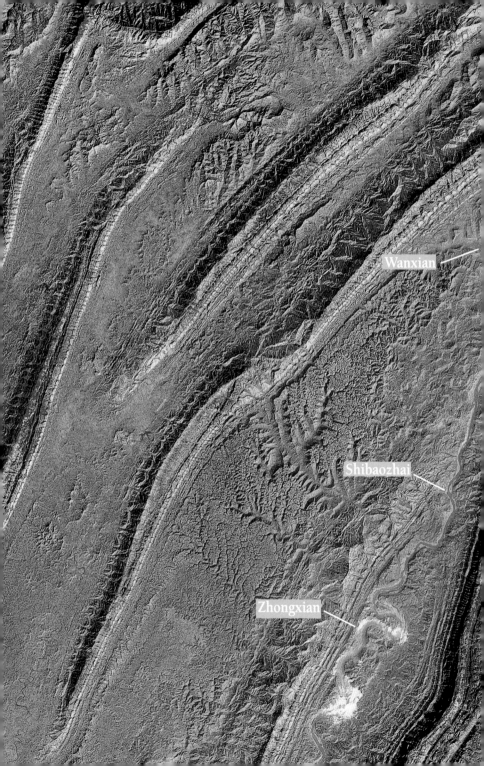

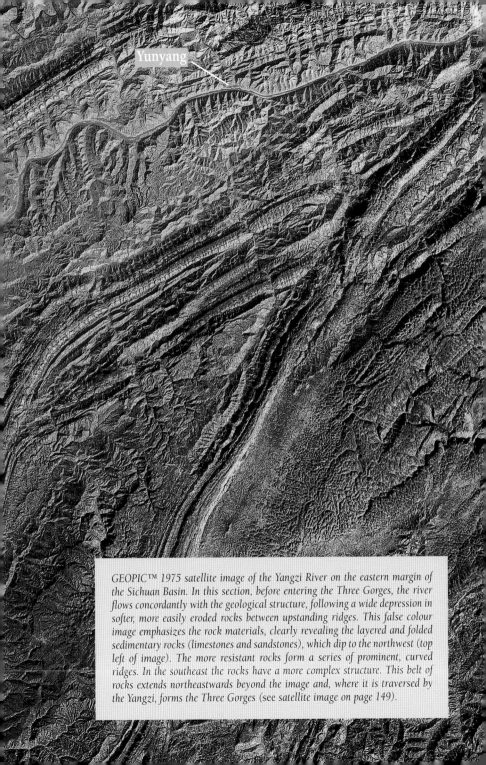

Yunyang

GEOPIC™ 1975 satellite image of the Yangzi River on the eastern margin of the Sichuan Basin. In this section, before entering the Three Gorges, the river flows concordantly with the geological structure, following a wide depression in softer, more easily eroded rocks between upstanding ridges. This false colour image emphasizes the rock materials, clearly revealing the layered and folded sedimentary rocks (limestones and sandstones), which dip to the northwest (top left of image). The more resistant rocks form a series of prominent, curved ridges. In the southeast the rocks have a more complex structure. This belt of rocks extends northeastwards beyond the image and, where it is traversed by the Yangzi, forms the Three Gorges (see satellite image on page 149).

CHONGQING

Chongqing

The bustling 'Mountain City' of Chongqing is centred on a promontory on the north bank of the Yangzi, rising above the confluence of the Yangzi and a main tributary, the Jialing Jiang, around the busy docks at Chaotianmen. The city has long since outgrown its original site and spilled over to the adjacent banks of both the Yangzi and Jialing. Cable cars glide across to opposite banks and giant bridges carry the city's burgeoning traffic. Caves perforate the steep hills, once carved out as bomb shelters and now busy as garages or naturally cool restaurants and hair salons.

For centuries it has been the main commercial and transportation centre for Sichuan Province. Hundreds of ships lined the muddy banks below the remaining old city wall at Chaotianmen—rusty ferries packed with commuters and barges heaped with goods plied the Three Gorges to the rest of China. Chongqing is the destination for most of the bulk transport that passed through the Gorges, which is likened to an eyedropper feeding the elephant of the populous region of Sichuan. The port bustle was impressive and sweat-soaked. Thousands of porters known as the *bang bang jun*—the pole- or stick-army—lined up with their bamboo poles and ropes to carry supplies up the staircases from the river into the heart of the city. Some 200,000 of these cheerful troops still ply their trade on any given day. Many laid-off workers become bang-bang jun of professionally organized agencies. Others work on the construction sites, camping in the muddy disarray of the crowded city.

Chongqing has undergone a rapid transformation. This is mainly due to the city being granted national status in 1997. It is now a municipal region similar to Beijing, Shanghai and Tianjin. Its authority extends to the eastern Sichuan counties down river, encompassing a total population of some 33 million people. Chongqing is now the world's largest metropolitan region. The city itself has a population of around six million. It is expected to grow to 10 million in the next decade, gobbling up nearby farmland for apartment complexes. Rural people can now move into the city and, with the purchase of an apartment, become full city citizens.

This area is bearing the brunt, and possible benefits, of inundation by the completion of the Three Gorges Dam, the world's largest dam, which has displaced more than 1.3 million people. Chongqing has seen an enormous amount of reconstruction, with the demolition of many old neighbourhoods that had previously been bombed by the Japanese and reconstructed as ramshackle warrens laced with sandstone staircases. These squalid conditions created cramped living conditions for the city residents, a people who are known for their habit of sitting outside on cool summer nights.

The People's Liberation Monument, originally the Victory Monument to commemorate the soldiers, sailors and pilots who helped overthrow the Japanese, stands before the modern alter of shopping, a large department store. The monument is a popular meeting point for locals. [Lu Jin]

The traditional lifestyle of Chongqing is being transformed by giant shopping and residential complexes that have all but eliminated the spicy street life, replacing it with glitzy boutiques for the parade of newly flush consumers. At the centre of the city is the *Jiefang Bei*, or Liberation Monument—a modern tower built in the 1950's to memorialize the martyrs of the civil war. The plaza area is closed to cars, making a vast pedestrian refuge for shoppers. The large Three Gorges Plaza, at the centre of the Shapingba area and west of the older downtown centre, is a marble-paved complex surrounded by tall office and residential buildings. It features a large bronze expressionist sculpture and a scale model of the great dam, with inscriptions from its chief advocate and a former resident, ex-Premier Li Peng.

The dam project initiated construction of massive new walls along the river shores and although the rise in water level has reduced the flight of steps to a minimum, *bang bang jun* still scurry eagerly to assist passengers with their luggage when they board or disembark from their cruise ships. While improved road and rail connections to the rest of the country reduced the importance of relatively slow river transportation and its associated frenzy of port activity, there are still some 80 docks lining the banks, about 20 of which are dedicated to handling passengers.

As the main industrial centre for southwest China, Chongqing is a top producer of iron and steel and boasts the largest aluminium smelter in China, as well as being an important pharmaceuticals centre. Chongqing Longcin, established in 1993, is one of the largest motorcycle manufacturers in the country and in 2002 moved to a newly built industrial park, where it employs more than 5,000 people and has a production capacity of one million motorcycles and two million engines annually. The popularity of the motorcycle has more than a little to do with the almost total absence of bicycles in this hilly city.

New express highways soar overhead and road tunnels penetrate the mountains in an effort to alleviate the thick crawl of traffic through the city. A new monorail line, running the length of the peninsula, opened in late 2004. Still, the landlocked port is plagued by some of the worst air pollution in China, as industry and traffic jams spew toxins into the still, humid air. However, the local government is taking steps to improve the situation such as introducing LPG-fueled public buses.

Air pollution aside, the folk cuisine of outdoor sidewalk dining remains popular: the *huo guo* or hot pot. These are basins filled with bubbling chili oil and *hua jiao*—flower pepper that causes the mouth to tingle—into which are dipped all kinds of meats and vegetables. Once the river boatmen's campfire meal of leftovers from the day's market, *huo guo* is now the local favourite, perhaps because opium pods are sometimes placed in the brew.

The Chongqing waterfront, 1944, taken by Cecil Beaton, official photographer to China for the British Ministry of Information at the time. [Cecil Beaton Collection, Imperial War Museum]

HISTORY OF CHONGQING

In the Fourth Century BCE, Chongqing (then called *Yuzhou*) was the capital of the State of Ba, whose men were renowned for their prowess in battle and their military successes. In the Southern Song Dynasty (1127–1279) the city's name was changed to Chongqing—meaning 'double celebration'—to mark the princedom and enthronement of Emperor Zhaodun in 1189. He was himself a native of the city.

Bustling with junks from Sichuan's hinterlands and neighbouring provinces, Chongqing was always an important collection point for an abundance of produce such as hides and furs from Tibet, hemp, salt, silk, rhubarb, copper and iron. The Qifu Agreement of 1890 opened Chongqing to foreign trade, prompting the exciting navigation of steamboats through the treacherous gorges to trade Chongqing's riches with the outside world. By the early 20th Century, a massive trade in southwest-China-grown opium had begun, abetted by warlord factionalism and greed.

Visitors to the city in the 1920s and '30s commented on its 30-metre high city wall, and the rough steps from the river up to the city gates 'dripping with slime from the endless procession of water carriers'. At that time, Chongqing, with a

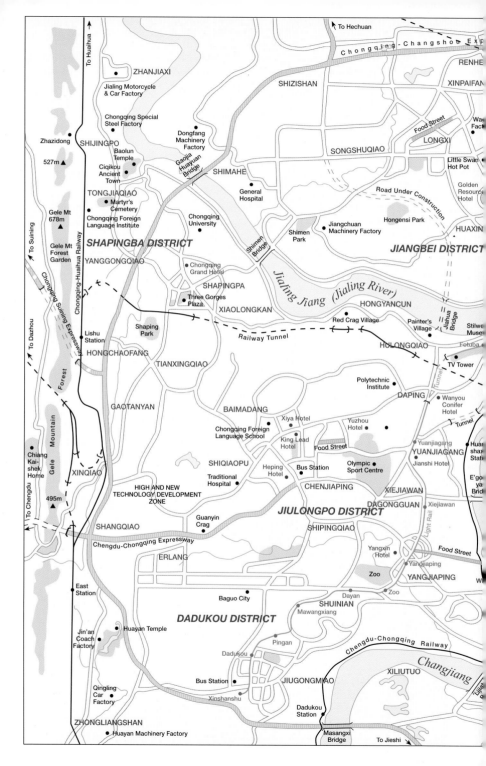

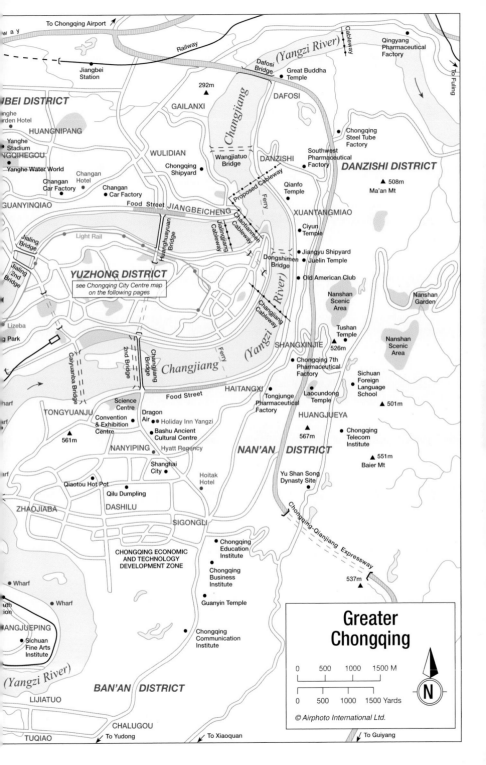

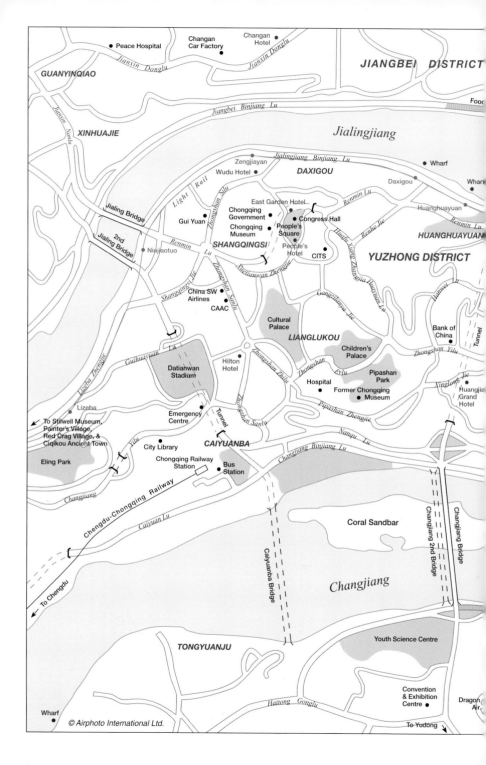

© Airphoto International Ltd.

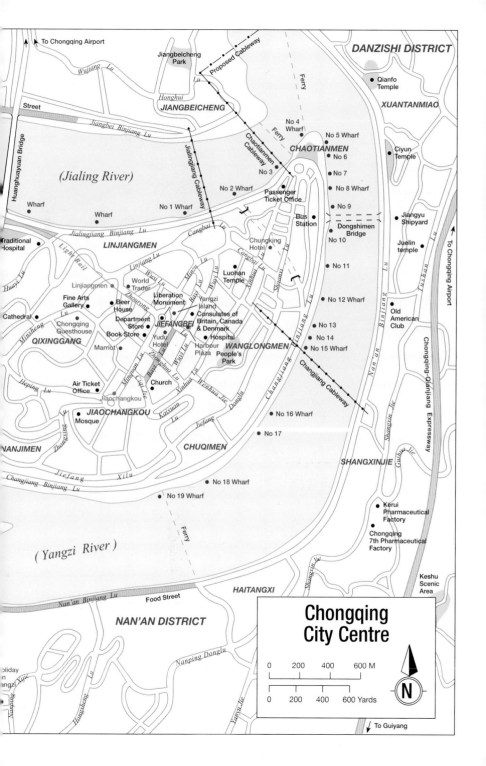

Mao Zedong and US envoy Patrick J Hurley at the start of the 1944 Chongqing coalition talks. Just one of many archive photographs in the Stilwell Museum. [John Colling]

population exceeding 600,000, had no other water supply. Between 10,000 and 20,000 coolies carried water daily to shops and houses through the steep and narrow lanes of the city. All portage was done by coolies as there were no wheeled vehicles in the city, only sedan chairs. The staircase streets have virtually disappeared, and all that remains of the city wall is the odd outcrop of masonry that props up a house here, or abuts a path there. The former gate of Chaotianmen, at the tip of the promontory overlooking the harbour, has been rebuilt into a plaza park. A funicular railway still descends to the docks below for passengers boarding the many boats to destinations near and far.

In 1939, during the Sino-Japanese War, the Guomindang government of China moved the capital from Nanjing to Chongqing, and on the south bank of the Yangzi foreign delegations built substantial quarters, which can be seen from the river. The airstrip used then can still be seen on the Shanhuba sandbar at times, particularly in winter, as one crosses the Yangzi River Bridge, in spite of the risen water levels from the Three Gorges Dam. The Guomindang government headquarters is now the People's City Government Offices (only the gateway is left of that period), situated just opposite the Renmin Hotel.

The Bombing of Chongqing

The bombing by the Japanese which began in 1939 continued in 1940 and in 1941 with increasing ferocity. As soon as the winter fogs lifted the planes came, and through the gruelling hot summer, until late in autumn, being bombed was part of the normal process of living. Our daily activities were geared to this predictable occurrence: one rose early, and since the nights were an inferno of heat and sweat, the rock exuding its day-stored heat, it was easy to wake when the sun rose, for dawn did not mean coolness, but another raging hot day. Quickly the fire was lit with sticks of wood and a fan to spurt the flame, water boiled for morning rice, and by nine o'clock the day's first meal (the before-the-bombing meal) had been consumed. The first alert then started. One went to the dugout, with some luggage in hand, kettle and iron pan (irreplaceable after 1940, as metal became almost non-existent); and there one spent the day. Sometimes the bombs fell very near and we came to know the peculiar whistling sound they made. At other times the drone was further away, and the explosions faint. Sometimes the bombers came over five or six times, on occasion up to twenty times a day. And once, in 1941, they continued without let for seven days and nights, and many people died, both in the bombings and also in the air-raid shelters, especially babies, from heat and exhaustion and diarrhoea.

The shelters were scooped-out tunnels in the rock, and since Chungking was all rock, with juttings and small hollows and hillocks almost everywhere, the bowels of these promontories could easily be utilized. But some of the common shelters had been dug in softer earth, and were unsafe. They caved in after a while. There was no ventilation in them, and the people who sat deep inside, away from the one and only outlet, the mouth of the tunnel, became anoxic if the raid was prolonged. They started to thresh about, or to faint. In between the explosions, there was respite. While awaiting the next batch of bombs, everyone would come out of the dugout, sit round the mouth of the cave, fan, gulp the hot air; but this was almost as gruelling as sitting inside the dugout because there was hardly any shade, and if there was a single bush, it was monopolized in its thin narrow coolness by some police squad or some self-important official and his family.

Han Suyin, Birdless Summer, 1968

During the Sino-Japanese War (1937–45), Chongqing's notorious foggy weather conditions probably saved the city from complete devastation, for only on clear days could the Japanese bombers, which flew over in 20-minute waves, succeed in accurately dropping their thousands of bombs. One survivor from that era is the old American Club located along the south-bank boulevard of the Yangzi. This elegant building from the early 1900s, with its wide porticos and view of the city, is constantly under threat from developers.

WHAT TO SEE IN CHONGQING

Chongqing, always a trading city, was never noted for its cultural heritage or architecture. However, unlike most northern Chinese cities, Chongqing and other Yangzi River towns are very lively at night. On summer evenings residents stroll about in the hope of a refreshing breeze, and dancing often takes place in People's Square, in front of the People's Congress Hall. Street markets and sidewalk restaurant stalls can be found along Xinhua Lu and Shaanxi Lu towards Chaotianmen. A bright and cheerful strip of restaurants and bars has sprung up along the south bank, on Nan'anbin Lu, just east of the Yangzi River Bridge.

Most visitors are taken to **Eling Park** at dusk to view the city. It is an attractive sight of steep lamplit streets sweeping down to the dark waters of the river below. First thing in the morning, walk down to the Chaotianmen docks; at the waterfront, a busy panorama unfolds—cruise ships, tugboats, rows of pontoons, and even a cable tramway to ease the ascent from shore to street of passengers as they disembark from their upstream cruise vessels.

The Jialing cable car starts its journey from Cangbai Lu to Xinlongqiao Jie on the north bank (*Jiangbei*). The five-minute ride is fun on a clear day. Another cable car, at Wanglongmen, on Xinhua Lu, spans the Yangzi to the south bank on Shangxin Jie.

While strolling around the city take note of the Chongqing banyan trees that line many of the streets. This large-leafed banyan (*Ficus lacor*, or *huang jiao shu* in Chinese) has been adopted as the city tree. It has no aerial roots as the traditional Chinese banyan, but instead its main roots twist around each other and are said to signify the united spirit of the Chongqing people, particularly during the war. The city flower is the camellia.

THE LUOHAN TEMPLE

This 19th-Century temple is glimpsed through an ornate passage whose walls are encrusted with rock carvings in the manner of Buddhist grottoes. Luohan are Buddhist saints; they traditionally number 500, although in this temple there are actually 524 statues of them. They are of recent vintage, the last of the originals having been destroyed during the Cultural Revolution (1966–76). The present statues were made by the Sichuan Fine Arts Institute in 1985.

PEOPLE'S CONGRESS HALL AND GALLERY OF SICHUAN FINE ARTS INSTITUTE

The institute was originally built as the administrative offices for southwest China in the early 1950s, but it is sometimes referred to as the Renmin Hotel as parts of it were converted to three-star accommodation. Its auditorium seats more than 4,200 people, making it the city's main venue for performances and meetings. The architectural style is a combination of Beijing's Temple of Heaven and the Forbidden City. It is certainly the most spectacular building in Chongqing and worth a look inside, if only to visit the gallery of the Sichuan Fine Arts Institute (*Sichuan Meishu Xueyuan*), which is housed in the two rooms either side of the entrance lobby. This is highly recommended, even for those with only a passing interest in Chinese art.

The institute is the only residential undergraduate- and graduate-level fine arts college in southwest China. Approximately 300 students per year enrol, coming from across China as well as from abroad. Founded in 1950, the college has sculpture, painting, crafts (including lacquerware, textile design, packaging design and ceramics) and teacher training departments. The institute itself is located at Huangjiaoping, on the Yangzi's northern bank, about half-an-hour's drive from the city-centre. However, the city-centre gallery is far more convenient for visitors and displays the best work of the institute's students teachers and professors. The work includes traditional Chinese and contemporary oil and water colour paintings and some woodcuts, which come in all sizes and styles, to suit a wide range of tastes. Helpful guides are on hand to answer questions and explain about the paintings and artists. There are frequently demonstrations of the various painting techniques.

Most of the items are for sale and prices are negotiable. Visitors are welcome to browse even if they have no intention to buy; the atmosphere is relaxed and thankfully free from the usual uncomfortable pressure to purchase that seems all too pervasive among arts and crafts shops frequented by tourists. Another reassuring difference is that the origin and quality of the artwork is guaranteed. It may even be possible to meet the artist who painted the work you wish to buy.

NEW CHONGQING MUNICIPAL ART MUSEUM & YANGZI THREE GORGES GALLERY

This museum, located on Renmin Lu opposite the People's Congress Hall, across from People's Square opened just a few years ago. Its numerous artefacts were transferred, taking some six months to do so, from the previous Chongqing Museum, located at 72 Pipashan Zhengjie. The new site has an exhibition area of 42,000 square metres and is divided into two main sections. They cover the development and culture of Chongqing itself as well as the Three Gorges and its history and culture. The displays include some of the archaeological treasures rescued from the Gorges before the rise in water level.

The People's Congress Hall, beside People's Square, bears a resemblance to the Temple of Heaven in Beijing. [Yin Chun]

The ground floor gallery exhibiting the history and culture of the Yangzi's Three Gorges consists of seven primary exhibition halls. The latter include a foyer followed by halls featuring the antiquity of the Three Gorges, legends and the history of ceramic writing, the mysterious Ba people, the power of Qin and Han, the cultural heritage of Jin and Tang, 1,000 years of cultural phenomena and the legacy of the Three Gorges.

The various subjects exhibited include the geological structure of the Three Gorges, natural scenery, famous sites, myths and legends, historic events, utilizing 500 photographs and reconstructed images, electric-powered maps, and various computerized programmes.

Of the 116 groups of objects on exhibit, the majority come from what had been accumulated in storage from excavations and collecting as of 1997, with the remainder from the old collections of the Chongqing Cultural Relics and Three Gorges units. The collection also contains some of the objects recovered from the Three Gorges area before it was flooded.

Extensive late-Neolithic remains in the principal Three Gorges region are from the Daxi culture (ca. 5000–3200 BCE) and the Chujialing culture (3200–2300 BCE), but it is the Ba culture sites that have most excited archaeologists. The Ba people can be traced from late-Neolithic origins to the Ming Dynasty (1368–1644 CE), when records of this people mysteriously cease.

The museum's relics include early Neolithic ceramics, Ba cultural bronzes, Han mythical birds and a Han-Wei period ivory chessboard, a Southern Song gold belt, and Song and Yuan porcelain caches.

Some of the highlights of the collection are: 1) a 7,000-year-old ceramic *fu* basin excavated in 1999 from the lower strata at Yuxi in Fengdu county—the earliest intact Neolithic artefact from southwestern China; 2) a bronze *hu* fermented-beverage container with swing handle and coiled dragon décor from the Warring States period, excavated from a Ba person's tomb at Lijiaba in Yunyang county in 2000; 3) an exquisite two-sided bird-decorated bronze sword from the Warring States period, excavated in 1997 from a Ba person's tomb at Lijiaba in Yunyang; 4) a unique Ba Yue ceramic bird holding a pearl in its mouth, with displayed tail feathers, unearthed in 2001 from a burial site in Fengdu; 5) an inscribed ceramic and ivory chess board, predating the earliest of its kind (Song Dynasty), dating to the Han-Wei period; 6) an exquisite gold belt, 107 centimetres long, of 14 pieces featuring grape motifs dating from the Song Dynasty, excavated in 1986 from a burial site at the Nanquan People's Hospital; and 7) a Qinliang jade crowned helmet, called *hu*, that belonged to Ma Qiansheng, a person of high rank from Zhongzhou, who died in 1595 at the end of the Ming Dynasty.

Ground floor exhibition halls are as follows:

Hall 1: Ancient Three Gorges exhibits include: a) the history of the formation of the Three Gorges; b–c) geological views of the walls of the gorges; d) reconstruction of Early Man; e) distribution map of the Three Gorges; f) site remains of Wushan Man; g) site distribution map of Palaeolithic settlements in the Three Gorges; h) discovery of the Gulf of Gaojiazhen.

Hall 2: The Goddess Legend and the history of ceramic writing exhibits including: a) the cultural type of Shaopengzui; b) reconstruction of a Shaopengzui culture village; c) representative Neolithic artefacts; d) Yuxi culture; e) Daxi culture; f) the legend of Great Yu; g) bronze vessels of the Ba people; h) photographs of Lijiaba; i) the excavation of Lijiaba; j) Excavated objects from Lijiaba; k) views of Wu and Qutang gorges; l) Wu Gorge's Goddess Peak and its legend; m) site remains at Shaopengzui.

Hall 3: The mysterious Ba people exhibits include: a) sketch map of the Ba realm; b) Shuangyantang site; c) legends of the Ba people; d) excavation of Shuangyantang; e) site of Zhongba; f) Zhongba and dragon kilns; g) cultural relics; h) brine springs; i) Chujiao burial and Chu culture; j) Ba Yue dancing and Ba music; k) replicas of Ba burials.

Hall 4: Qin and Han exhibits include: a:) Zhang Fei Temple; b) excavations at Jiuxianping; c) Ziyang City site; d) the Spirit Bird; e) Qutang Gorge; f) Baidi City; g) excavations at Zhuque; h) excavations of Han burials; i) excavated artefacts.

Hall 5: The culture of Jin and Tang exhibits include: a) Precious Pagoda site; b) contents of burial sites; c) Buddhist images; d) the Yu River and tracking roads of the Western Jin; e) the myth of Guicheng (Ghost City); f) Iron Pillar at Kuimen (Qutang Gorge); g) representative poetry and scenic arts; h) remains at the Tang site of Yuxi; i) remains at Mingyueba; j) two Jin burials and artefactual remains from Dayuba; k) questions concerning salt and its health value.

Hall 6: Cultural exhibits spanning the last 1,000 years include: a) tracking roads of the Three Gorges; b) the large stele at Kuimen; c) remains of the Yuan Dynasty; d) excavation of a Song city; e) views of the Precious Stone Fortress (Shibaozhai); f) peoples of the Three Gorges; g) Xinjia and Changshou Huoshenmiao kilns; h) ceramics and kilns from Zhongba and Kaixian; i) conservation of White Crane Ridge; j) preservation of the Three Gorges cultural relics; k) new cities of the remaining peoples; l) diagram of the storage areas of the Three Gorges.

Hall 7: Legacy of the Three Gorges exhibits include a) People's Hall and People's Auditorium; b) background of the Three Gorges Museum; c) map of China and Chongqing; d) relocation of Zhang Fei Temple; e) preservation of Precious Stone Fortress (*Shibaozhai*); f) preservation of Dachang residences; g) the historical and cultural legacy of New District cities.

PAINTERS' VILLAGE (*HUAJIA ZHI CUN*)

Painters' Village was established in the 1950s to nurture artists who would create paintings and lithographs to glorify the revolution. These state-sponsored artists came from all over China and included members of minority nationalities. They were paid a salary and their work was taken for use as propaganda, to exhibit overseas, or to give to foreign dignitaries as gifts. During the Cultural Revolution the artists were driven away and many of their works destroyed.

In 1984 the government established a gallery and invited overseas artists to visit and exchange ideas. Some of the work produced at the Village was purchased by overseas museums for their collections, other work appears in the China National Art Gallery. Only a few original artists survive today—aged 50-something to a sprightly mid-80s. Previously they enjoyed what, for China, were excellent conditions. Since China embarked on economic reforms, however, the artists have had to become commercial, as the government no longer buys all their work. A small percentage from what is sold supplements their meagre salaries.

In addition to the aforementioned challenges, the artists now face a new one. The site of the Village and its old buildings have given way to a river-crossing bridge and a new estate project respectively. Artists now have shops near the city zoo, inside People's Hall and in the Chinese Art Gallery near Chongqing airport. The Village itself may be relocated near the Red Crag Revolutionary Memorial Hall by late 2007, pending approval.

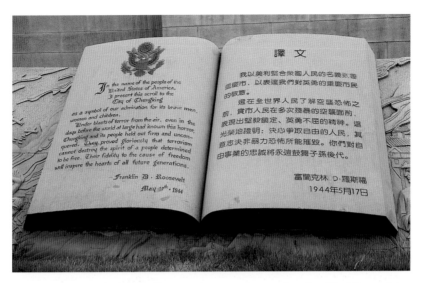

This memorial outside the Stilwell Museum bears an inscription from Franklin D Roosevelt in which he praises the 'brave men women and children' of Chongqing. 'They proved gloriously that terrorism cannot destroy the spirit of a people determined to be free.' [Kevin Bishop]

STILWELL MUSEUM

The museum, which was established in conjunction with the Stilwell Foundation in the United States and the Foreign Affairs Bureau in Chongqing, is dedicated to General Joseph Stilwell (1883–1946). Stilwell was sent to China in 1942 by then US President Roosevelt and served as Chief of Staff to Chiang Kai-shek and Commander-in-Chief of the American forces in the China-Burma-India theatre until 1944 when the threat of the Japanese Imperial Army was finally overcome. General Stilwell was instrumental in ridding Asia of that threat.

The museum is located at 63 Jialingxin Lu in the actual house occupied by General Stilwell during the war. The house is a tribute to his daughters, Alison and Nancy, who devoted so much time and effort in bringing this project to fruition in 1992. The building was re-opened in March 2003 after extensive renovation. The ground floor is a reconstruction of the layout during Stilwell's residence. Downstairs in the basement are several rooms displaying a wealth of archival photographs documenting such achievements as the Hump Flight Route over the Himalayas, the Dixie Mission, the exploits of the Flying Tigers, and the participation of Merrill's Marauders in the Burma campaign.

WARTIME POLITICS & POLITESSE

We landed at ten o'clock at Chungking. The air strip was a narrow island in the Yangtze, beneath the cliffs. For two months a year, this island lay under sixty feet of water and was subject to weird nightly rises in the river level. When we circled to land, I saw Chungking on the cliff top, looking like a greyish brown expanse of rubble ...

From the riverbed airstrip to the city of Chungking on the high bluff above, you toiled up a precipice of steps. I don't know how we reached the dreamed-of loaned house ...

We stayed in Chungking for several weeks but the place returns to me only in flashes. It was never meant to be a capital city, its sole advantage being that the Japanese couldn't reach it ...

Two visits stand out with rare clarity though I didn't know at the time how exceptional they were. The Generalissimo and Madame Chiang invited us to lunch, an intimate foursome. The Generalissimo wanted to hear news of the Canton front. Their house was modest, also furnished by Grand Rapids including doilies but clean and thug-free. Display in Chungking was useless. Madame Chiang did not stint herself when abroad, once taking a whole floor at the Waldorf. Madame Chiang, still a beauty and a famous vamp, was charming to UC and civil to me. Madame Chiang translated. UC and I agreed that the Generalissimo understood English as well as we did. He was thin, straight-backed, impeccable in a plain grey uniform and looked embalmed. I didn't take to him but felt rather sorry for him; he had no teeth. Reporting this later to an American Embassy wallah, he exclaimed over the honour showered on us, it was the highest compliment to be received by the Generalissimo with his teeth out.

I have been fascinated to find careless casual notes on that luncheon conversation. As I reconstruct it, the Generalissimo asked UC what he thought of some articles that had appeared in the Western press about the Chinese Communists; neither of us had read them and anyway had no opinions. The Generalissimo then went on to state that the Communists were 'skilful propagandists without much fighting ability. The CP doesn't possess the military strength and the government has no need to resort to force against them. If the CP tries to create trouble, injurious to the war, the government would use little measures to deal with them as disciplinary questions arose. The Fourth Route Army incident in China was very insignificant. Intensive CP propaganda in the

The river's rise hasn't put Chongqing's bang bang jung (stick or pole army) out of work. Steep slopes and long staircases are still part of the city's topography, despite the lessening of the initial haul from the river's edge, and porters continue to ply their trade. [Erik Potter]

US made America believe the CP was necessary to the war of resistance. On the contrary, the CP was hampering the Chinese army.'

He repeated this, according to my notes, in various ways, four separate times. Madame Chiang then said she got letters from the US saying the Kuomintang (Chiang's) armies fired at the backs of the Fourth Route Army (Mao's men) while it was withdrawing according to orders; the Generalissimo said this was not true, his soldiers never fired on the Fourth Route Army and the Communists disarmed Kuomintang forces whenever possible, to get more weapons and territory. Madame Chiang said, 'We are not trying to crush them.'

If UC understood this talk, he didn't mention it to me. I would have been bored but I expected powerful people to be boring; it comes from no one interrupting or arguing or telling them to shut up. The more powerful the more boring. With thirty-five years' hindsight, I see that the Chiangs were pumping propaganda into us, as effective as pouring water in sand. We had no idea of what was really going on in China, not that the Generalissimo and Madame Chiang, to whom power was all, feared the Chinese Communists not the Japanese. They were not fools. The Japanese would disappear some day; historically the Japanese were like an attack of boils. The true threat to the Chiangs' power lay in the people of China and therefore in the Communists who lived among and led the people. I didn't need political expertise to decide, in a few hours, that these two stony rulers could care nothing for the miserable hordes of their people and in turn their people had no reason to love them. An overlord class and tens of millions of expendable slaves was how China looked to me. War wasn't excuse enough for the terrible wretchedness of the people.

Madame Chiang and UC were hitting it off all right until I thrust my oar in. I asked Madame Chiang why they didn't take care of the lepers, why force the poor creatures to roam the streets begging. She blew up. The Chinese were humane and civilised unlike Westerners; they would never lock lepers away out of contact with other mortals. 'China had a great culture when your ancestors were living in trees and painting themselves blue.' Which ancestors? Apes or ancient Britons? I was furious and sulked. To appease me, Madame Chiang gave me a peasant's straw hat which I thought pretty and a brooch of jade set in silver filigree which I thought tacky. I didn't know how to refuse these gifts and was not appeased. UC behaved with decorum until we had done our bowing and scraping and departed. Then he said, laughing like a hyena, 'I guess that'll teach you to take on the Empress of China.'

'Why don't they do something for their people, instead of bragging about their past? All the big shots we've met don't give a damn about anything except their perks and their power. I wouldn't trust any of them. This is a rotten place. What's the matter with them?'

'Whatchumacallit. Maybe. More or less.'

In the market, a tall blonde Dutch woman, wearing a man's felt hat and a flowered cotton dress over trousers, approached me furtively and asked if we wanted to see Chou En-lai. The name Chou En-lai meant nothing to me; I said I would ask UC. I told UC that some sort of loon had sidled up to me in the market with this proposition and he said, 'Oh yes, he's a friend of Joris.' Joris Ivens, a darling man, is a Dutch documentary film maker who worked in China in 1938 or 1939. The Dutch woman had instructed me to return to the market with my answer. There followed a scene straight from James Bond but long preceding James Bond.

Our orders were to wander around the next day, until sure we were not tracked by our own thugs or any others, and meet in the market. The Dutch lady then led us through a maze of alleys, further throwing off pursuit. Finally we were bundled into rickshaws and blindfolded for the last lap. Blindfolds removed, we found ourselves in a small whitewashed cell, furnished with a table and three chairs, Chou En-lai behind the table. I was semi-stuffy, as I thought we were playing cops and robbers and was always quick to disapprove of silliness in others. I have no idea what Chou was doing or how he handled his life in Chungking where he was in constant danger.

Chou wore an open-neck short-sleeved white shirt, black trousers and sandals, the dress of an underpaid clerk. He too had a translator. We spoke French but knew by his brilliant amused eyes that he understood without translation. Unneeded interpreters may have been an inscrutable Oriental custom or maybe they served as living tape recorders. In any case, none of the stickiness of translation hampered us. For the first time and only time we were at home with a Chinese. We laughed at the same jokes. I suppose UC told him about the Canton front. Neither of us could have asked intelligent questions about the Long March, the Communists, where they were, and how they were operating, because we didn't know anything about these subjects, nor know who Chou was. He was a Communist living underground which made sense, thinking back belatedly and dimly to Malraux's La Condition Humaine, wherein Chiang was depicted ordering Communists to be thrown live into the boilers of locomotives. (I blush to remember my ignorance.)

UC was knowledgeable in exact detail about anything that interested him but China had not been on his list. Chou must have thought us brainless boobs of the first water, though that didn't affect our shared merriment. I wish I had Chou quotations to pass on to posterity but don't remember a word. Anyway we had listened to words until we were punch-drunk. It wasn't what Chou said, but what he was. He sat in his bare little room, in his nondescript clothes, and he was Somebody. We thought Chou a winner, the one really good man we'd met in China; and if he was a sample of Chinese Communists then the future was theirs. As for me, I was so captivated by this entrancing man that if he had said, take my hand and I will lead you to the pleasure dome of Xanadu, I would have made sure that Xanadu wasn't in China, asked for a minute to pick up my toothbrush and been ready to leave.

Months later, we were convoked to Washington to answer questions about China. We went surlily and told those desk Intelligence Officers that the Communists would take over China, after this war. Why? Because the Chiang lot were hell and it was hypocritical bilge to talk about Chinese democracy, there was less than none, and the people would welcome any change, even two-headed men from Mars, but as it happened the best man in the country was a Communist and it was safe to assume he had some comrades like him. We were called Cassandras as usual and branded fellow-travellers as usual. I was astonished when Chou surfaced as Foreign Minister of the new China, that lovely man from the whitewashed cellar in Chungking. All documentary films and travel books about Chou's China show that it is an immeasurable, almost inconceivable, improvement over Chiang's China. Never mind that it would be deadly for people like us; people like us were a drop in that remembered ocean of human misery.

Martha Gellhorn, Travels with Myself and Another, 1978

A gifted writer, Gellhorn (1908–1998) is more literarily noted for her war correspondence than for her five novels, 14 novellas and two collections of short stories. She took umbridge to being also noted for her brief marriage to Ernest Hemingway. Her refusal to be eclipsed by this association is evident in this recount of their 1941 adventures in China where he is simply referred to as "UC" (Unwilling Companion). Gellhorn, sent by Collier's to ostensibly cover the Sino-Japanese war, and UC gained the audience of opposing factions Generalissimo Chiang Kai-shek and Communist Chou En-lai.

(Right, far right) Scenes around the narrow streets of the ancient town of Ciqikou, beside the Jialing River in the northwest of Chongqing. [Kevin Bishop]

RED CRAG VILLAGE (HONGYAN CUN) AND GUI YUAN

Both these are now memorial museums to the 1949 revolutionary activities in the city. In the 1930s and '40s, during the period of co-operation between the Guomindang government and the Chinese Communist Party against the Japanese aggressors, these buildings were the offices of the Communist Party and the Red Army. Mao Zedong stayed in Gui Yuan House during his brief stay in Chongqing in 1945.

ANCIENT TOWN OF CIQIKOU

Situated on the south bank of the Jialing Jiang, in Shapingba District, about a half an hour's drive from the city centre, is the ancient town of Ciqikou (literally meaning 'porcelain mouth', or more accurately, port). The town used to be a centre for porcelain production and was located beside the river to facilitate its transportation.

Formerly known as Longyin (Hidden Dragon) Town, after the emperor's family fled here at the demise of the Ming Dynasty, the town has its origins in the Song Dynasty, although the present buildings date from the late Qing. It is very rare in modern China to find such a well-preserved example of an old town within a big city environment. What makes Ciqikou so interesting is that it is not a reconstruction or a tourist theme park, but a living town whose residents go about their daily lives, albeit under the gaze of visitors as they wander the tree-lined, flagstone-paved streets. It is inevitable that some of the shops should turn their attention to the tourist market, but there are just as many teahouses and restaurants that are clearly patronized by the local population.

Rock sculpture at Dazu Buddhist Grottoes, (above) the 'Revolving Wheel', Beishan;
(below) the keeper of hens. [Ingrid Morejohn]

CHONGQING ZOO

Chongqing Zoo (*Chongqing Dongwuyuan*), which can be found at 1 Xijiao Yi Cun, Juilongpo District, is well known for its Golden Hair Monkeys, South China Tigers and Lesser Pandas, but is most renowned for its Giant Panda exhibit. China reportedly has more than 180 pandas living in captivity. A 2002 census by Chinese authorities indicated there were nearly 1,600 Giant Pandas left in the wild, but a more recent study conducted by Chinese and British scientists suggests there may be as many as 3,000.

In 2006, Chongqing Zoo's famous Giant Panda Ya Ya was paired with an 11-year-old male Ling Ling, from Wolong Giant Panda Protection and Research Center in Sichuan Province. Ya Ya and Ling Ling reportedly watched a mating video and afterward they proceeded to breed. The pairing was successful and in September Ya Ya gave birth to a set of twins, they were her first cubs. However, tragedy struck when she lost one of her twin cubs just days after having given birth.

Apart from having one of China's best Giant Panda exhibits, if not the best exhibit, Chongqing Zoo has an assortment of other protected national animals, and the zoo is a favourite with locals and tourists alike.

SIGHTS AROUND CHONGQING

DAZU BUDDHIST GROTTOES

Dazu is famous for its monumental religious sculptures. This unassuming county town, 165 kilometres (103 miles) northwest of Chongqing, has 40 Buddhist grottoes secreted among its terraced hillsides containing about 50,000 carvings. The remoteness of the location has protected the caves from vandalism and the painted sculptures are in excellent condition.

None of the carvings date before the last two decades of the Tang Dynasty (618–907), when the more famous cave temples in northern China—at Dunhuang, Yungang and Longmen—had long since been completed. By that relatively late date, Buddhist sculpture had broken away completely from the Indo-Hellenistic influences so evident in the earlier Buddhist caves, and evolved a distinctly Chinese style. This development is amply illustrated in the grottoes at Beishan and Baodingshan, the two most stunning petroglyphic sites at Dazu.

Local legend has it that 'Dazu'—literally Big Foot—commemorates an outsize footprint left on the bed of a Baodingshan pond by Sakyamuni (the historical Buddha). 'Dazu' also means Great Sufficiency, and the county town is set amidst lush fields where grain, fruit, fish and pigs are farmed. Half the rolling, verdant, timeless landscape is water, with ribbons of irrigated terraces broken by spindly trees. The most comfortable way to reach the caves is to hire a car. The ride over hilly country will take about two hours, and the return journey can be easily made in one day.

OLD CHINA HAND ON DECK

Memorable experiences, and some unexpected problems, during a decade spent on China's Yangzi River.

By Bill Hurst

Few modern travellers who venture along the world's third-longest river would dispute the simple yet striking words of noted American author, Pearl Buck, whose writings still ring true: "There is no river in the world equal to the Yangzi for beauty and cruelty," she wrote. "The loveliest scenery is to be found along its curving shores. Islands feathery with bamboo and studded with alluvial deposits, little villages with cobbled streets running down to the river, cities whose walls guard them on three sides, and the Yangzi has them all. It has spoiled me for any other river."

Known to the Chinese as the Changjiang, or "Long River," the Yangzi is China's largest, forming a vital artery for trade and commerce over the centuries. But it is only in recent times that the Yangzi has been explored by Westerners such as Archibald Little, who introduced steam-powered ships to the upper reaches at the turn-of-the-last century, and the intrepid Victorian explorer Isabella Bird. What took them weeks of harrowing hardships and dogged endurance can now be accomplished in just a few days. Modern winches have replaced the teams of labourers who often risked life and limb hauling river craft weighing more than 272 metric tonnes (300 tons) past the worst of the rapids. Modern navigational aids have made traversing the river much safer. Sailing junks have all but disappeared. Yet despite these changes, the river itself remains the same, and the way of life of the people who inhabit its banks has hardly changed in 1,000 years. One other name must be added to the list of Western pioneers, that of Lars-Eric Lindblad. For it was he who opened up the river to the modern-day traveller, revealing towns and villages hardly known to the outside world and seldom seen by any foreigners. His farsightedness and faith in the future of tourism along the river encouraged the Chinese authorities to allow him the use of the MS Kun Lun, the now-famous vessel that was originally built for the late Chairman Mao. She carried some 36 passengers in magnificent, spacious accommodations (compared with the 700–900 passengers carried aboard her sister ships in the "East is Red" fleet). In the fall of 1979, the first group of adventurous travellers set sail on a remarkable river cruise from Nanjing to Chongqing.

It is difficult to be impersonal when writing about the Yangzi. My own involvement with the river began when I received a cable from Lars inviting me to be the expedition leader on that inaugural cruise. The last place on earth that I dreamed of visiting was China!

At that time I was conducting safaris in East Africa: little did I know then that the entire course of my life would be changed by a love for China and its peoples, which has brought me back to the river for the past few decades. Since then, many hundreds of cruises have come and gone, yet that maiden voyage remains the most memorable of all. The weeks of preparation and planning by the Chinese authorities had alerted the local inhabitants of our impending arrival. For most of them, it would be the first time that they had laid eyes on a foreigner.

There were many remarkable experiences during that first cruise, but the most overwhelming was our visit to the port of Wanxian, where many thousands of curious onlookers greeted our arrival. Coloured flags and banners proclaimed "Welcome" and "Friendship to American Friends." Loudspeakers blared out martial music. Deep feelings of warmth and friendship were exchanged with not a single word uttered. Our normally exuberant group fell silent, overcome by sheer emotion.

At the many banquets hosted by the Chinese along the river, endless toasts were made to the eternal friendship between the Chinese and American peoples—a friendship which, it was hoped, would flow as long and as deep as the Yangzi River itself.

The maiden voyage of the MS Kun Lun as a tourist vessel brought Caucasions to a generation of Chinese who had never witnessed such a spectacle, which thousands thronged to see wherever the vessel moored, such as here at Shibaozhai (see page 88). [Bill Hurst]

Special Topic

We enjoyed perfect weather during our passage through the spectacular Three Gorges. Their uncanny natural beauty has been an everlasting source of inspiration for countless poets and painters over the centuries. And the many faces of the river and its surroundings have been captured through the artistry of photographers such as Wong How Man.

But the most important aspect of travel on this great river is hard to truly capture on canvas or film. Not only on that maiden voyage, but on every voyage since, the most rewarding and lasting memories are of the Chinese people themselves: their courtesy, their generous hospitality, their quick smiles, and above all their friendship extended freely to us all. We have much to learn from this great culture, and the Chinese have much to learn from us. It will be a long process to bridge the abyss that separates our different cultures.

I felt strongly then—as I do now—that only through personal contacts between people can we ever hope for true understanding. Before each Yangzi River cruise it was necessary to bring on board essential supplies that were unobtainable in China (though the situation has improved greatly since 1979). For our first cruise, I lugged in 20 crates of such supplies, which completely mystified the Customs officials in Canton. Why, they wanted to know, was I carrying toilet brushes and detergents? What possible use would I have for an ice-making machine when the weather in China was cool? Perhaps the boxes of wines and liquors were easier to understand.

On arrival in Nanjing with my precious cargo I was met my Charlie Bozak, who was at the time Vice President of Lindblad Travel's China Division. He had seen the *Kun Lun* two months before, and noted that the bathrooms had become heavily stained during the many years the ship had lain idle. Only strong, Western-produced detergents could overcome this visible problem.

It was only later that the story filtered through to me of how the Chinese officials' concept of the capitalist West was totally shattered in a single moment when they gazed, aghast, at Charlie—a "high-ranking official" of a prominent foreign company, and one with the power to sign contracts-down on his knees scrubbing out bathrooms.

Even today, this first encounter with the strange ways of Westerners remains a talking point along the river, and is cited as an example for all officials to follow.

During the early 1980s the *Kun Lun* settled down to a series of cruises, some of which lasted 15 days, taking passengers along the entire navigable length of the Yangzi, from Shanghai to Chongqing, a distance of some 2,575 kilometres (1,600 miles). These were days of discovery and experimentation. As new ports were opened up to us, we had to devise new shore programmes that were designed to include as much contact with people as possible, in order to create a better understanding of the Chinese culture and way of life.

The Yangzi River offers an ideal opportunity to observe the Chinese country-side, where 80 per cent of the population still lives today. A visit to a small village or a local farmers' market often proves to be the highlight of a day's activities.

However, some of my attempts to introduce interesting new sightseeing programmes proved a disaster. For example, at the large industrial city of Wuhan the local travel service suggested we might like to visit a food processing factory. "Why not?", I thought, "Food has international appeal." The multi-storey factory was equipped with the latest technology. Live pigs entered the slaughterhouse on the fifth floor, to eventually emerge as sausages and canned pork on the ground floor. Surely it would be a fascinating visit. Only a few hardy souls made it past the slaughterhouse!

My efforts to broaden the ship's excellent Chinese menu, by introducing dishes to suit the Western palate, caused problems of a different kind. I never imagined that the addition of a simple fresh green salad, which most of us foreigners craved, would cause a major incident, but it did.

Returning to the *Kun Lun* one day with a large Chinese cabbage, I was asked by the chief dining room steward what I proposed to do with it. He was visibly horrified to learn that we were planning to eat it raw at dinner that evening. He immediately called the ship's Political Commissar, who decided that this was a matter for the Captain to investigate. The Captain, in turn, refused to accept any

The Kun Lun's *master chef would prepare delicious and sumptuous sculptures with themes such as butterflies, swans or pandas —a rarely found culinary expertise today. [Bill Hurst]*

Special Topic

responsibility and summoned the Doctor, who eventually admitted that if properly washed, green cabbage could safely be eaten raw. All agreed, however, that I was to be held personally responsible for the health of every passenger on board.

Needless to say, the salad proved a great success at dinner. However, the apprehension of the ship's crew was understandable, as no Chinese would ever eat raw vegetables, or use water that was not boiled.

Each voyage brings new adventures, and the constantly changing moods of the river bring new challenges. Landslides are a constant threat, and known geological faults are carefully monitored. Flood waters that regularly raise the river level in the Gorges by more than 30 metres (100 feet) demand exceptional skills of the river pilots. The low waters of winter expose dangerous shoals and rapids and the constricted flow leaves no room for error. The expertise of the pilots and ships' captains, many of whose forefathers were engaged in the same profession, did not come from any textbook: they were acquired through sailing these same waters for many years until every rock, every sandbar, and every eddy was indelibly etched in their minds.

Navigation of the Xiling Gorge improved as a result of the construction of the giant Gezhou Dam, built to meet the ever increasing demand for electricity in the region. The recent completion of the Three Gorges Project further improves river

Though built for Chairman Mao, he reportedly never actually sailed aboard the MS Kun Lun, *despite artistic renderings depicting him entertaining guests on its stern. [Bill Hurst]*

navigation; the dams bear testimony to the ingenuity and determination of the Chinese people. However, it was at the Gezhouba, passing through one of the giant locks, that I learned my most important lesson in Chinese logic. How much, I asked the Captain, does the ship pay for passage through the locks?

"Nothing," he replied, with a smile that indicated the question was absurd. He went on to explain that the Gezhou Dam authorities had indeed demanded payment from the various shipping companies, but these demands were refused on the grounds that before the dam was built the ships experienced no delays passing this point—but now that they suffered considerable inconvenience, the authorities should actually pay compensation to the shipping companies. Who could argue with that?

By the early 1980s, new cruise ships were being built to further develop tourism along the river. In the winter of 1984, when Lars was visiting Chongqing, the Chinese invited him to view the plans of a new 2,268-tonne (2,500-ton) ship under construction that incorporated the very latest ideas in hull design.

Ever eager to grasp an opportunity, Lars negotiated a joint-venture partnership which would ensure that the MS Bashan, as she was to be named, would be the most comfortable and sophisticated cruise vessel ever built in China to cater to the needs of the modern traveller.

The ship's interior was designed by Sonja Lindblad, and skilled craftsmen from the United States and Hong Kong were flown to Chongqing to supervise the internal construction and decoration. All plumbing fixtures and fittings, furnishings, fabrics, and lighting were imported, to insure the highest quality. The Bashan embarked on her maiden voyage. The extraordinary success of this shipsaw an ever increasing number of passengers on Yangzi River cruises. The future looked bright and promising. That was until one fateful summer day in the late Eighties.

The events of that day are still fresh in my mind. I was in China at the time, but left with the departing passengers from the Bashan immediately after our arrival in Chongqing. The situation was difficult at best, China seemed at odds with itself. It was with the deepest personal sadness that I bade farewell to the ship's crew. We wondered if we would ever see each other again.

Fortunately, the situation was not completely untenable. Lars was determined that we would never completely abandon China, and in early July I returned to Chongqing at his request to complete plans for 1990. I was delighted to be reunited with old friends again, and to learn how the Chinese felt about recent events.

On the surface it appeared that nothing had changed, but I was soon to detect an underlying sense of betrayal. Why, I was asked, do Americans want to punish and hurt the people of China?

This was the most difficult question I had ever been asked. How could I possibly explain sanctions to people innocent of punitive economics, knowing that these very same people would be the ones to suffer? In their view, the situation had returned to normal in China, but still the *Bashan* lay idle, and the crew's income had dropped, along with their standard of living. Why had Americans deserted China, and were all the pledges of friendship merely hollow words?

I explained, as best I could, that it was because of deep feelings of the American people towards them, the Chinese people, that the Americans had

decided not to visit China, in order to make their views known. This Western line of reasoning simply did not make sense to them.

The future is impossible to predict, but I feel particularly privileged to have had the opportunity to get to know the Chinese. I hope that tourists will continue to enjoy the Yangzi River, as there is much to see and learn during a voyage along this mighty waterway. I would encourage those who have not yet been to make the journey, to do so and for those who have already experienced the wonders of the Yangzi to return again.

Kenyan-born Bill Hurst is based in Hong Kong, but for a decade was Lindblad Travel's permanent Expedition Leader aboard the MS Kun Lun, *the* MS Bashan *and other vessels on the Yangzi River, voyaging often as much as 46 times per year. With Lars-Eric Lindblad, Hurst first explored the Yangzi in 1979 when China was re-opening itself after several decades of seclusion from the rest of the world. Affectionately known by locals all along the Yangzi as Gu Lau He (Old Man River), Hurst continues to travel along the Long River. His accomplishments are not only noted by his extended Chinese family and circle of friends, but many a Westerner who has been inspired to follow in his wake. This article has been edited from its first publication in* Intrepid, *the magazine of the Intrepids Club, spring 1990.*

(Left) *The large crews aboard even smaller vessels, as seen here circa 1979, are no longer required having been replaced by modern conveniences such as motors, winches and state-of-the-art electronic navigational systems. [Bill Hurst]*

(Following pages) *On a tributary of the Yangzi above Fuling, a schoolgirl does her homework in a village unfortunately slated for inundation. [Yin Chun]*

Special Topic

SAILING THE YANGZI

I sailed 1,500 miles downstream, from Chungking to Shanghai. Every mile of it was different; but there were 1,200 miles I did not see. It crosses ten provinces, 700 rivers are joined to it—all Yangtze statistics are hopeless, huge and ungraspable; they obscure rather than clarify. And since words have a greater precision than numbers, one day I asked a Chinese ship captain if he thought the river had a distinct personality.

He said, 'The mood of the river changes according to the season. It changes every day. It is not easy. Navigating the river is always a struggle against nature. And there is only one way to pilot a ship well.' He explained—he was smiling and blowing smoke out of his nostrils—'It is necessary to see the river as an enemy.'

Later a man told me that in the course of one afternoon he had counted nine human corpses bobbing hideously down the river.

The Yangtze is China's main artery, its major waterway, the source of many of its myths, the scene of much of its history. On its banks are some of its greatest cities. It is the fountainhead of superstition; it provides income and food to half the population. It is one of the most dangerous rivers in the world, in some places one of the dirtiest, in others one of the most spectacular. The Chinese drink it and bathe in it and wash clothes in it and shit in it. It represents both life and death. It is a wellspring, a sewer and a tomb; depthless in the gorges, puddle-shallow at its rapids. The Chinese say if you haven't been up the Great River, you haven't been anywhere.

They also say that in the winter, on the river, the days are so dark that when the sun comes out the dogs bark at it. Chungking was dark at nine in the morning, when I took the rattling tin tram on the cog railway that leads down the black crags which are Chungking's ramparts, down the sooty cliffs, past the tenements and billboards ('Flying Pigeon Bicycles', 'Seagull Watches', 'Parrot Accordions') to the landing stage. A thick, sulphurous fog lay over the city, a Coketown of six million… Doctor Ringrose, who was from Leeds, sniffed and said, 'That is the smell of my childhood.'

Paul Theroux, Sailing Through China, 1984

Literary Excerpt

Sails along the river are being gradually replaced by motorised vessels. While sailing sampans are still to be seen, their larger cousins, sailing junks, are now an unknown sight. [Lu Jin]

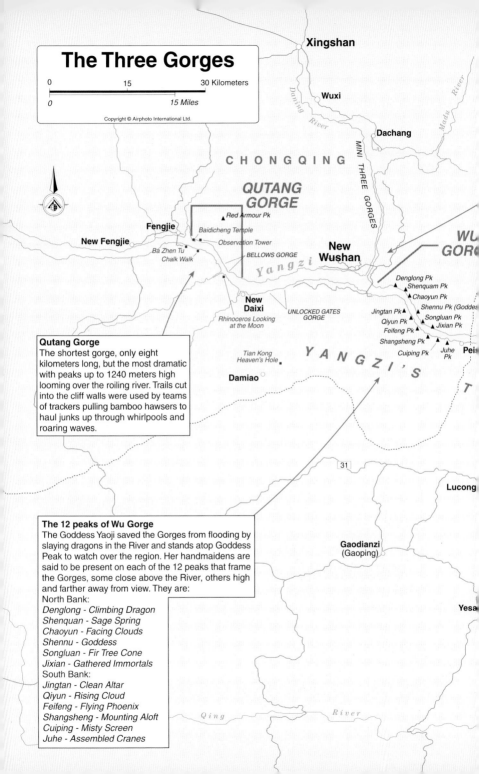

The Three Gorges

0   15   30 Kilometers
0   15 Miles

Copyright © Airphoto International Ltd.

Xingshan

Wuxi

Dachang

Daning River

Mady River

CHONGQING

QUTANG GORGE

MINI THREE GORGES

▲ Red Armour Pk

Baidicheng Temple

Observation Tower

Fengjie

New Fengjie

Ba Zhen Tu
Chalk Walk

BELLOWS GORGE

New Wushan

WU GOR

Yangzi

New Daixi

Rhinoceros Looking at the Moon

UNLOCKED GATES GORGE

▲ Denglong Pk
▲ Shenquam Pk
▲ Chaoyun Pk
Jingtan Pk ▲   ▲ Shennu Pk (Goddes
Qiyun Pk ▲   ▲ Songluan Pk
Feifeng Pk ▲   ▲ Jixian Pk
Shangsheng Pk ▲
Cuiping Pk ▲   Juhe   Pei
            Pk

Tian Kong
Heaven's Hole

Damiao

YANGZI'S

T

31

Lucong

Gaodianzi
(Gaoping)

Yesa

Qing River

Qutang Gorge

The shortest gorge, only eight kilometers long, but the most dramatic with peaks up to 1240 meters high looming over the roiling river. Trails cut into the cliff walls were used by teams of trackers pulling bamboo hawsers to haul junks up through whirlpools and roaring waves.

The 12 peaks of Wu Gorge

The Goddess Yaoji saved the Gorges from flooding by slaying dragons in the River and stands atop Goddess Peak to watch over the region. Her handmaidens are said to be present on each of the 12 peaks that frame the Gorges, some close above the River, others high and farther away from view. They are:
North Bank:
Denglong - Climbing Dragon
Shenquan - Sage Spring
Chaoyun - Facing Clouds
Shennu - Goddess
Songluan - Fir Tree Cone
Jixian - Gathered Immortals
South Bank:
Jingtan - Clean Altar
Qiyun - Rising Cloud
Feifeng - Flying Phoenix
Shangsheng - Mounting Aloft
Cuiping - Misty Screen
Juhe - Assembled Cranes

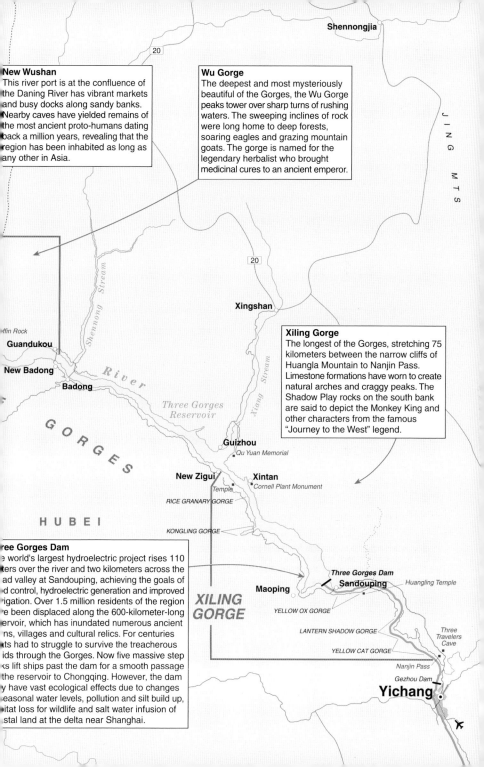

Shennongjia

20

New Wushan
This river port is at the confluence of the Daning River has vibrant markets and busy docks along sandy banks. Nearby caves have yielded remains of the most ancient proto-humans dating back a million years, revealing that the region has been inhabited as long as any other in Asia.

Wu Gorge
The deepest and most mysteriously beautiful of the Gorges, the Wu Gorge peaks tower over sharp turns of rushing waters. The sweeping inclines of rock were long home to deep forests, soaring eagles and grazing mountain goats. The gorge is named for the legendary herbalist who brought medicinal cures to an ancient emperor.

J I N G   M T S

20

Xingshan

Shennong Stream

ffin Rock

Guandukou

New Badong

Badong

R i v e r

Xiang Stream

Three Gorges Reservoir

G O R G E S

Xiling Gorge
The longest of the Gorges, stretching 75 kilometers between the narrow cliffs of Huangla Mountain to Nanjin Pass. Limestone formations have worn to create natural arches and craggy peaks. The Shadow Play rocks on the south bank are said to depict the Monkey King and other characters from the famous "Journey to the West" legend.

Guizhou
.Qu Yuan Memorial

New Zigui
Temple

Xintan
▪Cornell Plant Monument

RICE GRANARY GORGE

KONGLING GORGE

HUBEI

ree Gorges Dam
e world's largest hydroelectric project rises 110 ters over the river and two kilometers across the ad valley at Sandouping, achieving the goals of d control, hydroelectric generation and improved igation. Over 1.5 million residents of the region e been displaced along the 600-kilometer-long ervoir, which has inundated numerous ancient ns, villages and cultural relics. For centuries ts had to struggle to survive the treacherous ids through the Gorges. Now five massive step ks lift ships past the dam for a smooth passage the reservoir to Chongqing. However, the dam y have vast ecological effects due to changes easonal water levels, pollution and silt build up, itat loss for wildlife and salt water infusion of stal land at the delta near Shanghai.

XILING GORGE

Maoping

Three Gorges Dam
Sandouping

Huangling Temple

YELLOW OX GORGE

LANTERN SHADOW GORGE

Three Travelers Cave

YELLOW CAT GORGE

Nanjin Pass

Gezhou Dam

Yichang

THE EASTERN SICHUAN BASIN

Travellers using this guide should note that the riverside towns and historical sites are presented as they appear on the downstream journey from Chongqing. Although some description and background is retained for historical interest, readers should bear in mind that many of the towns have been at least partially, if not completely, submerged by the new reservoir. In some cases entire new towns were constructed above the final projected water level. The giant sluices of the Three Gorges Dam (*San Xia Ba*) were closed on 1st June 2003, and within about two weeks the water had reached the interim level of 135 metres (443 feet). It is planned to let the waters rise a further 40 metres (131 feet) to reach a final height of 175 metres (574 feet) by 2009. Meanwhile, most remaining old buildings that lie below this level are, if not in the process of being demolished, already razed to avoid them becoming submerged hazards to shipping.

FULING

The river Wu rises in distant Guizhou. Before reaching its confluence with the Yangzi, like many of the other tributaries it flows through remote and beautiful mountain scenery. Dams are planned, or being built, on a significant number of these tributary rivers with the subsequent disappearance of numerous picturesqe villages. Where the Wu feeds into the Yangzi, on the great river's south bank, stands the ancient city of Fuling, now immortalised in Peter Hessler's highly-acclaimed *River Town: Two Years on the Yangtze* (See Recommended Reading page 234). Hessler went to Fuling in 1996 as a 26-year-old Peace Corps volunteer, teaching English at a local college. His experiences there are encapsulated in *River Town* and, although he left Fuling, he continues to write about China. His experiences are related, and observations of Chinese culture captured, in *Oracle Bones: A Journey Between China's Past and Present*.

Some 2,000 years ago Fuling was the political centre of the Kingdom of Ba (fourth to second centuries BCE) and the site of its ancestral graves. Fuling is the connecting link in the water transportation routes between northern Guizhou and eastern Sichuan. The town and its surrounding area are rich in such produce as grain, lacquer and tung oil, and the local culinary specialities are hot pickled mustard tuber, Hundred-Flower sweet wine and pressed radish seeds. In 1972 archaeologists excavated graves from the Kingdom of Ba, and among the finds were ancient musical instruments. Today the city has a population exceeding 1.1 million, though only about 300,000 live within Fuling proper, due to its lower levels being submerged. A high wall faces the reservoir to hold the waters back.

The most important archaeological site in Fuling is a set of ancient carvings and inscriptions on what is known as **White Crane Ridge**. This lies about one kilometre (a half mile) west of the town, near the south bank of the river. It was saved from a watery grave, having been preserved *in situ* in a specially constructed, 250-metre long, underwater museum, that was slated for completion in late 2006.

On the ridge of hard, purple sandstone are carved ancient water level marks in the form of 14 scaled fish and inscriptions of nearly 30,000 characters referring to the hydrology of the river at this point. There is also a sculpture of Guanyin, the Goddess of Mercy. The earliest of the stone fish, two of which are carp exceeding one metre in length, were carved in the Tang Dynasty (618–907). They used to be visible only at the lowest water level, which occurred perhaps once every decade or so. It was said that when the eye of the carp appeared there would be a bumper harvest. Other inscriptions date from the Song Dynasty. The inscriptions contain valuable hydrological data covering a span of 1,200 years, from the first year of the Tang Dynasty to the early 20th Century, and describe 72 different years when the water in the Yangzi River fell to record levels.

The carved-stone carp of White Crane Ridge were used to measure the rise and fall of the river level. The Three Gorges Reservoir has permanently submerged this ridge and its carp. [Lu Jin]

Sichuan Basin

BOATS GREAT AND SMALL   by Judy Bonavia

The traditional Chinese boats that navigated the Yangzi were *sampan* (meaning three planks), the larger-sized *wupan* (five planks) and junks. Their sails were tall to capture any welcome breeze, and stiffened by bamboo battens. The sculling oar, or *yulo*, was extremely long with normally four men working it. Mats overhead provided shelter for passengers; decks were covered with coils of bamboo rope. Local pilots were hired to negotiate the most difficult rapids. Their instructions were relayed to the harnessed trackers pulling the long hauling ropes—often far ahead of the boat—by a drum beaten at different rhythms. Large freight junks often required 300 or 400 trackers as well as groups of strong swimmers who would loosen the ropes should they snag on rocks along the way.

An eighth-century poem gives a compelling picture of the gruelling drudgery of a boat puller's life:

A Boatman's Song
Oh, it's hard to grow up at the way-station side!
The officials've set me to pullin' station boats;
Painful days are more, happy days are few,
Slippin' on water, walkin' on sand, lake birds of the sea;
Against the wind, upstream, a load of ten thousand bushels—
Ahead, the station's far away; behind, it's water everywhere!
Midnight on the dykes, there's snow and there's rain,
From up top our orders: you still have to go again!
Our clothes are wet and cold beneath our short rain cloaks,
Our hearts're broke, our feet're split, how can we stand the pain?
Till break of dawn we suffer, there's no one we can tell,
With one voice we trudge along, singing as we pull;
A thatch-roofed house, what's it worth,
When we can't get back to the place of our birth!
I would that this river turn to farm plots,
And long may we boatmen stop cursing our lots.
                                        Wang Qian (768–833)

They were truly beasts of burden, as observed by an American, William L Hall, and his wife, who spent several weeks on a small Chinese cargo-boat in 1922:

If the boat happens to turn about when it is struck by a cross-current,
a call from the pilot brings all the trackers to their knees or makes

them dig their toes into the dirt. Another call makes them either claw the earth or catch their fingers over projecting stones. Then they stand perfectly still to hold the boat. When it is righted, another call makes them let up gradually and then begin again their hard pull.

Passengers usually took *kuaize*—large *wupan*—and paid for the Yichang–Chongqing trip 185 cash for every 100 *li* (18 cents for every 50 kilometres). They would also supply wine for the crew, and incense and fireworks for a propitious journey. Going upriver, this journey used to take as long as 40–50 days in the high-water period and 30 days in low water, depending on the size of the boat, while the downriver trip could be completed in five to 12 days. At the end of the journey the passengers might buy some pork as a feast for the crew.

River life was varied along the Yangzi and its tributaries. Big junks, fitted out as theatres, sailed between the towns to give performances of Chinese opera or juggling. Some boats were built as hotels, offering accommodation to travellers arriving too late at night to enter the city gates. Others were floating restaurants and tea-houses, not to mention boats which were a source of livelihood as well as home to the numerous fisherfolk and their families.

Peasants along the lower and middle Yangzi first set eyes on foreign men-of-war and steamers when Britain's Lord Elgin journeyed as far as Wuhan (Hankou) in 1842. Although the Chinese had in fact invented the paddle wheel (worked probably by the treadmill system) for driving their battleships as early as the eighth century, paddle boats were not widely used. In an incident on Dongting Lake in 1135, they were proved positively useless when the enemy threw straw matting on the water and brought the paddle wheels to a stop. They seem not to have been used since.

With the opening up of the Yangzi ports to foreign trade in the latter half of the 19th century, foreign shallow draught paddle steamers and Chinese junks worked side by side. But the traditional forms of river transport slowly became obsolete, and were confined to the Yangzi tributaries for transporting goods to the distribution centres.

Early Western shipping on the Shanghai–Wuhan stretch of the river was dominated by Americans, whose experience of paddle steamers on the Mississippi and other rivers had put them to the fore. The American firm of Russell and Company was the leading shipping and trading concern in those years. A fifth of the foreign trade was in opium shipped up to Wuhan. By the late 1860s, British companies such as Jardine & Matheson and Butterfield & Swire had successfully challenged the American supremacy. Accommodation on the companies' river boats was luxurious, and trade was brisk.

Special Topic

The Wuhan–Yichang stretch was pioneered by an English trader, Archibald Little, who established a regular passenger service in 1884 with his small steamer Y-Ling. In his book *Through the Yangtse Gorges*, he described the bustling scene on the river:

The lively cry of the trackers rings in my ears, and will always be associated in my mind with the rapids of the Upper Yang-tse. This cry is 'Chor-Chor', said to mean 'Shang-chia', or 'Put your shoulder to it', 'it' being the line which is slung over the shoulder of each tracker, and attached to the quarter-mile-long tow-rope of plaited bamboo by a hitch, which can be instantaneously cast off and rehitched. The trackers mark time with this cry, swinging their arms to and fro at each short step, their bodies bent forward, so that their fingers almost touch the ground... Eighty or a hundred men make a tremendous noise at this work, almost drowning the roar of the rapids, and often half a dozen junks' crews are towing like this, one behind the other. From the solemn stillness of the gorge to the lively commotion of a rapid, the contrast is most striking.

Other companies soon followed, but none dared travel this route at night. Again, it was Archibald Little's perseverance that brought about steamship navigation through the gorges above Yichang to Chongqing. Acting as captain and engineer, he successfully navigated his 17-metre *Leechuan* up to Chongqing in 1898, though he still needed trackers to pull him over the worst rapids.

During the heyday of the Yangzi in the 1920s and 1930s, travel by steamer from Shanghai all the way up to Chongqing was luxurious though not entirely safe. Halfway, at Wuhan, passengers had to change to smaller boats for the rest of the journey.

After the establishment of the People's Republic of China, priority was placed on making the Yangzi safe for navigation all year round, and major rock obstructions were blown up in the Gorges. The Yangzi today is the vital economic artery of central China, with a highway network and many new bridges complementing the traditional port activites.Thousands of regular ferries and small river boats, offering a range of accommodation, overflow with passengers. The great lumbering river liners of the old 'East is Red' fleet are now mostly idle or scrapped, as air and bus transport is faster and competitive in price. There are now many luxury river cruise ships which ply the route from Chongqing to Wuhan or Yichang, with a few going to Nanjing and Shanghai.

Along the Yangzi are numerous styles of vessels and it is said that when sails were predominant, a trained eye could tell where a vessel was from by its sail rigging. [Bobby Chan sketches]

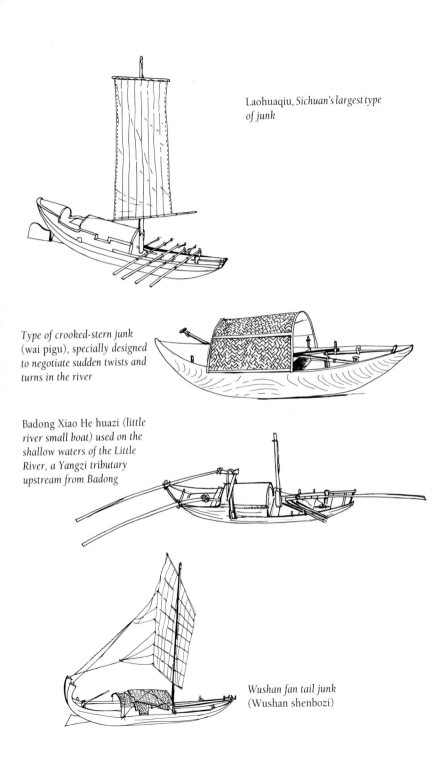

Laohuaqiu, *Sichuan's largest type of junk*

Type of crooked-stern junk (wai pigu), specially designed to negotiate sudden twists and turns in the river

Badong Xiao He huazi (*little river small boat) used on the shallow waters of the Little River, a Yangzi tributary upstream from Badong*

Wushan fan tail junk (Wushan shenbozi)

FENGDU

Fengdu, on the north bank of the river, 172 kilometres east of Chongqing, was in the past more popularly known as the 'City of Ghosts'. There is a temple here dedicated to the God of the Underworld.

The origin of the town's extraordinary reputation dates back to the Han Dynasty (206 BCE–220 CE) when two officials, Yin and Wang, became Daoist (Taoist) recluses here and eventually Immortals. When combined, their names mean 'King of the Underworld'. For many centuries, Fengdu was well known as a pilgrimage site, especially for the deceased, some of whom were said to be able to walk zombie-like to Fengdu for their judgment and rebirth. Less ambulatory souls would fly over the clouds and land at the 'Looking Back Pavilion' (*Huijing Lou*), to watch the funeral rites of their family. They would then drink a 'tea of forgetfulness' to erase all human memories before being reborn. The tea is still served in the tower, but without much effect on the living.

Today the upper town is thronged with tourists attracted by temples and shrines dedicated to the demons of the underworld. There is a new entrance to the original temple complex on **Minshan**, mid-mountain, which can be reached by cable-car. The temple overlooks the watery grave of the demolished lower old town, which is now completely submerged. However, the historical temples located on Minshan remain accessible, protected by a long dike at the foot of the mountain. A large new town has been established opposite, on the south bank.

A pilgrim to the old temple used to be able to purchase, for the sum of one dollar, a 'Passport to Heaven', stamped by the local magistrate and the abbot. Landmarks in the temple complex bear horrific names—Ghost Torturing Pass, Last Glance at Home Tower, Nothing-to-be-done Bridge. Fengdu's temples display instruments of torture and wild demon images. Shopkeepers kept a basin of water into which customers threw their coins: if they sank they were genuine, but if they floated the coins were ghost money and unacceptable. Boats would anchor in midstream rather than by the bank in case of attack by ghosts.

A large building in the likeness of the God of the Underworld rises over the old town, with a restaurant in his head. This monument overlooks the old temple complex on Minshan hill. An amusement park in the higher valley gives cart tours of the ghoulish imagery of the underworld, with automaton animation. It is pure kitsch, a daily Halloween, Chinese style. The town government also initiated a new attraction, on a mountain slope 15 kilometres (9 miles) northeast of the old town, the largest rock carving in the world. Hand cut from red sandstone, it depicts the God of the Underworld and is some 400 metres (1,312 feet) high, such that one can walk in one ear and out the other of the low-

Within Minshan's Gui Cheng (Ghost City) are these three arches of Nai He Qiao (The Bridge of No Return). Here, departed souls cross to the underworld to receive their judgement. [Yin Chun]

relief sculpture. A statue of the Goddess of Mercy stands on the top of his head, as if to keep away the ill omen of such an immense demonic visage. Boats now sail directly to this new attraction thanks to the raised reservoir water levels.

DINGFANG TOWERS

Just before reaching the town of Zhongxian, on the north bank, are the Dingfang Towers, or *que*. This monument was constructed during the Eastern Han Dynasty (25–220 CE). A *que* is a kind of ornamental tower, not uncommon during this period, which was usually constructed in front of religious buildings or royal tombs to show a person's status. The monument at Dingfang is a double *que* with two eaves and is of particular archaeological importance. It is planned to move the towers before they are inundated by the river. There are only 31 *que* still in existence in China, mostly in Sichuan and Chongqing.

ZHONGXIAN

There are two moving stories about how Zhongxian (Loyal County) was named. In the Warring States Period (475–221 BCE), Ba Manzi, a native of Zhongxian, became a general in the army of the Kingdom of Ba. Towards the end of the Zhou Dynasty the Kingdom of Ba was in a state of civil war, and Ba Manzi was sent to the Kingdom of Chu to beg for military assistance to put down the rebellion. The price demanded by Chu was the forfeit of three Ba cities. Once Chu's troops had helped restore stability to Ba, the King of Chu sent his minister to demand payment. Ba Manzi, however, said: 'Though I promised Chu the cities you will take my head in thanks to the King of Chu, for the cities of Ba cannot be given away', whereupon he cut off his own head. Receiving his minister's account, the King of Chu sighed: 'Cities would count as nothing had I loyal ministers like Ba Manzi.' He then ordered that Ba Manzi's head be buried with full honours.

The second tale is of another man of Zhongxian, the valiant general Yan Yan, who served the failing Eastern Han Dynasty (25–220 CE). Captured by the incumbent Shu general of the Three Kingdoms Period (220–265 CE) Zhang Fei, he refused to surrender, saying boldly: 'In my country we had a general who cut off his own head but we do not have a general who surrendered.' Enraged, Zhang Fei ordered Yan Yan's beheading. The doomed general remained perfectly calm as he asked simply, 'Why are you so angry? If you want to cut off my head then give the order, but there is no point in getting angry and upsetting yourself.' Zhang Fei was so deeply moved by Yan's loyalty and bravery in the face of death that he personally unbound him, treating him as an honoured soldier.

Traditionally, the thick bamboo hawsers used to haul junks over the rapids were made in this area, as the local bamboo is especially tenacious. Bamboo handicrafts are still a thriving industry today, while the local food speciality is Zhongxian beancurd milk. Part of the original town was submerged by the rising waters.

SHIBAOZHAI (PRECIOUS STONE FORTRESS)

Shibaozhai's Zhailouge Pavilion represents the first gem of Chinese architecture to be encountered on the downstream journey. From afar, the protruding 220-metre hill on the north bank appears to resemble a jade seal, and is so named. The creation of the hill is attributed to the goddess Nuwo, who caused a rock slide while she was redecorating the sky after a fierce battle between two warring dukes.

Shibaozhai Village was demolished prior to the completion of the Three Gorges Dam in 2003, though the Zhailouge Pavilion (pictured right, circa 1979) was saved. Before the final rise in water level, a protective coffer dam is being constructed around the pavilion and the rock against which it stands, and is to be completed October 2007. Ships can still dock nearby and Shibaozhai remains a popular tourist attraction. [Tom Nebbia]

A red pavilion hugs one side of this rock, which was detached from a cliff a kilometre-and-a-half away. The rock mass is in fact still migrating, moving a perceptible amount every year as it slides down the flanks of an anticline. The rising waters of the reservoir require a small coffer dam be built around it to protect Zhailouge, though it may have been cheaper, and perhaps even wiser, to raise and relocate the pavilion elsewhere. The migrating rock on which the temple is situated would make a protective dam susceptible to leaks, perhaps even failure. When the reservoir waters reach their maximum height, they will be level with the pavillion's first storey, the dam blocking the the ground level as viewed from the water. At the time of this printing, the protective dam was being built and the pavilion was not open to tourists. The Zhailouge pavilion's tall yellow entrance gate is decorated with lions and dragons and etched with an inscription inviting the visitor to climb the ladder and ascend into a 'Little Fairyland'.

The temple on top of Yuyin Shan was built during the reign of Emperor Qianlong (1736–96). Access was originally by an iron chain attached to the cliff. A nine-storey wooden pavilion was added in 1819 so that monks and visitors to the temple would not have to suffer the discomforts of the chain ascent. In 1956 three more storeys were added. Each floor is dedicated to famous generals of the Three Kingdoms Period (220–265 CE), local scholars and renowned Chinese poets.

In front of Ganyu Palace at the top of Jade Seal Hill is the Duck Hole. It is said that as spring turns to summer, if you take a live duck and drop it through the hole, it will quickly reappear swimming in the Yangzi. In the past the monks apparently drew their drinking water from this hole, using a pipe made of bamboo.

The spirit wall in the temple's main hall is constructed of excavated Han Dynasty (206 BCE–220 CE) bricks. The hall behind is dedicated on the right to Generals Zhang Fei and Yan Yan of the Three Kingdoms Period (*see* page 182), and on the left to General Qin Liangyu (1576–1648 CE) who fought bravely against the Manchu forces. A mural shows the goddess Nuwo repairing the sky.

In the rear hall are the remains of the Rice Flowing Hole. Legend has it that, long ago, just enough husked rice would flow up from the small hole each day for the needs of the monks and their guests. One day a greedy monk, thinking he could become rich, chiselled a larger hole, and the rice flow ceased forever. His effigy may be seen in the last room of the temple complex.

Cruise vessels usually dock near Zhailouge for a few hours' visit. An array of souvenir stands greets visitors off the docks. The new town of Shibaozhai is located directly above the site of the old town, which was demolished and the site subsequently submerged by rising water levels.

WANXIAN

About two hours below Shibaozhai the boat reaches Wanxian, which was recently renamed Wanzhou. It is guarded by two nine-storey pagodas for good fortune. Of the three main regions affected by the proposed Three Gorges Reservoir—Yichang, Wanxian and Chongqing, Wanxian has been affected the most. Two-thirds of its total population of 1.2 million were relocated in Wanxian prefecture and the reservoir has already inundated 60 per cent of the city. More than 900 factories were located below the new waterline; many were relocated to higher ground and others simply shut down and were demolished.

Wanxian has a number of silk-weaving and spinning factories supported by intense silkworm cultivation—operated on a family basis—that continues year round in Wanxian County. Other light industries include tea, bamboo and cane goods, cotton clothing, leather and Chinese medicines. The local paper mills utilise wheat and rice straw from the surrounding countryside.

HISTORY OF WANXIAN

Known as the Eastern Gate to Sichuan, the city is 2,000 years old, receiving its present name during the Ming Dynasty (1368–1644), and becoming a foreign Treaty Port in 1902. In 1926, after the local warlord commandeered foreign vessels for the transport of his troops, two British gunboats bombarded the city, causing massive fires. This became known as the Wanxian Incident. Following this event, which sorely angered the local populace, a boycott on the loading and unloading of British vessels was enforced for several years. The city later suffered aerial bombardment by the Japanese in their unsuccessful attempt to conquer the region.

As the halfway city between Yichang and Chongqing, Wanxian was a main port for East Sichuan merchandise (including large quantities of tung oil, used for treating wooden junks). The town once had a thriving junk building industry; the boats being constructed from cypress wood found in the nearby hills. Early travellers commented on the huge number of junks anchored at Wanxian.

WHAT TO SEE IN WANXIAN

The town is famous for its rattan and cane market where buyers and sellers mingle in a frenzy of bargaining for handmade summer bed mats, fans, hats, straw shoes, furniture and basketry. Small, round, red-trimmed baskets with lids are the most popular item and are well known throughout China. Roadside stalls trade in spicy noodles and cooling, opaque soyabean jelly and fresh fruit. In the mornings, local produce and seasonal delicacies such as mountain mushrooms or live eels are sold in the market.

Sichuan Basin

Since this photo was taken just a few decades ago, traditional boat-building methods have all but disappeared. Then, even with the advent of steam-driven boats, the gorges would rustle with the sound of sails being unfurled in the breeze. Though sailing sampans may still ply the waves, the sails of the river's Kuize (junks) have long since been replaced by motors while their tung oil-treated, cypress-wood hulls have been replaced by fibreglass or aluminium hulls. [Bill Hurst]

There was a community of foreign missionaries in this region (formerly part of Sichuan Province) before 1949, and two churches—Catholic and Protestant—continue to draw sizeable congregations of country folk.

In 1983 a small workshop was set up, employing two teenage boys and a few part-time workers to paint and varnish river stones from the Three Gorges. These make attractive mementos and can be bought at the Arts and Crafts Store. Visitors may also visit silk-weaving and cane-furniture factories.

LU POND AND XISHANPAI PAVILION

This small pool, originally dug by a locally revered Song Dynasty official, Lu Youkai, was once a very large lotus pond surrounded by decorative pavilions. Now it is not much more than a traffic roundabout. Nearby stands an ancient two-storey, yellow-tiled pavilion that houses a huge rock carved by the calligrapher Huang Tingzhen. Around the Xishanpai Pavilion once flowed a winding freshwater channel. Local literati would spend their evenings here, floating full wine cups along the channel. When a wine cup stopped in front of one of them, that person's forfeit would be to compose a poem.

WESTERN HILL PARK

A clock tower, which dominates the town's skyline from the river, was built in this large park in 1924. The upper part was damaged by Japanese bombs in 1939. There is a memorial to a Russian volunteer pilot whose plane crashed in the river in the same year. During the summers, people would relax in bamboo deck-chairs under the leafy trees, sipping tea and listening to Sichuan-style opera. The rising water level has reached the base of the tower, which is preserved by a small isolating wall in similar fashion to Shibaozhai.

TAIBAI ROCK

The poet Li Bai (701–62) lived here for a time; in the Ming Dynasty a memorial hall was built to commemorate him. Stone inscriptions dating back to the Tang Dynasty are still to be seen.

THE THREE GORGES MUSEUM, WANGZHONG HIGHWAY

This small museum, on the Wanzhong Highway, is a repository for some of the artefacts that were collected in advance of the flooding of the area upon completion of the new dam. Han tomb effigies and a Ba period hanging coffin are featured. The museum's exhibits are rudimentary, but the shop is extensive—the usual tourist trap with no local products.

Sichuan Basin

YUNYANG OF YORE

The original county town of Yunyang (Clouded Sun) used to be situated 64 kilometres (40 miles) below Wanxian, on the north bank. This is already completely underwater, and a new town has been constructed three kilometres (1.8 miles) upstream on the same side.

The Tang Dynasty poet, Du Fu (712–70), banished to a minor position in Sichuan, fell ill while travelling through Yunyang and stayed for many months, recuperating and writing poetry.

Prior to the town-consuming river-cum-reservoir, a significant archaeological site was discovered in 1987 at Yunyang, **Lijiaba**. By 1993 it was being excavated intensively by the archaeological unit of Sichuan University's Department of History. The 50-acre settlement yielded artefacts from the Shang through Han periods (ca. 1700 BCE–220 CE).

Weapons from the Warring States period (476–221 BCE) were identified as Ba because of their unusual shapes. Ceramic evidence points to settlement by both the Ba and their eastern neighbours the Chu, during the Spring and Autumn period (771–476B CE). Discovery of a cemetery and excavation of some of its tombs revealed a strong Ba cultural presence in the area and may provide more information about Ba origins, historical development and their relations with the Chu. Further excavation at Lijiaba is of course no longer possible. However, the famous Zhang Fei temple complex, built in the Northern Song period (960–1126), was spared.

ZHANG FEI TEMPLE

Zhang Fei, the 'Tiger General' of the Kingdom of Shu during the Three Kingdoms period (220–65 CE), is revered as a man who kept his word (*see* page 182). In 221, Guan Yu, Zhang Fei's sworn brother, was killed by the armies of the Kingdom of Wu. The Tiger General, then an official in Langzhong County, swore revenge and prepared to attack Wu with his army arrayed in white armour and carrying pennants—white being the colour of mourning. He ordered Commanders Zhang Da and Fan Jiang to lead the attack and avenge his brother, under pain of death.

The two pusillanimous officers got Zhang Fei drunk and cut off his head. They then fled by boat to Yunyang, intending to surrender to Wu. Here, however, they heard of a peace settlement between Wu and Shu, and threw Zhang Fei's head into the river, where it circled a fisherman's boat. Zhang Fei appealed to the fisherman in a dream to rescue his head and bury it in Shu. The fisherman obeyed, and the head was interred on Flying Phoenix Hill. A temple was built to commemorate the bold warrior on the south bank of the river, opposite the site of the original town. It is said that, before internment, the head was placed in a vat of oil, and when copper cash was thrown into the vat, the head would float up to give advice to the lovelorn and childless.

The temple was partly damaged in the flood of 1870, so most of the present ensemble of buildings dates from the late 19th Century. It was extensively restored.

Baidi Cheng's Western Pavillion contains these modern statues depicting Lui Bei entrusting his sons to Zhuge Liang, in the first hall of this Ming Dynasty complex. [Lu Jin]

Sixty per cent of the temple's rich collections of paintings, tablets and inscriptions were lost during the Cultural Revolution. Such items that were reversed and inscribed with Mao's sayings on their backs were spared and these can be viewed today. In front of the main hall are giant statues of the three famous sworn blood brothers—Liu Bei, Guan Yu and Zhang Fei. Inside the hall sits the wild-eyed, red-faced Guan Yu; on either side are scenes from his life. The Helpful Wind Pavilion contains steles and huge portraits of the general and his wife. It is said that his spirit, in the form of a helpful wind, frequently assisted passing boats. Junkmen used to stop at the temple to light firecrackers and burn incense in appreciation.

The relocated temple now sits opposite the new town. Piers were built to accommodate tourist ferries and cruise ships may also dock here.

FENGJIE

Fengjie stands on the north bank, just above the western entrance to Qutang, the first of the three great Yangzi gorges. Fengjie town, the county seat for the area, was an attractive town, with part of its Ming Dynasty city wall intact and stairways from the ferry pontoons leading up through three old city gates.

Fengjie was typical of many of the Yangzi River towns. Its markets were filled with local produce, clothing, mountain herbs and fruits—especially peaches, pomelos and snow-pears—for which it was famous. Leafy trees and traditional whitewashed two-storeyed houses lined the main street. Outside the city wall, above the river, used to be makeshift mat-shed teahouses where the local men and travellers would relax in bamboo deck-chairs, drinking tea and eating sunflower seeds or eggs boiled in tea.

Sadly, much of the old town was demolished in preparation for the rise in water level. Chinese director Jia Zhang-ke's film *Sanxia Haoren* (Three Gorges People, but titled *Still Life* in English) tells the storey of displaced Fengjie residents. In the fall of 2006, it was the surprise winner of the Venice Film Festival's top award, the Golden Lion. The town is now still very lively with Chinese tourists who have come to visit the famous historical site of Baidi Cheng nearby (*see* page 100).

HISTORY OF FENGJIE

Called Kuifu during the Spring and Autumn period (722–481 BCE), the ancient town became known as Fengjie after the Tang Dynasty (618–907). It has long been famous as a poets' city, as many of China's greatest poets commemorated their visits here with verses. The Tang Dynasty poet Du Fu (712–70) wrote some 430 poems while serving as an official here for two years.

Liu Bei, the King of Shu during the Three Kingdoms period (see page 182), died of despair in the Eternal Peace Palace after being defeated by the armies of Wu. Two ancient tablets unearthed in recent years indicate that the Fengjie Teacher Training Institute stands on the site of the palace. On his deathbed, Liu Bei entrusted his sons to the care of his loyal adviser, Zhuge Liang, entreating him to educate them in wisdom and to choose the most talented one to succeed him as king.

It was here that Zhuge Liang trained the troops of Shu in military strategy. He constructed the Eight Battle Arrays, 64 piles of stones 1.5 metres high erected in a grid pattern, 24 of which represented the surrounding troops. The principles of Zhuge Liang's manoeuvres have long been studied by China's military strategists and continue to be relevant to present-day concepts of Chinese warfare.

Nearby was the small village of Yufu (now submerged), which means 'the fish turns back' and relates to the legend of Qu Yuan, China's famous poet and states- man of the Third Century BCE. During his service at court, the country was riven by factions and discord. His political enemies had him exiled; eventually, in despair, he drowned himself in Dongting Lake. His body was allegedly swallowed by a sacred fish which then swam up the gorges to Qu Yuan's birthplace, near Zigui, where the fish intended to give Qu Yuan an honourable burial. However, so great were the lamentations and weeping of the mourners along the shore that the fish also became tearful and swam past Zigui. It was not until it reached Yufu that the fish realized its mistake and turned back. (*See* page 134 for more about of Qu Yuan.)

The Great Karst Funnel, a large limestone sinkhole, and its surrounding area (see following pages) makes a great day trip from Fengjie. [Lu Jin]

THE GREAT KARST FUNNEL AND VALLEY SCENIC AREA

The Great Karst Funnel, which is also known as The Heavenly Pit, or Xiaozhai (Small Dwelling) Karst Pit and Tiankeng (Sky Hole), is the largest karst sinkhole in the world. The Valley Scenic Area (Difeng) contains one of the largest geosutures in the world, The Great Crack.

The Sky Hole is situated on the east bank of the Jiupan River, with a north-westerly trending limestone valley, the Great Crack, extending to the south. Located near Xiaozhai village on the Daxi River in Fengjie County, access is by vehicular ferry from the City of Fengjie, 56 kilometres (35 miles) north.

These karst (limestone) features occur in the Wushan and Qiyanshan mountains, a landscape of low hills, plateaus, gorges, and scattered peaks. They are part of a larger scenic area comprising the Jiupan River, the Longqiao River valley and underground river, and the Macao Dam area.

Elevations in the region range from 237 to 2,084 metres (778 to 6,837 feet) above sea level. A warm and wet subtropical climate prevails, supporting more than 2,000 species of plants, including about 100 rare species peculiar to the region. Wildlife abounds, and numerous species of fish inhabit the rivers. Colourful Han and Tujia minorities live in the valleys, distinguished by their distinctive costumes, customs and dishes.

The Great Karst Funnel

Sinkholes form where a stream flows from impermeable rocks onto permeable limestone. Consequently, the stream enters the limestone through joints, and dissolves a vertical shaft or tube. Concurrently, underground streams within the limestone erode sub-horizontal passages. Where a widening sinkhole encounters a large cave chamber below, the cavern roof will eventually collapse, forming a huge depression such as the Sky Hole.

The Great Karst Funnel is eroded through a sequence of creamy coloured limestones up to 1,130 metres (3,707 feet) thick. Topographically, the sinkhole comprises an upper elliptical section, 626 metres long, 537 metres wide, and 320 metres deep, (2,054 by 1,762 by 1,050 feet respectively) and a lower rectangular section, 357 metres long, 268 metres wide, and 342 metres wide (1,171 by 879 by 1,122 feet respectively).

A narrow path, 2.7 kilometres (1.7 miles) long, descends to the floor of the sinkhole. The path to the base of the upper section includes 800 steps, with a further 2,000 stone steps in the lower section. Two dry-stone thatched cottages on the middle terrace are used as rest-houses. Historically, local villagers sought refuge in the pit to escape from bandits that roamed the countryside during periods of civil unrest. Thus, the area is known locally as Xiaozhai, meaning small villages. Numerous caves in the walls of the sinkhole contain evidence of human occupation, and ancient hanging coffins have been found on the cliffs in the district.

Springs emerge from the bedding planes and caves in the pit walls. One waterfall is 100 metres (328 feet) high. Large limestone boulders litter the floor of the pit. On the downstream (northern) side of the pit, the stream enters a 10-metre (33-feet) high passage. Daylight penetrates for about 500 metres (1,640 feet) from the entrance, and a vast underground lake occurs about 500 metres (1,640 feet) further along. Underground chambers, narrow side passages, grotesquely-shaped rocks, and circular potholes bear witness to the erosive action of water.

The Great Crack (Long Dry Valley or Tianjing)

The Great Crack (also known as the Earthly Ditch or Kaijingxia Geosuture) is a 37-kilometres-long (23-miles-long) karst valley, lying between undulating peaks to the south of the Sky Hole. The upper (southern) reaches of the valley are broad and forested, between 200 to 400 metres (656 to 1,312 feet) wide and 300 to 400 metres (984 to 1,312 feet) deep, containing a turbulent stream. In contrast, the middle reaches range from about one metre to 70 metres (three to 230 feet) wide, and are up to 900 metres (2,953 feet) deep. In the middle section, the stream sinks at a feature called the "Dark Eye". Part of the middle section, where the top of the gorge is between 10 to 30 metres (33 to 98 feet) wide, and the bottom only half-a-metre to 15 metres (1.6 to 49 feet) wide, is called the Great Valley (Tianjing). The lower section is known as the Dark Valley.

The valley contains many scenic features including clear streams, deep pools, waterfalls, an underground river, dry valleys, numerous caves, Elephant Trunk Hill, a natural bridge and an historic Guanyin Temple. An eight-kilometre (five-mile) section of the dry valley between Tianjingxia and Huitoushi has been developed for tourism with the construction of a plank road.

The Maze River

The Maze River follows a 4,326-metres-long (14,190-feet-long) underground passage that extends from the floor of the Sky Hole to a large pool below a 40-metres-high (131-feet) limestone cliff. A three-kilometres-long (1.8-miles-long) gorge continues downstream. Up to 400 metres (1,312 feet) deep, the gorge contains swift currents, dangerous shoals, and deep pools, before it opens into the Jiupan River.

To the north of the Maze River, around Yizishang, are many deep caves, including Fairy Cave, Sifang Cave, and Swallow Cave. These are rich in stalactites and stalagmites. (See recommended reading page 234.)

Special Topic

BAIDI CHENG (WHITE EMPEROR CITY)

The local ferry from Fengjie takes about 20 minutes to reach Baidi Cheng on the north bank of the river, passing several pagodas on the surrounding peaks.

Opposite Baidi Cheng, at **Laoguanmiao**, a previously unknown neolithic cultural settlement and cemetery was discovered and excavated in 1995 by the Sichuan Fengjie County Museum and the Baidicheng Cultural Relics Institute. The late Neolithic–Shang (ca. 3500–1100 BCE) site yielded stone tools and potshards. The earliest shards are associated with handmade red-clay ceramics decorated with diamond patterns that date between 3500–3000 BCE.

Because of its strategic position, Baidi Cheng was chosen in the First Century CE by Gong Sunshu, an official turned soldier, as the site of his headquarters. The legend goes that in 25CE white vapour in the shape of a dragon was seen rising from a nearby well. Taking this as an auspicious omen, Gong declared himself the 'White Emperor' and the town 'White Emperor City'. Remains of the city wall can still be seen on the hill behind Baidi Mountain. The 12-year reign of the White Emperor was regarded as a time of peace and harmony, so after his death a temple was built to commemorate his reign. This temple dates back more than 1,950 years.

The climb up the wooded Baidi Mountain to the temple complex used to involve a flight of several hundred steps. The rise in the water level of the river means that this climb has been greatly reduced; it has also turned Baidi Mountain into an island. Fine views of the entrance to Qutang Gorge can be seen from the temple.

The **Western Pavilion** on the slope is believed to have been occupied by the great poet Du Fu, who wrote numerous poems at this site. The pavilion (at one time known as *Guanyin Dong*) overlooks what Du Fu described as 'the limitless Yangzi'. Further up the hill is a *stupa*, marking the grave of a much-loved literary monk who served at the temple during the Qing Dynasty (1644–1911).

A red wall with an imposing yellow dragon-head gateway surrounds the temple complex. Though the temple was originally dedicated to Gong Sunshu, the White Emperor, his statue was removed in the Ming Dynasty (1368–1644) and replaced with images of Liu Bei, Zhuge Liang, Guan Yu and Zhang Fei, heroes of the Shu Kingdom during the Three Kingdoms period. The present halls date from the Ming Dynasty.

The front hall contains large modern statues that depict Liu Bei on his deathbed entrusting his sons to the care of Zhuge Liang. To the left is the handsome, winged **Observing the Stars Pavilion** (*Guanxing Ting*), where a large bronze bell can be seen hanging in the upper storey. From this pavilion Zhuge Liang observed the stars and made accurate weather forecasts, which together helped him plan his victorious battles. The two Forest of Tablets halls contain several rare engraved

White Emperor City temple's entrance at Baidi Cheng. [Lu Jin]

stelae, some being more than 1,300 years old. The Phoenix Tablet is particularly finely engraved. The Bamboo Leaf Poem Tablet is one of only three in China. It is considered a fine work of art, combining as it does poetry and calligraphy, for the tablet is engraved with three branches of bamboo, each leaf forming the Chinese characters of a poem.

The **Wuhou Hall** is dedicated to Zhuge Liang, his son and grandson. The bodies of the statues are of the Ming Dynasty (1368–1644), but the heads, smashed in the Cultural Revolution (1966–76), are new. **Mingliang Hall** is dedicated to Liu Bei, who is shown surrounded by four attendants, as well as the black-faced Zhang Fei and the red-faced Guan Yu on one side, and Zhuge Liang on the other. Adjoining rooms display furniture, scrolls, porcelain and other cultural relics.

In 1987, several buildings were converted to form a museum displaying the many cultural relics found within the area, including two coffins from the Ba culture. One of these dates back to the Western Han Dynasty (206 BCE–8 CE).

At the foot of Baidi Mountain, Yanyu Rock—exceeding 30 metres in length, 20 metres wide and 40 metres (132 feet) high—used to be a constant hazard to boats riding the swift current and heading into the narrow entrance of Qutang Gorge. Over the ages, countless vessels perished. In 1959 it took a work team seven days to blow up this gigantic rock.

QUTANG GORGE

Immediately below Baidi City is **Kuimen**, the 'Dragon Gate' entrance to the first of the three gorges of the Yangzi River—the eight-kilometre (five-mile) long Qutang Gorge. The shortest but grandest of them all, the gorge's widest point is only 150 metres (492 feet). Mists frequently swirl around the mysterious limestone peaks, some 1,500 metres (4,921 feet) high. It was also known by early Western travellers as the Wind Box Gorge or Bellows Gorge, as the ancient local folklore mistook the Ba coffins to be the wind bellows of the gods.

Prior to the Three Gorges Dam, this gorge was a particularly dangerous stretch during high-water seasons and was known to rise to 50 metres (164 feet). It was as if, in the words of the poet Su Dongpo, 'a thousand seas were poured into one cup'.

An upper Yangzi steamboat captain recalled how in September 1929 the level of water was 75 metres (246 feet), and likened the passage to a trough, with the water banked up on both sides. His ship became quite unmanageable, and was carried down, broadside on, only coming under control again at the lower end. He would never, he vowed, try to negotiate it again at such a level.

Two mountains—**Red Armour Mountain** (*Chijia Shan*) to the north, once compared to a celestial peach, and **White Salt Mountain** (*Baiyan Shan*) to the south—form Kuimen's entrance, their steep precipices like two giant doors guarding the tumultuous waters. It is a picture of the entrance to Qutang Gorge that appeared on the reverse of the old five-yuan banknote (which are still to be found in circulation), and now decorates the latest ten-yuan note.

In the Tang Dynasty (618–907), chains were strung across the river as an 'iron lock' to prevent the passage of enemy boats. In the Song Dynasty (960–1279) two iron pillars nearly two metres (6.5 feet) tall were erected on the north side, and seven chains, some 250 metres (820 feet) long, were used to block the river passage. Although the original purpose was defensive, the chain locks were later used to enable local authorities to gather taxes from all boats travelling downriver. This system continued until the middle Qing Dynasty (1644–1911). The iron posts are now placed at the entrance to the viewing pavilion on the north bank.

On the precipice of Baiyan Shan (south side) are a series of holes nearly a metre (three feet) apart and about one-third of a metre (one foot) deep, forming a 'Z' shape. These are known as the **Meng Liang Stairway**. According to legend, Yang Jiye, a Song-Dynasty general, was buried on a terrace high up on the mountain. His loyal comrade-in-arms, Meng Liang, decided secretly to take the bones back for burial in Yang's home town. In the dead of night he took a small boat into the gorge

Kuimen, the famous entrance of Qutang Gorge. Red Armour Mountain (Chijia Shan), which is also known as Peach Mountain, looms over the gorge high above in the background. [Yin Chun]

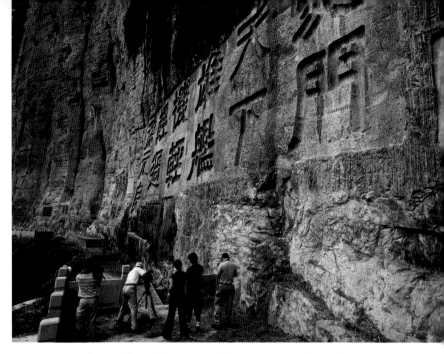

The orginal carved inscriptions of Fenbi Tang, now submerged,
were copied onto a cliff face higher up the side of the mountain. [Lu Jin]

and began to hack out a pathway to the terrace. Halfway up the rock face he was discovered by a monk who began crowing like a cock. Meng Liang, thinking that dawn was breaking and fearing discovery, abandoned his task. When he later discovered the monk's mischief, he was so provoked that he hung the monk upside down over a precipice. The rock he dangled the monk from became known as **Hanging Monk Rock** (*Daodiao Heshangshi*), but it is now submerged. History records, however, that General Yang was not buried here and the steps are probably the remains of an ancient river pathway. Sections of a city wall, 1,400 years old, have been found on top of Baiyan Shan so it is possible that the pathway led to this early settlement. Another theory about the stairway suggests that it was built to provide access to the rare medicinal herbs that grow high on the cliff faces.

At the highest point above Meng Liang Stairway, one can see **Armour Cave** (*Kuangjia Dong*) where it is said a female Song-Dynasty general hid her weapons. In 1958 the cave was explored and found to contain three 2,000-year-old wooden coffins from the Kingdom of Ba, in which were bronze swords and lacquered wooden combs.

Nearby used to be the **Chalk Wall** (*Fenbi Tang*) where 900 characters, dating from the Song Dynasty, were carved by famous calligraphers on the rock face. The site derived its name from the limestone powder that was used to smooth rock surfaces before being carved. Although this site has now been submerged, copies can be seen nearby on a higher cliff face.

Across on the north bank is the **Bellows Cave**, which is a large, deep cave named after Bellows Gorge. A Ba hanging coffin may be seen in the cliff crevice to the east of the cave.

East of Armour Cave (on the south side), on the top of a black rock, is a huge stone that the Chinese say resembles the body of a rhinoceros looking westwards as if forever enjoying 'the autumn moon over the gorge gate'. They call this rock 'Rhinoceros Looking at the Moon'. As one sails by the formation, seen directly from the side, it is said to resemble Liu Bei, the King of Shu during the Three Kingdoms period, sitting on his throne.

From Baidi Cheng to Daixi, through the whole length of Qutang Gorge, visitors may see on the northern bank the old towpath. Once high up on the cliff face, the path was hand-hewn in 1889 by the local people. Prior to this there existed a smaller towpath that was often submerged at high water. Travellers had to abandon their boats and climb over the peaks, a dangerous and time-wasting detour. Boats going upstream had to wait for a favourable east wind; if the wind was in the wrong quarter, boats could be stranded for ten days or more.

The sandstone walls of the gorges have become pitted by natural erosion, creating lines of holes, some of which are several metres deep. The town of **Daixi**, at the mouth of a stream bearing the same name, marks the eastern end of Qutang Gorge. More than 200 burial sites have been found here, and excavations have revealed a rich collection of bone, stone and jade artefacts and pottery as well as various burial forms of the middle and late New Stone Age period (*see* page 174).

Below Daixi the river widens out. About five kilometres downstream, on the south bank, are two sharp, black peaks that form the **Unlocked Gates Gorge** (*Suokai Xia*). On the west side of the gorge, midway up the mountain, is a semi-circular stone shaped roughly like a drum—this is the **Beheading Dragon Platform** (*Zhanglong Tai*). Facing this on the opposite side of the gorge is a thick, round stone pillar, the **Binding Dragon Pillar** (*Suolong Zhu*). Once upon a time, the Jade Dragon, a son of the Dragon of the Eastern Sea, lived in a cave on the upper reaches of the Daixi Stream. One season he decided to visit his family by way of the Yangzi, but shortly afterwards found himself lost. Changing into the form of an old man, he asked his way of a herder boy. The boy pointed north with his sickle. The dragon rushed off in that direction but again got lost, whereupon he flew into a mighty rage and rushed at the mountains, causing them to crumble and dam up the river; farmlands were flooded, earthquakes toppled houses, and men and animals perished. At this moment the Goddess Yao Ji rushed to the spot on a cloud. She rebuked Jade Dragon, but he was unrepentant. In response, she flung a string of pearls into the air, which changed into a rope that bound the dragon to the stone pillar. Yao Ji then ordered the great Da Yu, controller of rivers, to behead the murderous dragon on the nearby platform. He then diverted the river by cutting the gorge. The people of this valley have lived happily ever since.

WUSHAN

Wushan County is situated above the Yangzi on the north bank. It is embraced by lovely mountain peaks where in flourishes the tung tree, whose oil was used for the caulking, oiling and varnishing of junks and sampans. A two-million-year old fossil of an ape man was discovered in a cave in these mountains in the 1980s. This important archaeological find is now in the Beijing Museum of Chinese History.

The town of Wushan dates back to the latter part of the Shang Dynasty (c. 1600–1027 BCE). In the Warring States period (475–221 BCE), the King of Chu established a palace west of the city. During the First Century, the faith of the Buddha had reached China and many temples were built here; almost all the temples have been destroyed over the years. The name of the town originates with Wu Xian, a successful Tang-Dynasty doctor to the imperial court, who was buried on Nanling Mountain, on the south bank opposite Wushan. A winding path—with 108 bends—leads from the foot of the mountain to the summit where there is a small temple. This path was an official road through to Hubei Province in ancient times.

A shepherd's goats have ample grazing on Wushan (Witch Mountain) after a spring rain. [He Zhi Hong]

Much of the original town was situated on a low-lying flood plain on the north bank of the river and was demolished in preparation for the rise in water level. A new road bridge arches over the river and leads to Wu Mountain, a new marker for the entrance to the Wu Gorge.

The energetic visitor may climb to the summit of **Wushan** (Witch Mountain), a two-hour hike. Worshippers still come to a small shrine here, built within the ruins of an old Buddhist monastery. From the summit the views of Wu Gorge and the river are spectacular. A less strenuous outing may be made to the newly opened limestone cave complex in Wu Gorge high up on the cliff face above the north bank of the river. This involves a short boat ride from Wushan town, an easy scramble up the rocky slope and then a walk along the old towpath. Around the cave complex there are the usual ornamental pavilions and a teahouse. The cave complex, **Luyou Dong**, is named after a Song-Dynasty official who visited Wushan and left an appreciative record of his stay. The lower parts of this cave are now submerged.

Wushan was, until its demolition in 2002, a rough market town with worn steps from the mud flats and docks to the narrow streets packed with farmers selling their produce. A lively market was built along the remains of the old city wall. Old homes were crowded with families and 'beauty salons' catered to the visiting sailors. It was the epitome of a steamy and spicy river port. Today all that has gone, with the large new boulevards and pretentious buildings of the new town cut higher into the mountain slopes. The park that runs from the new dock area to the government centre high up the hill is the future site of the world's largest 'people mover', a 400-metre escalator that will make the climb up to town an attraction.

DANING RIVER & THE LITTLE THREE GORGES

Some of the cruise ships stop at Wushan to allow their passengers to take a trip up the crystal-clear Daning River through its magnificent Little Three Gorges (*Xiao Sanxia*), whose total length is only 33 kilometres (20 miles). However, a similar excursion is now possible along the Shennong Stream, a tributary at the eastern end of Wu Gorge, and it has become a popular inclusion to the itineraries of cruise patrons (*see* page 128 for more details).

The Daning River excursion is undertaken in low motorized sampans or aboard new larger excursion boats. About three kilometres from the mouth of the river, at its confluence with the Yangzi, the entrance to the first of the gorges is reached. This is the **Dragon Gate Gorge** (*Longmen Xia*), three kilometres long. The mouth of the gorge is like a massive gateway through which the river rushes like a green dragon, hence its name. The gateway appears to shut once one has passed through. On the east side is **Dragon Gate Spring** (*Longmen Quan*) and above it **Lingzhi Peak**, topped by the Nine-Dragon Pillar. On this peak, it is said, grow strange plants and the fungus of longevity (*lingzhi*), guarded by nine dragons. On the western bank, two rows of 15-centimetre square holes, continuing the entire length of the small gorges and numbering over 6,000 are all that remain of an astonishing plank walkway, which was first constructed in the Han period and recorded in the Annals of Wushan County in 246 BCE. Wooden stakes inserted into these hand-hewn holes supported planks and large bamboo pipes, which stretched for 100 kilometres along the river. This pipeline conveyed brine, while the planks provided an access for maintenance. In the 17th Century the pathway, used by the peasant leader Li Zicheng in his uprising against the Ming Dynasty, was destroyed by the imperial army.

After leaving the gorge the boat passes the Nest of Silver Rapid (*Yinwo Tan*). In the past, rich merchants trading in the hinterland often came to grief here; perhaps there are caches of silver under the bubbling surface still! In 1958 work began on clearing major obstacles from the river.

The Daning then meanders through terraced hillsides before entering the ten-kilometre (six-mile) long **Misty Gorge** (*Bawu Xia*), with its dramatic scenery of rocks, peaks and caves, including Fairy Maiden Cave, Fairy Throwing a Silk Ball, and Guanyin Seated on a Lotus Platform. A long, layered rock formation, hanging in plates like a scaly dragon, can be seen on the eastern cliff. Suspended upon the precipice is a relic of the ancient inhabitants of eastern Sichuan 2,000 years ago, an 'iron' coffin (which is actually made of wood that has turned black with age). This gorge is accordingly also known as **Iron Coffin Gorge**.

The former village of Double Dragon or **Shuanglong** (population 300), above Bawu Gorge, was the halfway point. The village, with houses dating from the 1700s, during the early Qing Dynasty, was demolished in 2002. The lush valley is now inundated. Excursion boats previously then proceeded upstream to visit Dachang, a Ming era village. It too, was emptied and demolished prior to the second level inundation in 2006.

Emerald Green Gorge (*Dicui Xia*), 20 kilometres (12 miles) long, is inhabited by wild ducks and covered with luxuriant bamboo groves from which rises a deafening cacophany of bird-song. There are also many types of monkey still to be seen if you are lucky. Once their shrill cries resounded throughout the Yangzi gorges, but today they can be seen and heard only along some of the tributaries. River stones of an extraordinary variety and colour can be gathered from the river bed.

The scenery of the Three Little Gorges on Daning Stream is as spectacular as ever. The songs and shouts of trackers echoed throughout Daning's Longmen and Bawu Gorges as boats were hauled through strong currents over dangerous shoals, but no more. However, Ducui Gorge's scenery remains much as it was prior to the innundation. [Yin Chun]

The Iron Coffins of the Ba people, found throughout the Three Gorges area including Daning and Shennong streams, are actually made from wood that has been well-weathered. [Yin Chun]

In 2002, an old man sits among the ruins of his house in the village of Shuanglong (Double Dragon) and sings aloud from a cartoon booklet of classic mythology, as if singing could stop the demolition. [Richard Hayman]

UNDERWATER
THE WORLD'S BIGGEST DAM FLOODS THE PAST

by Peter Hessler

At six-thirteen in the evening, after the Zhou family has already moved their television, a desk, two tables, and five chairs onto a pumpkin patch beside the road, I prop a brick upright at the river's edge. On new maps for the city of Wushan, this body of water is called Emerald Drop Lake. But the maps were printed before the lake appeared. In fact, the water is a murky brown, and the lake is actually an inlet of the Yangtze River, which for the past week has been rising behind the Three Gorges Dam. On Zhou Ji'en's next trip down from his family's bamboo-frame shack, he carries a wooden cupboard on his back. A small man, he has a pretty wife and two young daughters, and until recently they were residents of Longmen Village. The village does not appear on the new maps. A friend of Zhou's carries the next load, which includes the family's battery-powered clock. The clock, like my wristwatch, reads nearly six-thirty-five. The water has climbed two inches up the brick.

Watching the river rise is like tracking the progress of the clock's short hand: it's all but imperceptible. There is no visible current, no sound of rushing water-but at the end of every hour another half foot has been gained. The movement seems to come from within, and to some degree it is mysterious to every living thing on the shrinking banks. Beetles, ants, and centipedes radiate out in swarms from the river's edge. After the water has surrounded the brick, a cluster of insects crawl madly onto the dry tip, trying desperately to escape as their tiny island is consumed. The people knew that the flood was coming, but they did not know that it would come so fast. Most residents of Longmen left last year, when the government relocated them to Guangdong Province, in the south of China. But a few, like Zhou Ji'en and his family, stayed behind to work the land for one final spring. Lately, things have been happening very fast. Two days ago, the elder daughter, Zhou Shurong, completed first grade. Yesterday, her mother, Ou Yunzhen, harvested the last of their water spinach; today, those plots are underwater. All that remain are pumpkins, eggplants, and red peppers.

More than thirty feet above Zhou's pumpkin patch, a neighbor named Huang Zongming is building a fishing boat. Huang has told me that it will be "two or three more days" before the river reaches the boat. Chinese peasants tend to speak about time in an indeterminate manner, even at a moment like this, when the river is a very determined two and a half days ahead of schedule; the government says that it will ultimately rise by more than two hundred feet.

The Zhou family has rented a three-room apartment on the hillside above, and they are moving today because several inches of water have crept across the only road out. At 7:08 P.M., the brick is half submerged. Zhou Shurong has carried out her possessions-an umbrella, an inflated inner tube, and a Mashimaro backpack that contains a pencil box and schoolbooks. As the adults continue hauling furniture, the little girl sits at a table in the pumpkin patch and calmly copies a lesson:

The spring rain falls softly,

Everybody comes to look at the peach blossoms.

At seven-twenty, a young man arrives on a motorcycle and catches black scorpions that are fleeing the rising water. "Usually they're hard to find," he tells me. "They're poisonous, but they can be used for medicine. In Henan Province, I've seen them sold for a hundred yuan—'twelve dollars'— a pound."

By seven-fifty-five, when a flatbed truck appears with two moving men, the brick has vanished. Only a small stretch of road remains dry, and that is where they park the truck. The river hits the vehicle's left front tire at 8:07 P.M. The men start to load the furniture; the sky grows dark. "Hurry up!" Ou Yunzhen says. Nearby, Zhou Shurong and her five-year-old sister, Zhou Yu, stand the way children do when they sense anxiety in adults: perfectly still, arms straight at their sides, eyes unblinking. At eight-twenty-three, the water reaches the left rear tire. The television is the last object to be loaded; it is placed with care in the front seat, next to the girls. At eight-thirty-four, the driver turns the ignition. As the truck rumbles off, the water reaches the top of the hubcaps. Ou Yunzhen stays behind to harvest the last of the pepper crop in the dark.

The next day, in the hard light of the afternoon, I visit the remains of the shack to see what the family abandoned to Emerald Drop Lake: a man's left boot, half a broken Ping-Pong paddle, an empty box that says, in English, "Ladies Socks," a math examination paper, written in a young girl's hand, with the score at the top in bright-red ink-sixty-two per cent.

From 1996 to 1998, I taught English to college students in Fuling, a small city on the Yangtze some two hundred miles upstream from Wushan. Every winter, along with the other seasonal changes, the river shrank. Rain became less frequent, and the snowmelt stopped coming off the western mountains, until eventually the Yangtze exposed a strip of sandstone known as the White Crane Ridge. The ridge was thin and white and covered with thousands of inscriptions. For centuries, local officials had used it to keep track of low water levels. When I visited the ridge in January of

1998, the river was exactly two inches lower than it had been at the time of the earliest dated carving, 763 A.D. The inscriptions made it clear that, in these parts, the Yangtze's own cycle mattered more than the schedules of any authority. One carving, completed in 1086 A.D., commemorated the ridge's emergence during the ninth year of the reign of Yuanfeng, an emperor of the northern Song dynasty. In fact, Yuanfeng had died the year before, but news of the death—and of the new emperor—had yet to reach the river.

Fuling was still remote when I lived there. The city had no traffic lights and no highway. There was one escalator in town, and people concentrated hard before stepping onto it. The only fast-food restaurant bore the mysterious name California Beef Noodle King U.S.A. It was a poor region, and it got poorer as you went downstream toward Wushan, which was at the end of the Three Gorges—a hundred-and-twenty-mile stretch of narrow mountains and cliffs through which the Yangtze passes, creating a landscape of stunning beauty, hard farming, and fast currents.

I could see the river from the classroom where I taught writing. Our government-provided textbook included a model essay, in the chapter "Argumentation," entitled "The Three Gorges Project Is Beneficial." The essay cited a few drawbacks—flooded cultural relics, displaced populations—but the author went on to assert that these were easily outweighed by the benefits of better flood control, a greater supply of electricity, and improved river transportation. Given the fact that the Chinese government had strictly limited public criticism of the dam, we could go only so far with the "Argumentation" unit. I spent more time teaching the proper form of an American business letter.

The idea of building a dam in the Three Gorges was conceived by Sun Yat-sen in 1919. After Sun's death, in 1925, the vision was kept alive by dictators and revolutionaries, occupiers and developers, all of whom saw the project as an important step in modernizing the nation. Chiang Kai-shek promoted the idea, as did Mao Zedong. When the Japanese occupied parts of the river valley in 1940, their engineers performed surveys; when the Kuomintang regained control of China, officials from the U.S. Bureau of Reclamation helped the Chinese continue the planning. After the Kuomintang was defeated, the Communists turned to the Soviet Union for technical assistance. But the Russian advisers left after the Sino-Soviet split in 1960, and during the political chaos of the next two decades the project was put on hold. (The dam's history is explored in a recently published book, *Before the Deluge*, by Deirdre Chetham.)

Special Topic

By the time construction finally began, in 1994, the era of big dams had passed in most parts of the world. Both the United States government and the World Bank refused to support the project, because of environmental concerns. Many critics of the dam believed that one of its main goals-protection against the floods that periodically ravage central China—would be better served by the construction of a series of smaller dams on the Yangtze's tributaries. Engineers worried that the Yangtze's heavy silt might back up behind the Three Gorges Dam, limiting efficiency. Social costs were high: an estimated 1.2 million people would have to be resettled, and low-lying cities and towns would have to be rebuilt on higher ground. Once completed, the dam would be the largest in the world—as high as a sixty-story building and as wide as five Hoover Dams. The official price tag was more than twenty-one billion dollars, roughly half of which would be funded by a tax on electricity across China.

But in Fuling I never heard any of this. When I left the city, in the summer of 1998, the only visible indications of the project were a few altitude markers that had been painted onto buildings in the lower sections of town. The signs said, in bright-red paint, "177 M"—supposedly, the future height of the reservoir. It was precisely forty metres higher than the White Crane Ridge's inscription from 1086 A.D.

During the next five years, I often returned to the Three Gorges; more red signs had cropped up along the river. Most identified metre marks of either 135 or 175, because the reservoir was scheduled to be filled in two stages, first in 2003, and then at the higher level in 2009. Some of the red signs had an odd specificity: 141.9, 143.2, 146.7. They reminded me of the ridge—the whole valley was being marked and inscribed in preparation for the flood.

Down near the riverbanks, the old cities and villages were left virtually unimproved. Even though the rest of China was in a construction frenzy, there was no point in building anything new where the water was certain to rise. These settlements gave a rare glimpse into the past: untouched landscapes of gray brick and dark tile. Higher up, on the surrounding hillsides, new cities and towns were being built with cement and white tile. From the river, the Yangtze's evolving history could be read at a glance, in a series of horizontal bands: the dark riverside settlements that belonged to the past, the green stretch of farmland that would be claimed by the reservoir, and the clusters of white looking toward the future.

The new cities went through distinct stages of creation. In the beginning, the inhabitants were mostly young men: construction workers, bulldozer operators. Shops soon appeared, but they stocked almost nothing that you could eat or wear. They sold tools, windows, lighting fixtures. Once, in the new city of Fengdu, I walked down a half-built street where virtually everybody was selling doors. Women generally appeared once the local market economy took hold. After that, children materialized, and then the city was alive.

The old settlements died quickly when the government began demolishing them in 2002. Most residents were given housing compensation, which they could use to purchase apartments in the new cities. But an estimated hundred thousand rural villagers were relocated to other parts of China. Generally, they were moved in blocs: sometimes an entire hamlet was loaded onto a boat and sent downstream to another province, where the government provided small land allowances. I knew a cop who escorted an entire village by train to the southern province of Guangdong. After the old villages had been reduced to rubble, many of the residents who remained were elderly. They delayed the final move, living in tents and lean-tos. Makeshift shops sold mostly products that people could eat or wear.

A few younger people stayed behind to earn a bare living. Scavengers sold scrap metal, and peasants tried to coax one final crop out of the doomed soil. Neat rows of vegetables were cultivated amid the rubble, like gardens in a war zone. I arrived in the village of Dachang last year just as the first row of houses was being torn down. A middle-aged man sat in the wooden frame of his ruined home. It wasn't yet eleven o'clock in the morning, but he was quite drunk. "I'm like a man hanging from a nail," he told me.

Some of the stragglers were like that—they had slipped outside the valley's evolution. Often, they didn't belong to traditional Communist work units, or they were migrants who weren't eligible for compensation. When I visited the old city of Wushan in September of 2002, after most of the structures had been torn down, there were still a number of beauty parlors where prostitutes waited patiently behind blue-tinted windows. I had a sudden vision of the women, nine months later, sitting with the water up to their necks. In the tiny village of Daxi, one old man pulled out form after form, showing me how he had lost his resettlement funds—more than ten thousand yuan (around twelve thousand dollars)—on a bad investment in coal. The region was rich in doomed cultural artifacts: ancient villages that would disappear, temple sites that would be drowned. In Dachang, which had the most intact Ming- and Qing-dynasty architecture, I was shown around by a man in his early twenties named Huang Jun. At the old dock, underneath a massive banyan tree, he pointed out two stone lions that guarded the steps leading down to the water. The lions' faces were chipped and scarred; their backs had been worn smooth from decades of being sat on. In the future, the site would be underwater.

"During the Cultural Revolution, Red Guards threw the lions into the river," Huang said. "It was chaotic, and nobody knew what had happened to the statues. But years later an old man dreamed one night that they were out in the water. He told the other villagers, and they searched in the river and found them. That was in 1982—I remember it. The story is very strange, but it's true."

June 8th

At nine-forty in the morning, the river is almost empty. Tourist ships have been cancelled for weeks-first because of the outbreak of SARS, and more recently because the reservoir has been filling up. The water rises at roughly six inches an hour. Some friends and I are in a small speedboat, powered by an outboard motor, and we head in the direction that used to be downstream. But now the river has no heart; it lies slack between the walls of the Wu Gorge. The water comes to life only in the bends, where the sky opens and the wind kicks up waves.

Eight months ago, I hiked this route on a series of century-old footpaths. The trails had been carved directly into the limestone cliffs, and they hung more than two hundred feet above the water. I travelled with a friend, camping along the way, and in the middle of the gorge we followed a tributary called the Shennu Stream. The Shennu came from the southern mountains and it was too shallow for boat traffic. The valley rose around us as we hiked upstream, until at last we were in a deep canyon, hopping from boulder to boulder. Ferns covered the cliffs; there weren't any red metre markings in this unpopulated place. We tried to guess how high up the cliffs the water of the new reservoir would rise.

This morning, the pilot heads to the Shennu. We move east through the Wu Gorge, where virtually all of the cliff trail is underwater. The mouth of the Shennu is wide and still; tree branches float near the banks. But upstream, where the water is flowing, the debris begins to disappear, and the river's color starts to shift. The water turns dark green, then green-blue. Long-stemmed ferns trail directly into the river-the current hasn't yet pulled them off the cliffs. We zip around one sharp bend, then another. The landscape still has the character of a water route carved by a smaller stream—it meanders wildly, taking abrupt turns—and it is mesmerizing to flash through it on a speedboat. The boat doesn't belong here; the water doesn't belong here: this is a brand-new gorge. The stream color shifts to deep blue. The sound of rapids ahead joins the motor's roar.

There is a horrible scraping sound and the boat lurches to a stop; everybody grabs the side. The engine cuts off. We sit in stunned silence for a moment while the pilot checks for damage. The boat and the motor are intact. Drifting backward, the rapids suddenly loud now, we see the boulder, its tip glistening beneath a foot and a half of water. Looking at the submerged shape-enormous, tan-colored, the hard curve of its back disappearing into deeper water—I think of the stone lions and the old man's dream.

At two-fifty in the afternoon, I return to Emerald Drop Lake. Yesterday, I walked on the road; today I have to take a boat. I visit the Zhous' former residence with Huang Po, the nine-year-old boy from the fishing family next door. When Huang sees the sixty-two-per-cent math examination lying in the rubble, he folds the paper carefully and puts it into his pocket.

"Why do you want that?" I ask.

"If I see her, I'll give it to her," Huang Po says.

"I don't think she wants it," I say.

The boy grins slyly and touches his pocket.

His father, Huang Zongming, has finished building the fishing boat a day earlier than he predicted. It is forty-two feet long, made of the wood of the Chinese toon tree. Eventually, Huang plans to sell it. The labor required several family members and more than twenty days of work; recently they caulked the cracks with a mixture of lime, hemp, and tung oil. This morning, they treated the entire surface with a coat of the oil. Tung oil is a natural sealant, as well as an effective paint thinner-in the late nineteen-thirties, it was China's single most valuable trade product. The tung oil gives the wood a reddish shine; the shape has a rough, simple beauty. The boat sits on wooden struts. It has never touched water. I ask Huang when he plans to move it.

"Whenever the water reaches it," he says. Huang is shirtless, a skinny, square-jawed man with efficient ropelike muscles. Later, when I ask if he's worried about the boat's not being tested before the water rises, he gives me the slightly annoyed look of a shipwright hassled by diluvian reporters. Huang Zongming is a righteous man, and he knows that his boat will float.

I first met the Huang family in September of last year, when Longmen Village was still on the map. By local standards, the place was relatively prosperous; residents fished the waters of the Daning River, the tributary that entered the Yangtze at Wushan, and farmed the rich floodland. When most of the villagers were relocated to Guangdong, Huang Zongming and his brothers, Huang Zongguo and Huang Zongde, stayed behind. The government had organized the Longmen transfer, but it was unable to insure that everybody actually went. In today's China, despite official registrations, people who are determined to live in a place can generally find a way to do so.

Huang Zongguo told me in September that the relocated peasants often complained about the scarcity of farmland in Guangdong. He added that they struggled because they couldn't understand Cantonese. Huang was disappointed with his family's resettlement allowance-roughly ten thousand yuan per person. We spoke in his simple gray brick home; the water and the electricity had just been cut off. In two weeks, Huang Zongguo said, the demolition crews would arrive.

Since last fall, Zongguo and Zongming have paid for the construction of a two-story building high above Emerald Drop Lake. The home is almost completed, but Zongming tells me that he doesn't want to move there until later in the year; during the summer he prefers to be close to the river. He lives in a shack topped by an old fibreglass boat cover, along with his wife, Chen Cihuang, and their two children, Huang Po and Huang Dan, a twelve-year-old girl. Zongming is thirty-five years old, and he has worked a fishing boat since he was ten. Unlike his former neighbors the Zhous, who grew up in the highlands and migrated to Longmen to farm, Zongming is completely at ease around water. His response to the rising river is simply to move the makeshift home thirty feet higher up the hillside. But he feels no need to undertake this project until the last possible moment. At five-fifteen in the afternoon, the water is about eight feet below the Huang home. I ask Zongming when he expects the river to reach his new boat. "Probably about noon tomorrow," he says.

In the new city of Wushan, which has been constructed on the hillside directly above the former site, there are parallel streets called Smooth Lake Road and Guangdong Road. Smooth Lake refers to a poem that Mao Zedong wrote in 1956, when he swam across the Yangtze and dreamed of a new dam:

Walls of stone will stand upstream to the west
To hold back Wushan's clouds and rain
Till a smooth lake rises in the narrow gorges.

The poem is familiar to people along the river, and it's not unusual for them to speak of the project in terms of national achievement and welfare. In 1997, when the Yangtze was diverted at the dam site to prepare for construction, President Jiang Zemin proclaimed, "It vividly proves once again that socialism is superior in organizing people to do big jobs." Once, in the new village of Qingshi, I saw a restaurant whose owner had posted a handwritten sign in the form of a traditional Chinese New Year's couplet:

Honorable migrants leaving the old home and moving to a new life
Giving up the small home, serving the nation, building a new home.

Guangdong Road takes its name from the southern province that was the first part of China to boom after free-market reforms were implemented, in 1979. Funding from this area has supported part of the Three Gorges Dam development, and in the new towns it's not unusual to see names that pay respect to the south. The new city of Wushan has a school called the Shenzhen Bao'an Hope Middle School. Shenzhen is a thriving Special Economic Zone that borders Hong Kong, and seeing its name on a school in Wushan is like coming upon Silicon Valley Inspiration High in the middle of Appalachia. New Wushan itself seems like a vision of prosperity that has arrived from far away. The town's central square features an enormous television screen, before which crowds gather at night to watch martial-arts films. Guangdong Road is lined with plastic palm trees that are illuminated after dark. There is a coffee shop called Starbucks (with no official link to the American chain). Other shops bear English names: Well-Off Restaurant, Gold Haircut, Current Bathroom. There is a clothing boutique called Sanity.

In the new cities I rarely heard criticism of the dam. Even in rural areas, where people have received far fewer benefits, complaints tend to be mild and personal. Generally, people felt that they hadn't received their full resettlement allowances, often because of the corruption of local Communist Party cadres. But those who complained almost never questioned the basic idea of the dam. When I asked Huang Zongming what he hoped his children would do when they became adults, he said he didn't care, as long as they used their education and didn't fish. He told me that the dam was "good," because it would bring more electricity to the nation. In Wushan, I met a cabdriver who told me that his home town had leapfrogged a half century. "If it weren't for the dam, it would take another fifty years for us to reach this stage," he said.

But later in the same conversation he told me that the city wouldn't last another half century, because of landslides. The new Wushan, which has a densely concentrated population of fifty thousand, is a vertical city: high buildings on steep hillsides that have never been heavily settled. Concrete erosion controls prop up many of the neighborhoods. The cabbie drove me to Jintan Road, where there had been a recent landslide. An apartment building had been evacuated; piles of dirt still pressed against the street. I asked the cabbie if he was concerned about the fifty-year limit. "Why worry about it?" he said. "I'll be eighty by then."

During my years along the Yangtze, I had always been impressed by the resourcefulness of the people, who responded quickly to any change in their surroundings. They took the revolution of the market economy in stride; if a product became available and was in demand, shops immediately stocked it. But there was almost no long-term planning. When people spoke of the future, they meant tomorrow.

One afternoon last year, I discussed this shortsightedness with Jiang Hong, a Chinese-born geographer who teaches at the University of Wisconsin at Madison. She has studied communities in the deserts of northern China where generations of government policies have been implemented to convert the region into arable land. Many of these practices were environmentally unsound, and local residents generally resisted them. But she had noticed that in recent years there has been less opposition to such schemes, partly because free-market reforms gave people more incentive to try to change their environment. In the past, government campaigns often touted abstract goals, like the attempt to surpass the United States and Britain in steel production in the late nineteen-fifties. Such a target can inspire a peasant for only so long; nowadays everybody wants a better television set. And the lack of political stability has kept people from developing long-term expectations.

"Since 1949, policy has changed so often," Jiang Hong told me. "You never knew what would happen. In the nineteen-eighties, people saw the reforms as an opportunity. And you had to seize the opportunity, because it might not last."

Whenever I travelled along the Yangtze, I sensed that the dam's timing was perfect, because the parallel drives of Communism and capitalism had bent just enough to intersect. Building the world's biggest dam appealed to the dreams of the Communist leaders, but they never could have achieved it in the days of isolation and chaos, before the market reforms. And if the reforms had been around long enough for locals to get their bearings and look beyond satisfying today's immediate desires, they would have questioned and possibly resisted the project. In the future, when people look back at China's transition period, one of the lasting monuments may well be an enormous expanse of dead water in central China.

June 9th

At nine-thirty in the morning, after Huang Zongming has drunk a single glass of grain alcohol, the waters of Emerald Drop Lake reach a corner of the wooden frame that is propping up the fishing boat. Most of the family's belongings have yet to be carried up the hill. Offshore, a snake glides through the reservoir, its head up like a periscope.

A resident of Wushan has commissioned Huang and his nephew to caulk a long rowboat, and Chen Cihuang has been left to organize the evacuation. At nine-forty-six, the water touches another corner of the boat frame. The family has loaded the craft with a few possessions: a power drill, a basket of fishing gear, a carton of Magnificent Sound cigarettes. They throw spare lumber into the stern. An inch of water has flooded the former home; Chen, her sister-in-law, and the children wade through as they carry their possessions. Huang Po splashes his sister whenever possible.

By ten-forty-seven, Huang Po has made enough of a nuisance of himself to be excused from moving duties. He strips off his clothes and goes swimming.

At ten-fifty-nine, a sampan floats past and the pilot shouts out, "Do you have a boat to sell?"

Chen snaps back, "We're this busy and you think we're selling boats?"

By eleven-forty, all four corners of the frame are underwater. Sixteen minutes later, another sampan drifts past; somebody is selling coal. The move is complete when Huang Zongguo helps the women dismantle the roof. Huang Po suns himself, stark naked, on the prow of the new boat.

At one-thirty-four in the afternoon, the wake of a passing craft rocks the fishing boat, which lurches, creaks, and finally swings free. It floats.

Peter Hessler's highly acclaimed 2001 novel River Town *details his Peace Corps years in Fuling. After spending more than a decade in China sharply observing its people and their culture, his latest book explores the subtle nuances of what it means to be Chinese in a modern context while reflecting China's significant history. Its title was appropriately inspired by the archaeological site at Anyang, where inscriptions on shell and bone found there are the earliest known writing in East Asia, it is:* Oracle Bones: A Journey Between China's Past and Present.

Special Topic

WU GORGE

Below Wushan the river approaches the entrance to the 40-kilometre (25-mile) long Witches Gorge (*Wu Xia* or *Wu Gorge*), the middle Yangzi gorge that straddles the boundary between Chongqing Municipality and Hubei Province. So sheer are the cliffs that it is said the sun rarely penetrates. The boat passes, on the south side, the **Golden Helmet and Silver Armour Gorge** (*Jinkuang Yinjia Xia*) shaped, it is said, like an ancient warrior's silver coat of arms crowned by a round golden helmet. Ahead are the 12 peaks of Wu Gorge, famed for their dark and sombre grace.

> Six peaks grace the north side:
> Climbing Dragon Peak (*Denglong Feng*)
> Sage Spring Peak (*Shengquan Feng*)
> Facing Clouds Peak (*Chaoyun Feng*)
> Goddess Peak (*Shennu Feng*)
> Fir Tree Cone Peak (*Songluan Feng*)
> Gathered Immortals Peak (*Jixian Feng*)
>
> Three peaks flank the south side:
> Flying Phoenix Peak (*Feifeng Feng*)
> Misty Screen Peak (*Cuiping Feng*)
> Assembled Cranes Peak (*Juhe Feng*)
>
> Three more peaks may be glimpsed behind these:
> Clean Altar Peak (*Jingtan Feng*)
> Rising Cloud Peak (*Qiyun Feng*)
> Mounting Aloft Peak (*Shangsheng Feng*)

The most famous peak is **Shennu Feng** (Goddess Peak)—also called Observing the Clouds Peak—which resembles the figure of a maiden kneeling in front of a pillar. She is believed to be the embodiment of Yao Ji, the 23rd daughter of the Queen Mother of the West. Yao Ji, at the age of 18, was sent to oversee the Jade Pool of the Western Heaven, accompanied by 11 fairy handmaidens. However, she found life there lonely and cold, and took to rambling among the mountains and rivers of the mortal world. Wushan became her favourite place, and there she established a small palace.

Once, returning from a visit to the Eastern Sea on her floating cloud, she came upon 12 dragons playing havoc with the river and the mountains, and causing flooding and hardship in their wake. She summoned Da Yu the Great from his work

Wu Gorge

The Goddess Yao Ji saved the people of the gorges from flooding by slaying dragons terrorising the region. She continues to watch over the region in the form of this pillar of rock. [Yin Chun]

on the Yellow River and, alighting from her cloud, presented him with a heavenly supernatural book. This endowed him with powers to call upon the wind, rain, thunder and lightning to move the earth, thus enabling his sacred ox to slash open the gorges (which is why all oxen have bent horns), and permit the waters to drain into the Eastern Sea.

Yao Ji resolved to stay here with her 11 maidens to protect the boats from the dangerous rapids, the peasants' crops from damage, the woodcutters from wild animals, and to grow the fungus of longevity for the sick. Eventually these 11 maidens and Yao Ji became the 12 sentinel peaks of Wu Gorge. There are, of course, many variations to this story. For example, it was said that if the Goddess can be seen from the river the journey will be safe; or if she is veiled in mist or rain, this is because she is bathing and shy.

More often than not these green-clad peaks are hidden by swirls of cloud and mist, and are difficult to distinguish, though each has its own characteristics and posture. Poets have attempted to evoke both their bleakness and beauty:

"Autumn Thoughts"—Du Fu (712–770)

Jade dews deeply wilt and wound the maple woods;
On Witch Mountain, in Witch Gorge, the air is sombre, desolate.
Billowy waves from the river roar and rush towards the sky
Over the frontier pass, wind and clouds sink to the darkening earth.
These clustered chrysanthemums, twice blooming, evoke the tears of yesteryear;
A lonely boat, as ever, is moored to the heart that yearns for home.
To cut winter clothes, women everywhere ply their scissors and foot-rulers
Below the White Emperor's tall city is heard the urgent pounding of the evening wash.

As the river twists and turns, a mountain comes into view, appearing as if it will block the way. This is **Gathered Immortals Peak**. Five kilometres below this peak is a small tributary that marks the boundary between the municipality of Chongqing and Hubei Province.

This tributary has served as a boundary over the ages. During what could be considered China's chivalrous era, the Three Kingdom period (*see page 182*), it was the boundary between the Shu people to the west and the Wu to the east.

Just above the north-bank town of Guandukou—marking the end of Wu Gorge—was the site of the Flint Rapid (*Huoyan Shi*), which was very violent at high water, with limestone rocks jutting into the river like huge stone gates beckoning helpless craft. These obstacles, along with all the dangerous rocks in the shipping channel, were blown up in the 1950s.

Steeply inclined bedding is clearly visible in the lower left of this photograph of the entrance to Wu Gorge. Shennu Feng can be seen just above the crest of the bedding. The lighter-hued waters of Shengnu Brook merge with, and are lost to, the Yangzi's darker waters at the tributary's mouth. [Huang Zhengping]

(Top) *The Qing dynasty Wuduo Qiao (No Capture Bridge), which probably originated in the Ming dynasty, would nearly disappear during spring flooding.* (Above) *As water levels receded, more of it would become visible. [Bill Hurst].*

(Right) *Travellers along the old plank road could stop on Wuduo Qiao to watch sampans sail beneath it into this tributary. The bridge has now been demolished to prevent it from being a submerged hazard to vessels navigating the new reservoir. [Pat Morrow]*

Over time, the trackers' bamboo hawsers have cut grooves into many of the rocks along the Yangzi and its tributaries such as the Daning River and Shennong Stream. [Huang Zhengping]

SHENNONG STREAM

Shennong Xi (Shennong Stream) is a tributary of the Yangzi that rises in the Shennongjia. This mountain basin hosts a variety of unique flora and fauna, the source of many traditional herbal medicines. Great slopes of arrow bamboo in snowy valleys used to support many pandas, together with white-furred bear, fox and rabbit. A legendary primate, *ye ren*, a nocturnal vegetarian that nests in high trees, is said to inhabit the thick cloud-wrapped forests.

Since the completion of the dam, the water level has risen from about one metre deep (three feet) to about 40 metres (131 feet) deep, meaning the Shennong Stream is navigable further up its course. Cruise vessels once moored beneath the suspension bridge at Guandukou, at the mouth of the tributary, but the town is no more. Vessels now dock at a new pier just above the former Guandukou, and passengers then transfer to a smaller vessel for a journey upstream to Bamboo Gorge.

Badong, the county seat and the westernmost county town of Hubei Province, has been relocated three kilometres (1.8 miles) upstream on the south bank from its original site, which has been submerged under the risen waters. The town now stands opposite the former Guandukou and is linked to the far bank by means of a new cable-stayed bridge, which is part of the newly constructed Hubei–Chongqing trunk road that runs through the Gorges.

In ancient times, Badong was situated on the northern side of the Yangzi and belonged to the State of Ba; in the Song Dynasty (960–1279) the town was moved to the southern bank. Local products include tung oil, lacquer, tea, medicinal herbs and animal skins. Labourers, pitch black with coal dust, used to be a common sight in Badong as they loaded and unloaded river lighters, negotiating the steep steps above the river with staff in hand, humping baskets of coal. Houses with wooden balconies huddled together on pillars embedded in solid concrete foundations above the bank of the river.

A short distance after leaving Guandukou a single coffin belonging to the Ba people can be seen perched in a small cave high up on the right-hand side. Some distance beyond, as the river meanders through tranquil scenery of verdant river cliffs and terraced fields, is a large cave on the left-hand side called **Swallow Cave**. The entrance is 100 metres (328 feet) high and 40 metres (131 feet) wide and extends for eight kilometres (five miles) into the mountain. Well-developed rectilinear joints in the rock control the vertical sides and horizontal roof of the cave, and a number of large stalactites hang above the entrance. The cave is populated by a very unusual species of bird, the Himalayan swiftlet (*Aerodramus brevirostris*), called in Chinese *duan zui jin si yan*, literally short-billed, gold silk swallow. Normally only found in coastal areas in Southeast Asia, it is for some unexplained reason also to be found in caves on the Shennong Stream and its source mountains, the Shennongjia.

The region is famous for rare medicinal herbs and it is not uncommon to see local tribesmen in their boats gathering plants growing among the rocks at the edge of the river.

On reaching **Bamboo Gorge**, passengers board small, traditional wooden boats known as *wan dou jiao*, or peapod boats, due to their shape. The boats are 13 metres (43 feet) long, 1.8 metres (six feet) wide and 0.7 metres (2.3 feet) deep. Teams of trackers—local Tujia people—skillfully paddle the boats upstream through the narrow, steep-sided limestone gorge. Stalactites are suspended from overhanging cliffs and large-leafed Chinese parasol trees shade the water, by now running almost clear. As brown dippers hop from rock to rock, butterflies sip nectar from pink hibiscus flowers. Eagles can sometimes be spotted soaring overhead.

The stream gradually becomes shallower and, before long, the boats reach stretches of fast-flowing rapids. Here the boatmen jump into the water and haul the craft using traditional bamboo ropes, accompanied by the chants used for centuries by trackers on the Yangzi, their cries echoing around the cliffs above. A rare species of yellow lily can be seen clinging to the rock walls. Flowering only during the autumn months, their habitat is restricted to the limestone cliffs of the Three Gorges. The flowers, growing on a single stem with no leaves, are shaped rather like

(Top left) *The 110-metre-high Swallow Cave on Shennong Stream. [Kevin Bishop]*; (top right) *on reaching Bamboo Gorge passengers board traditional, small, wooden peapod boats to travel further upstream, paddled by local Tujia boatmen. [Kevin Bishop]*

(Bottom) *The trackers still use traditional bamboo hawsers as opposed to synthetic ropes. [Yin Chun]*

Wu Gorge

(Top) *Clothes are not always worn by trackers, as they may be swept off by the strong currents of the main river or even the Shennong stream.* [Lu Jin]; (Below) *A tracker jumps into the water to help his comrades on shore. The surrounding limestone gorge is renowned for its unique flora and fauna.* [Yin Chun]

Local Tujia people have hauled boats through the region's rapids for centuries.
The world is truly a team effort, and the dangers of any one failing is shared by all. [Yin Chun]

A large steering oar, a yulo, is placed on the bow of any boat heading downstream.
This helps to guide the craft through the rapids. [Yin Chun]

a bulb of garlic, hence the local name 'stone garlic'. They are used as a snake-bite remedy. In the quieter reaches of the gorges, golden monkeys (*Rhinopithecus roxelana*) still roam in chattering bands. These are a very colourful, bright orange-yellow, hence the name. Since it shares its habitat with the panda, it is well-protected and, happily, not an extremely rare species.

After a short rest for the boatmen and a chance for passengers to stretch their legs, the boats turn around and rush back downstream, aided by the skilful use of the long *yulo*, a heavy steering oar placed over the bow to guide the boat through the swirling rapids. Once back on the more placid stretches the boatmen are able to relax and it is a customary for them to sing Tujia trackers' songs or, if there are women aboard, to sing love songs that echo in the canyons.

The peapod boats are solidly built and very stable in the water, each carrying 12 passengers and five or six crew. Although passengers are obliged to wear lifejackets as a precaution, the deftness of the boatmen leaves you in no doubt that you are in safe hands.

Wu Gorge

Traditionally, trackers would make their own rope sandals, which give good grip even on slippery stones. They are still worn by the Shennong Stream trackers. [Erik Potter]

POETRY AND PADDLING

Qu Yuan, one of China's greatly loved patriotic poets, was born in 340BCE in the Qu family village very near Zigui. The fame of the walled town that stood on the north bank dates from this period long ago. **Qu Yuan's Memorial Hall**, with its distinctive white gateway and walls edged in red, has been relocated to a higher site, safe above the final water level. It contains a Ming-dynasty (1368–1644) statue of the poet, as well as stone inscriptions. The old town has been demolished and its residents moved to New Zigui near Maoping on the south side of the river, not far from the Three Gorges Dam site.

Zigui's gift to the world: Dragonboating! [Yin Chun]

The great poet served as a chancellor to King Huai of the Kingdom of Chu, with special responsibility for the royal clans. The king had complete trust in him until discord developed among the clans and Qu was falsely slandered. Banished from the capital, he wandered about in Hubei Province, deeply sad and bitter. His poetry and essays reveal his romanticism, loyalty and patriotism. Qu had vigorously advocated that the State of Chu stand firm against attack by the Qin state, but his advice had gone unheeded, and in May of the year 278 BCE, he drowned himself in Dongting Lake at the age of 62.

According to historical records, the local people scoured Dongting Lake for his body, beating drums and racing their boats in the course of their search. This event came to be commemorated each May, and to this day the Dragon Boat Festival (*Duanwu Jie*) is held in the river towns up and down the Yangzi and in many other parts of China. *Zongzi*—packets of glutinous rice steamed in leaves and tied with reeds—were thrown into the water as a sacrifice to Qu Yuan. The tradition of eating *zongzi* at this festival continues in Chinese communities the world over.

There are many fairy tales about Qu Yuan. East of Zigui is a bay named after him. It is said that when he died, a huge fish swallowed him up and swam all the way from Dongting Lake past Zigui to Yufu and back again, where it disgorged the body, amazingly still intact (*see also* page 96). It is said that he never forgot his ancestral home; to the farmers there he introduced a jade-white rice that was soft and fragrant. Locals remember him at each new rice harvest.

XIANG XI (FRAGRANT STREAM)

In the tree-shaded seclusion of her ancient courtyard home above the Xiang Stream is a statue of the Han Dynasty beauty Wang Zhaojun, a virtuous patriot who, through her honesty, was denied Imperial-favour. [Raynor Shaw]

A small stream just below Zigui and above the entrance to Xiling Gorge is well known to all Chinese as the home of the beautiful Han-Dynasty (206 BCE–220 CE) heroine Wang Zhaojun. Her story is the quintessence of virtuous patriotism.

Zhaojun, a maid of honour to the emperor, refused to bribe the painter from whose portraits of court ladies the emperor traditionally chose his concubines. In revenge, the painter portrayed her as quite hideous, and so imperial favour was denied her. In 22 BCE the emperor, wishing to make a marriage alliance with the northern Xiongnu king, chose Wang Zhaojun. Only then did he set eyes on her; he was captivated but it was too late. Married to the Xiongnu king, Zhaojun was able to exert a good influence on relations between the Xiongnu and Han peoples, which gained her great respect. The emperor, in his rage at having lost her, decreed the beheading of the corrupt court painter. Local people say that before her marriage, Wang Zhaojun returned to her home town and, when washing in the stream, dropped a precious pearl that caused the stream to become crystal-clear and fragrant. Tradition names a pavilion-topped mound to the south of Hohhot in Inner Mongolia as her burial site.

Zhaojun's ancient courtyard home overlooks the Xiang Stream above the town of Xingshan. Trees line the opposite shore, with guest cabins built in the branches.

Wu Gorge

(Following pages) Xiling Xia with a frosty winter coating. Consider an off-season visit to China, it is often much quieter, and prices can be more attractive. [Lu Jin]

XILING GORGE

Xiling Gorge starts at Xiang Xi and zigzags for 76 kilometres (47 miles) down to Yichang. It is the longest, and historically the most dangerous, of the Yangzi gorges. Before the passage was made safe in the 1950s, 'the whole surface of the water was a swirling mass of whirlpools sucking the froth they created into their centres'. Xiling comprises seven small gorges and had two of the fiercest rapids in the stretch of the Yangzi between Chongqing and Yichang.

On entering the western entrance the boat passes through the four-kilometre (2.5-mile) long **Military Books and Precious Sword Gorge** (*Bingshu Baojian Xia*). The gorge is named after an exposure of stratified rock, now underwater, that resembled a stack of books. There are two stories told of these rock formations, both concerning heroes from the classical novel *Romance of the Three Kingdoms* (*see* page 182).

One legend has it that Zhuge Liang (181–234), military adviser to the King of Shu, became seriously ill while passing this way. Unwilling to entrust his valuable military treatises to any member of his entourage, he placed them up here on this inaccessible ledge, to be kept safe for later generations. The second tale is also about Zhuge Liang. It was he who devised the stratagems that enabled Liu Bei, the king, to defeat Cao Cao at the Red Cliff Battle (208 CE). Afraid that he would eventually fall out of favour, Zhuge Liang retired from official life and went into seclusion, hiding his military writings and sword here.

A large cleft rock stands at the mouth of a ravine—Rice Granary Gorge (*Micang Xia*)—on the south side. Fine sand, blown by river winds, piles up on this rock, and slowly sifts through a hole underneath. People call this Zhuge Liang's Granary.

Further on was the site of the perilous Xintan (new rapids) that rushed over submerged rocks. In 1524, rock slides from the northern mountainside created this 3.2-kilometre (2-mile) long, triple-headed rapid. The fall of the riverbed was estimated at about six metres (19.7 feet). When the water level was low, junks would unload their cargo and be hauled over by 100 or more trackers. Passengers would re-join their boat beyond the rapid after walking along a winding mountain track and passing through the village of Xintan. In 1941 the steamboat Minxi came to grief and several hundred people perished. The swift current carried boats downriver through Xintan at the rate of seven metres (23 feet) per second.

In 1854 a local merchant collected subscriptions from river traders and built three life-saving craft to patrol the Xin Tan rapids, and to salvage boats and

In the heart of Xiling Gorge at the Three Gorges Project, a ship takes the maiden voyage through the newly completed dual-channel, five-step locks, 15 June, 2003. [Lu Jin]

survivors. This was the beginning of the Yangzi River Lifeboat Office, which eventually maintained its Red Boats at all the danger spots along the Chongqing–Yichang stretch until the 1940s (see page 147).

An earthquake in 1984 triggered a rockslide that slid half of the ancient town of Xintan into the current. A new town has been constructed higher up on the north bank above the final water level. In the town and visible from the river is an obelisk, which is a memorial to Cornell Plant, an Englishman who lived here for about 20 years during the early 20th Century. He served as river inspector for the Chinese Imperial Maritime Service and was responsible for setting up the navigation system on the Yangzi. This system continues today, with over 500 new buoys being placed in the reservoir, following Plant's original marking plan of white-north shore and red-south shore.

Beyond Xintan the channel winds east and then south, towards **Ox Liver and Horse Lungs Gorge**, apparently named after yellow stalactite formations that used to be on the north side. These were removed to save them from the rising waters and are on display in the museum in New Zigui. One of the 'Horse's Lungs' was said to be shot away by British gunboats during the reign of Guangxu (1875–1908).

In the middle stretch of Xiling Gorge, the strange and lovely **Kongling Gorge** towers above the iron-green rocks of the 2.5-kilometre (1.5-mile) long Kongling Tan, which were the worst of all the Yangzi rapids. Seventeen catastrophes involving steamships occurred here between 1900 and 1945. The larger boulders choking the channel had names such as 'Big Pearl', 'Monk's Rock' and 'Chickens' Wings', but the deadliest of all was known as 'Come to Me'. Apparently the only way for riverboat captains to successfully negotiate this rock was for them to sail straight for it and then turn at the last possible moment; the current would carry the boat safely past. But should the skipper be too timid and turn too soon, the boat would be dashed on the rocks.

Thankfully for the modern day traveller, the rise in water level behind the Dam has made such experiences a thing of the past. Today, one can only try to imagine the previous dramas and terrors while sailing along the new 'peaceful lake' of the reservoir.

Downriver from the Dam, the boat enters **Yellow Ox Gorge** (*Huangniu Xia*)—said to look like a man riding an ox. Here the passage widens out and sweeps past the ancient **Huangling Temple** (*Huangling Miao*), nestled on the south bank amid orange and pomelo trees. The great poet Du Fu wrote of his journey through this gorge:

Three dawns shine upon the Yellow Ox.
Three sunsets—and we go so slowly.
Three dawns—again three sunsets—
And we do not notice that our hair is white as silk.

(Right) Ox Liver and Horse Lung Gorge was once famous for its impressive stalactites, which were claimed by the 139-metre rise in the level of the Yangzi. [Lu Jin]

Huangling Temple, on the south bank, is said to have been first built during the Spring and Autumn Period (770–476 BCE), is dedicated to the great Da Yu who, with his yellow ox, controlled the flood waters and dug the gorges (*see* page 123). The present hall was built in the Ming Dynasty (1368–1644) and houses a statue of Da Yu, as well as stone inscriptions. Zhuge Liang is also said to have dug the Yellow Ox Spring (or Toad Rock, as it is sometimes called) nearby. Its clear water, according to the Tang-Dynasty *Book of Teas*, was excellent for brewing tea, and Yellow Ox Spring was classified as the Fourth Spring under Heaven.

After one passes below Huangling Temple, near a pavilion, a natural stone arch bridge may be seen with a white 'aspara' angel statue on top. From here downstream is the last stretch of natural scenery of the Gorges—the **Bright Moon Gorge** (*Mingyue Xia*) and the **Lantern Shadow Gorge** (*Dengying Xia*) loom ahead. The latter is overlooked on the south side by peaks in the shape of four figures from the 16th-Century Chinese novel, *Pilgrimage to the West* (also known as *The Monkey King*). When the rays of the evening sun fall upon these peaks, the figures do appear lifelike—Xuan Zang standing on the precipice edge; Monkey (*Sun Wukong*) peering into the distance; Sandy (*Sha Heshang*) carrying the luggage; and Pigsy (*Zhu Bajie*) riding a horse, all silhouetted against the fading light like characters in a shadow play.

At the last turn of the Xiling Gorge is the village of Shibei with a prominent pillar—a memorial to the 1939 battle with Japanese troops who were stopped here during their invasion. Just upstream, below the Lantern Shadow rocks, is a new guest house in traditional style, 'Home of the Gorges' (*Sanxia Ren Jia*), with a clear stream flowing out of a canyon and some wooden junks tied at a dock. This small enterprise is a new piece of nostalgia in the face of nearby massive developments.

The last of the smaller gorges is **Yellow Cat Gorge** (*Huangmao Xia*), so named from the yellow cat-shaped rock on the riverside. Qi Taigong Fishing is the name given to a rock beside a cave on the south face, because of its fanciful resemblance to a bearded old man wearing yellow trousers.

Now the boat reaches the strategic **Southern Crossing Pass** (*Nanjin Guan*), with Three Travellers' Cave above (*see* page 171), marking the end of Xiling Gorge and the three great Yangzi gorges. From here the river widens dramatically and ahead lies Gezhou Dam and Yichang.

The Gezhou Dam (*see* page 150), impressive if first seen cruising up-river, is now an anticlimax for those sailing down. Nevertheless, it was China's largest before the construction of the Three Gorges Dam, and is still the third largest dam in the world and the world's largest low-water dam. It produces 2.715 million kilowatts of electricity per hour. A single stage lock allows ships to descend to the level of Yichang.

RIVER RITES

By Madeleine Lynn

Life on board a junk was hard and dangerous work. Cornell Plant, River Inspector for the Chinese Imperial Maritime Service in the 1900s, wrote about the risks of travelling through the Three Gorges: Chinese say that one junk in ten is badly damaged, and one in 20 totally wrecked each trip. Probably not 20 per cent reach Chungking unscathed, and never one without experiencing some hair's-breadth escape.

It was common for trackers to fall from the towpaths to their deaths or to break a limb and be left behind by their junk. Thus Yangzi boatmen had a wealth of rites and taboos that had to be observed to ensure a safe passage.

At the beginning of a voyage and also before entering the Three Gorges, the most dangerous stretch of the river, it was the cook's task to light incense, set off firecrackers and, most importantly, to kill a rooster and sprinkle the blood on the bows of the junk. Writing in 1880, Captain Gill described how to get through the Xintan Rapids safely. The junk could hire a shaman who would come on board with a yellow flag inscribed 'Power of the Water! A happy star for the whole journey'. As the boat ploughed through the waves dragged by the straining trackers, the shaman would stand at the bow, waving the flag in a regular motion to appease the powers of the water. It was also essential to sprinkle rice on the water all the way through the rapids.

Like fishermen everywhere in China, many Yangzi boatmen still believe that it is very bad luck to turn over a fish at table: 'capsize fish, capsize boat'. Another taboo is resting chopsticks on top of a rice bowl in a position that suggests a junk ran aground. Unlike Western sailors, however, there is no taboo against women aboard ship and junk owners usually brought their wives along.

Sometimes fish swimming upstream used to jump onto the decks. They were considered demons and had to be taken ashore and buried. Boatmen also had to contend with the ghosts of the drowned, who would string themselves in a line behind a boat, preparing to board the vessel and cause trouble. The way to shake them loose was to cut quickly in front of another boat, so that the ghosts would lose their grip and attach themselves to the boat behind. Not a very neighbourly thing to do! Describing this to explorer Wong How Man in 1986, a boat captain recounted that, 'In the past, it was a game that often left the trailing boat's owner jumping, cursing and shooting off firecrackers to pacify his increased string of ghosts.'

Meanwhile those living on shore had floods to contend with. The lovely pagodas all along the river were built for flood prevention. It was believed that floods were often caused by dragons (since they have the power to control the waters), or by evil demons. A pagoda built on top of the hill inhabited by one of these creatures could prevent him from coming out and causing trouble. A pagoda could also prevent the wealth of the nearby town from being swept away by the current.

After the disastrous flood of 1788, which inundated over 30 counties in Hubei Province, the Emperor ordered nine iron oxen (*see* page 15) to be placed along the banks of the river. According to the court record: 'The Sea Dragon submits to Iron and the Ox belongs to Earth, Earth controls Water, the Iron Ox can suppress the flood.' This was following Chinese theories of the properties of the elements: fire, metal, earth, water and air.

The present Huangling Temple was constructed during the Ming Dynasty, although the original is thought to have been built in the Spring and Autumn Period (770–476 BCE). Inside the hall is a statue of Da Yu, and in a nearby courtyard is a statue of his yellow ox he employed to control flood waters. As the temple is downstream of the Three Gorges Dam it has not been affected by the rise in water level. [Lu Jin]

TRACKING THROUGH THE RAPIDS

*T*hough the junk was now apparently safe, for it breasted the smooth, swift water of the second sluice and was no longer being thrown from side to side, the heaviest work still remained to be done. I turned to watch the trackers, for theirs was now the heavy work of making many tons of cypress go uphill on a fiercely resisting roadway of water. It was a moving sight—horribly depressing, to see more than three hundred human beings reduced to the level of work animals, blind-folded asses and oxen; yet thrilling too, to see the irresistible force of their co-operation, for the three hundred and fifty cloth shoes of their each step up the slope were planted in the same moment, and the sad trackers' cries, 'Ayah!... Ayah!,' were sung in a great unison choir of agony and joy, and the junk did move.

It moved, however, more and more slowly, as the last and hardest test of the trackers' labor began—heaving the junk over the head of the rapid, over the round, swift crest of the sluice. The bow of the junk seemed to dig into the water there. The rope grew taut. The great crowd of towing men hung for a long time unable to move. I saw the cook look down toward the junk, obviously at a loss what to do.

Then suddenly from midstream, from the very center of danger, came a lovely, clear, high-pitched line of song.

It was Old Pebble. I looked out and saw him standing on the deck, himself leaning as if to pull, hurling a beautiful song at the crowd on the bank.

On the proper beat the many trackers gave out a kind of growl and moved their feet forward a few inches, and the bow of the junk dug deeper into the head of the sluice. They took a second, firmer step. And a third, and a fourth.

I had never heard Old Pebble sing such a haunting melody. I saw that he was in a kind of ecstasy. His face shone in a grimace of hard work and happiness. I remembered my doubts about his credo of 'simplicity', which he had recited to me in our first evening on the river, and I remembered my distress that such a sturdy young man did not avow personal goals of wealth, love, honor, and fame. Now I saw from his face that this was his life's goal; this instant of work, this moment's line of song, this accord with his poor fellow men, this brief spurt of useful loyalty to the cranky, skinny, half-mad owner of the junk on which he had shipped, and above all this fleeting triumph over the Great River.

At last the junk raised its head, shivered, and shot suddenly forward into the still water of the pond above the rapids.

When it was over, and the junk was pulled up to the loading platform, Old Pebble was streaming sweat, but he looked very happy.

I walked down to the river's edge to see what he would say. He jumped ashore and bent down to the river and scooped up double handfuls of the brown water and washed his face, sloshing and snorting like a small boy. I moved near him. He looked up. All he said was, 'Ayah, this river is a turtle.'

John Hersey, A Single Pebble, 1914

Teams of trackers appear strangely like penguins on an iceflow as they haul heavily laden cargo junks through the treacherous rapids of the Three Gorges in this historical photograph taken in the late 19th century. [Joseph Dautremer]

HOW MUCH FOR A LIFE?

In 1854, a rich merchant living near Xin Tan, one of the most dangerous of all the rapids in the Three Gorges, raised subscriptions to build three life-boats. Painted red to distinguish them from regular craft, they soon became known as the Red Boats. More money was raised over the years to increase the fleet and in the 1880s the running of the service was taken over by the government, although funds still came from public subscription. By the early 1900s there were almost 50 boats stationed along the river. In 1800 alone they saved 1,473 lives from 49 wrecked junks.

A Red Boat would accompany each vessel on the most perilous parts of the journey—being dragged upstream by the trackers over the different sets of rapids. Downstream voyages were not as dangerous, so a special escort was not deemed necessary. When a wreck occurred a gun was fired as the summons for all Red Boats to come and help.

The life-boats were not allowed to salvage cargo from the wrecks. However, there was a reward system for the salvaging of human beings. W E Geil, who travelled along the Yangzi in 1904 on his way to Burma, describes how it worked:

On life-saving the Chinese have curious notions. While eating cakes cooked in lamp oil in a tea house in Chintan village [Xintan], the skipper of the Red Boat came in and I asked him certain questions about the pagoda for destitute souls. He told me that for the recovery of a dead body from the water, a reward of eight hundred cash is given by the emperor. It used to be eight hundred cash for saving a live man and four hundred for a dead one. but it was soon discovered that this did not pay, so it was reversed, and now four hundred cash are given to save a live man and eight hundred to recover a dead one. This allows four hundred cash to bury the man if he dies after being taken out of the water. This interesting fact was further explained to me by another of the Red Boat men—that the dead man involves funeral expenses and the live man none! This is good Celestial reasoning. It would be more profitable to drown a man before pulling him out. I found out afterwards that the reward of four hundred cash is given provided the rescuer gets his clothes wet; otherwise he gets but two hundred.

W E Geil, A Yankee on the Yangtse, 1904

*Rafting on Juiwan stream is extremely popular due to its scenic placid green shoals
(20 in all) and heart-pumping roiling rollercoaster-like whitewater. Rafters descend
90 metres (295 feet) in the course of the 13 kilometres-long (8 miles-long) journey.
Jiuwan Stream is not far from New Zigui and the Three Gorges Project.
The poet Qu Yuan wrote about the stream in "Laments at Parting" ... "I grew orchids
beside Juiwan Stream, and planted many scented grasses of a hundred mu". [Huang Zhengping]*

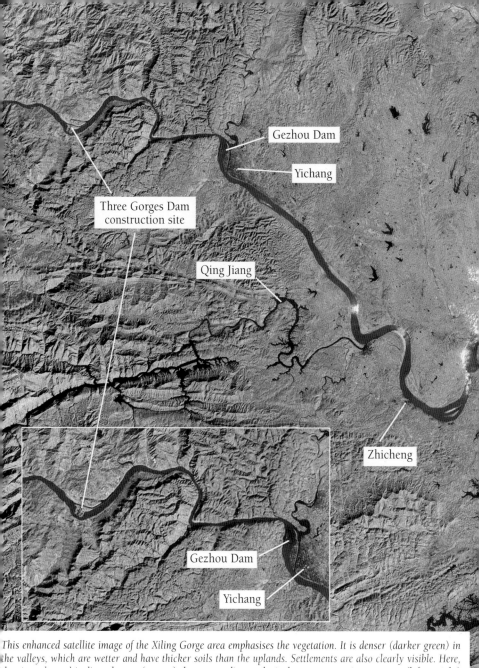

This enhanced satellite image of the Xiling Gorge area emphasises the vegetation. It is denser (darker green) in the valleys, which are wetter and have thicker soils than the uplands. Settlements are also clearly visible. Here, the river channel is discordant to (crosses) the surrounding geological structure, cutting a course (left to right) across a complex pattern of ridges and folds (Contrast this pattern with the situation shown on the satellite image on pages 40–1). The Three Gorges Dam and the Gezhou Dam can be seen on the main image, and enlarged on the inset. The Qing Jiang, a major Yangzi tributary, crosses the centre of the photograph and joins the main stream near Zhicheng. [Landsat-7 satellite data acquired by USGS. This fusion image was processed and supplied by Geocarto International Centre, Hong Kong. Copyright © 2001 Geocarto and Airphoto International Ltd.]

THE YANGZI RIVER DAMS

The concept of damming the Yangzi River is not new. In 1919 Dr Sun Yat-sen published a paper titled *A Plan to Develop Industry*. The paper contained a section on *Improvements to Navigable Rivers and Canals*, which recommended the construction of several large dams to enhance flood control, provide irrigation, and to generate electricity. Geological surveys to determine suitable locations for a dam in the Yangzi valley began in the 1930s. By 1947 a team of 50 American geologists and engineers were working at one of the potential sites. Following the Communist victory in 1949, work was suspended.

During the 20th century most of the large rivers in the world were dammed—the Ganges, Indus, Nile, Niger, Danube, Zambesi, and Parana. Only the Congo, Amazon (although the Tocantins tributary was dammed) and Yangzi remained un-dammed. The first dam across the Yangzi, the Gezhou Dam, was constructed between 1970 and 1989. However, plans for a larger dam across the Yangzi River were still being made.

Many of the Yangzi tributaries have already been harnessed by smaller dams and diversion structures. The power of the waters falling from the Tibetan Plateau are an inducement to build electrical industrial complexes such as the large Ertan Dam on the Dadu River feeding the extensive smelting and metal refining centre at Panzhihua in Sichuan Province. The Chinese Ministry of Water Resources has proposed eight more dams in the upper Yangzi. Two are under construction near Lijiang and the Great Bend of the Yangzi.

THE THREE GORGES DAM

Following extensive surveys, two potential sites for a large dam were selected at Sandouping and Taipingxi. Both are areas of granite in a region of folded sedimentary rocks. The site finally selected for the Three Gorges Dam is at Sandouping, 27 kilometres upstream from the Gezhou Dam and the widest point in the gorges, where the channel was 1,000 metres wide. Zhongbao Island, 1,000 metres long by 200 metres wide, was located in the middle of the channel.

Strong citizen opposition to the Three Gorges Project forced the People's Congress to temporarily suspend plans for the dam in March 1989. However, the project was swiftly resurrected by Premier Li Peng in the aftermath of the Beijing massacre in June 1989. In 1993, almost 75 years after Sun Yat-sen's paper was published, 49 years after site selection surveys were initiated, and four years after the Gezhou Dam was commissioned, work began on the Three Gorges Project.

Construction was planned in three phases over a period of 17 years between 1993 and 2009, at a total cost of 90 billion yuan. The Three Gorges Dam and associated infrastructure was estimated to cost 50 billion yuan. A further 40 billion yuan was allocated for resettlement of the population living below the final reservoir level of 175 metres asl (above sea level). During the peak of construction activity, the project occupied a security-controlled construction area of 15.28 square kilometres, employed 27,000 labourers working 24 hours a day in three shifts, and was overseen by 200 local and overseas engineers. The final phase employs 15,000 workers. When completed the Three Gorges Dam will be the largest hydroelectric dam in the world. The concrete gravity dam stretches for 2,309.47 metres across the valley, reaches a height of 185 metres asl, which is a maximum of 181 metres (equivalent to a 60-storey building) above the deepest part of the river bed, and is 80 metres wide at the crest. Water will be impounded to a final height of 175 metres asl, which is 113 metres above the level at the Gezhou Dam. Water storage will amount to 70 billion cubic metres in a reservoir extending for about 600 kilometres upstream to a point 65 kilometres above Chongqing.

During the First Phase, from 1993 to the end of 1997, the southern river channel was closed off with a reinforced concrete coffer dam. A diversion channel was excavated and a temporary ship lock was constructed on the north bank. The temporary lock was 240 metres long, 24 metres wide and four metres deep. Navigation continued through the middle channel, by-passing the main channel in which construction of the dam was carried out.

The Second Phase, between 1998 and 2003, involved constructing the second stage coffer dams and rerouting the river through the diversion channel. These works allowed the permanent five-step ship lock, the spillway, the intake dam and the northern power station to be constructed. Two flights of ship locks, each of five stages, have been installed. The northern flight for upstream vessels and the southern flight is for downstream vessels. Each lock measures 280 metres long, 34 metres wide, and five metres deep. They are designed to accommodate vessels up to 10,000 tons. Passage through the lock takes about two hours. The locks are closed at both ends by a pair of mitre gates. Each gate is 20 metres wide, 39.5 metres high and weighs 900 tons The lower sluice gate of the spillway has a slot for sediment flushing. Opening of the fifth step will coincide with raising the reservoir to the final height of 175 metres asl. Upon completion, passage through the five steps will take from three to five hours.

The Third and final Phase, between 2003 and 2009, commenced on 16 June 2003 with the closing of the diversion channel and temporary ship lock, rerouting the river through the spillway dam and raising the water level to 135 metres asl. Following the water level rise, the first four steps of the five-step permanent ship lock, the spillway and the sluice gate were opened on 16 August 2003. During this phase the ship elevator will be constructed. The lift will be 120 metres long, 18 metres wide and 3.5 metres deep to accommodate vessels up to 3,000 tons. Passage time will be between 30 to 45 minutes. The third stage reinforced concrete coffer dam was erected, allowing construction of the northern power station that is 643.7 metres long and houses 14 generators. Work began in July 2003 and will be completed by 2009. A second power station, 584.2 metres long and housing 12 generators, is being constructed at the southern end of the dam.

Included in the project is a new 28-kilometre-long expressway, opened in 1996, connecting the Three Gorges Dam site with Yichang and the Gezhou Dam site. The road has five tunnels, the longest being 3.6 kilometres. Journey time is now reduced from two hours to 30 minutes. Immediately downstream from the dam is a 900-metre-span suspension bridge, built between 1994 and 1996. The bridge weighs 290 tons, cost 390 million yuan to build and is supported on two British-manufactured cables costing 100 million yuan each.

During the 16-year project, 102.83 million cubic metres of rock and soil will be excavated and 31.98 million cubic metres of earth and rock embankments built. A total volume of 27.94 million cubic metres of concrete will have been placed, incorporating 463,000 tons of reinforcing bars. In addition, 256,500 tons of steelwork will have been erected.

The four main objectives of the dam are flood control, electricity generation, and improvements to navigation and irrigation.

Because 70 per cent of the tributaries are in the upper reaches of the river the majority of the seasonal runoff from the Yangzi river basin can be intercepted at Sandouping, thereby protecting the flood lower reaches. The reservoir has a flood storage capacity of 22.15 billion cubic metres and is designed to accommodate the one in 100 year frequency flood, rather than the one in ten year flood of the Gezhou Dam. During normal years December, January and February are the main dry season months and July, August and September are the peak flooding season. The flood control strategy is based on this seasonal pattern. From early December to early February the reservoir will be maintained at the maximum 175 metre level, but between February and May the reservoir will be lowered to the 155 metre level, allowing a 20-metre flood control capacity to contain the initial flood. During May and June the reservoir will be lowered by a further ten metres to the 145 metre level, creating a 30-metre flood control capacity. The reservoir will be maintained at the 145 metre level during the flood season months of July to September.

With 33 per cent of China's 1.2 billion population concentrated in the Yangzi valley, the demand for electricity is high. Hydroelectricity will, in future, be generated within the region. This will avoid the need for expensive power transmission and reduce the current reliance on coal fired generation, which is polluting. Currently between 40 and 50 million tons of coal are used each year, transported from the Wei River valley in Shaanxi Province, or from Inner Mongolia.

Electricity generation will be carried out at two power stations. The 700 megawatt (MW) generators, driving Francis-type turbines, have been ordered from

Installation of the Francis-type turbines for hydroelectric generation at the Three Gorges Dam.
[China Yangtze Three Gorges Project Development Corporation]

Yangzi Dams

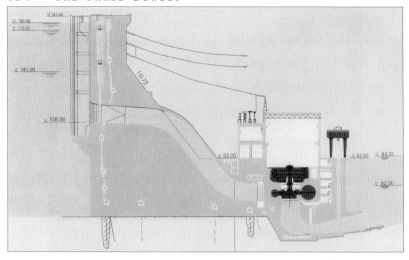

Cross-section of the intake dam and powerhouse of the Three Gorges Dam.
[China Yangtze Three Gorges Project Development Corporation]

General Electric (Canada), ABB (Switzerland), Siemens (Germany) and Alstom (France). Total generating capacity from the initial 26 sets of generators will be 18,200 MW. An area on the south bank has been reserved for six additional generating sets. Four 700 MW generators will be commissioned each year until 2007. Eventually there will be a total of 40 power generators at the main dam, with a total generating capacity of 28,000 MW. When fully operational the Three Gorges plant will generate 84.7 Terawatt hours (TWh—one trillion or 1012 watt hours) or 15 per cent of China's electricity needs. Distribution will be by 15 transmission lines. Supply to Hubei and Sichuan provinces and Chongqing Municipality in central China will be by 500 kilovolt alternating current lines and to the cities of Shanghai and Guangzhou by 500 kilovolt direct current lines.

Because of the marked seasonality of the rainfall, prior to construction of the dams river levels fluctuated markedly. Thus navigation was very seasonal. When the dam is filled to the final 175 metre level the water level at Chongqing will be raised by 45 metres, allowing year round navigation to reach the city. The ship locks on the dam are designed for an annual one-way movement of 50 million tons.

In recent decades North China has become drier, the discharge of the Yellow River has decreased to crisis levels, the problem of desertification has increased and Beijing has experienced severe water shortages. Related to the Three Gorges Project is a project known as the South to North Water Transfer Scheme, which is designed to convey surplus water from the Yangtze River north to the Yellow River and Beijing (*see* page 14). This requirement was an important factor in designing the final height of the Three Gorges Dam.

ENVIRONMENTAL AND SOCIAL CONCERNS
OF THE THREE GORGES PROJECT

Construction of the massive Three Gorges Dam clearly will have an immense impact on the regime of the Yangtze and on the surrounding region. Many of the potential problems have been addressed in wide-ranging environmental impact assessments and other studies carried out during the planning stages of the dam. Safety of the dam structure and ensuring water quality are the two overriding concerns.

Since the 1970s, earthquake studies have been carried out in the dam and reservoir area to assess rock characteristics, geological structures, fault activity, and potential water seepage. Rock stress measurements have been made in 300- to 500-metre-deep boreholes. These studies have concluded that both the dam site and the reservoir area are seismically stable. A magnitude six earthquake is the maximum predicted in the region. However, the dam has been designed to resist an earthquake of magnitude seven. Large landslides occur in the reservoir area, but studies have shown that most of the banks are composed of hard rock, major faults are few, and neotectonic activity (recent earth movements) is low. Therefore, it was concluded that the reservoir banks are stable and that landslides would not adversely affect navigation or the dam structures.

The annual average sediment load of the Yangzi River is about 490 million tons. Reduction of the current velocity caused by the dam could create undesirable sedimentation problems that would ultimately fill up the reservoir, rendering it worthless. For example, prior to the construction of dams along the Colorado River in the USA, the measured annual sediment load was 135 million tons a year at the mouth. This was reduced to 0.1 million tons a year after the dams were built, indicating retention of eroded sediments within the drainage basin.

Consequently, studies of the Yangzi River began in the 1960s using observation, analogue analyses, mathematical modelling, and physical modelling to assess the optimum design for flushing the sediment through the dam. Altogether 14 physical models were built—five of the dam area and nine of the upper reaches—at scales of between 1/100 and 1/300. Modelling results concluded that because about 84 per cent of the annual sediment load is carried during the flood season from July to September the reservoir level should be kept at the lower level of 145 metres to allow the flood waters to flush the reservoir. In addition, several planned water conservancy projects on the major tributaries, including shelter-belt forestry schemes, will reduce incoming sediment loads. Calculations indicated that after 80 to 100 years of operation the reservoir will still have between 86 per cent to 92 per cent of its original capacity.

This aerial view of the dam clearly showns the central spillway that separates the generating stations on each side of it. In this picture one of the coffer dams remains. (bottom of the photograph) This has since been demolished and the dam is now complete. At the top of the photograph, the

double-lane, five-stage ship lock can be seen. The lock began operating in mid-2003, when some of the generators were also first pressed into service. By the end of that year, six generators, each capable of generating 700 megawatts, were producing electricity. [Lu Jin]

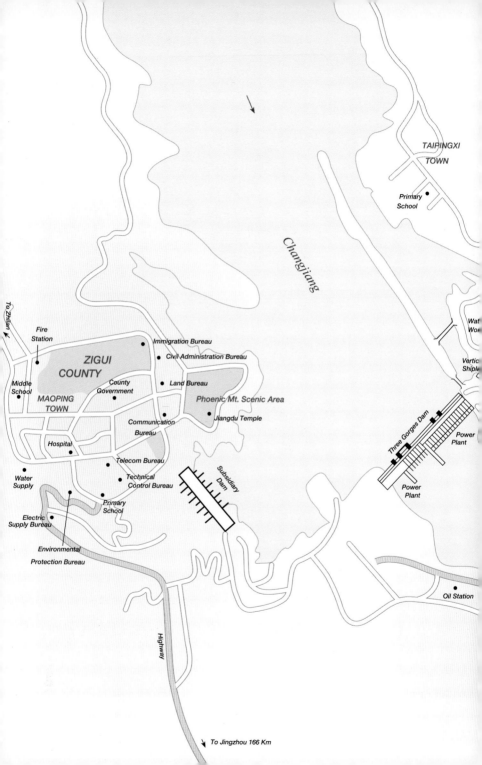

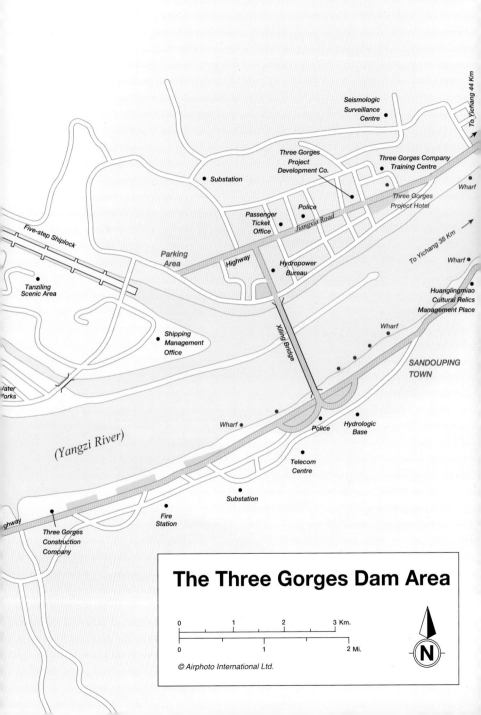

The Three Gorges Dam Area

© Airphoto International Ltd.

Regular flooding is a beneficial process that deposits silt over lowlands, replacing the soil and replenishing fertility. Flood control measures will prevent this natural process and artificial fertilization may need to be introduced to compensate. However, long-term, possibly detrimental, effects of flood control on soil fertility are difficult to assess. An overall reduction in flow in the lower reaches has raised concerns about possible saltwater intrusion in the delta area around Shanghai. Discharge in the lower reaches will have to be carefully managed.

Active measures taken to preserve water quality are many and varied. Slopes above 25 degrees in the reservoir catchment area must, by law, be restored to grassland. During the 1950s and 1960s, in order to achieve national iron production quotas, large areas of trees were felled as fuel for furnaces. Today a ban has been imposed on tree felling, and tree planting is being promoted. Polluting factories have been closed down and the opening of new factories is strictly controlled. Measures have been taken to control the 1.35 billion tons of wastewater discharged annually into the Yangzi River.

Within the reservoir area 49 rare or endangered species were identified. Fish migrations through the dam have been considered and the ecology of the freshwater carp studied. The Gezhou Dam project included a study, between 1981 and 1988, of the effects of the dam on the freshwater sturgeon and the effects of changing water quality on the freshwater dolphins (*see* page 173).

Social consequences of the dam are wide reaching. Close to 1.9 million people living below the projected 175 metre final reservoir level have been compulsorily displaced to places as far apart as Shanghai, Qingdao (in Shandong Province), western Sichuan Province and Guangzhou. Two cities, 11 county towns, and 116 townships will have been destroyed, along with 24,500 hectares of farmland. Studies for the resettlement scheme were conducted in an eight year, 237-million-yuan project, and 40 billion yuan was allocated to implement the resettlement plans. Almost 33 per cent of the population were moved to different provinces. About 60 per cent of the remaining rural population will continue in agriculture and 40 per cent will need to find new jobs.

A total of 44 archaeological sites and ancient monuments will be inundated by the reservoir. These have been the subject of rescue surveys and excavations, but the cultural and heritage losses to the nation, and to the world, are immense (*see* A Flood of Artefacts, page 174).

(Left) The Three Gorges Hydropower Station's single unit capacity and total installed capacity are both the largest of their kind in the world. Soon to have 40 generators with a total capacity of 28,000 megawatts, the Three Gorges Project currently has 26 sets of generators capable of 18,200 megawatts. Reaching its full potential, it will be capable of generating an annual average output of 84.7 Terawatt hours—equivalent to the power generated by six Gezhou Dams or four Grand Coulee Dams. The service area extends to a 1,000 kilometre radius, reaching south to Guangzhou, east to Shanghai, almost to Beijing in the north and nearly to the Myanmar border to the west. [Huang Zhengping]

Yangzi Dams

THE GEZHOU DAM

Where it leaves the confines of the Xiling Gorge at Nanjinguan (the Nanjin Pass), the Yangzi River dramatically widens from 300 metres in the gorge to 2,000 metres, and abruptly turns to the south. Three kilometres downstream, near the city of Yichang, the Gezhou and Xi islets formerly divided the main river channel into three channels: the southern Dajiang (Grand Channel); the central Erjiang (Second Channel); and the northern Sanjiang (Third Channel) between Gezhou Islet and the north bank of the river. This locality was selected for the first dam across the Yangzi River, the Gezhouba ('ba' means dam in Chinese) Water Control Project.

Construction of Gezhouba took 19 years, employed 100,000 workers, and cost 4.85 billion yuan. The ground breaking and foundation laying ceremony was held on 26 December 1970, Mao Zedong's birthday, and the completed dam was finally commissioned in October 1989. Work was carried out under three projects.

The Sanjiang (Third Channel) Project, begun in May 1971 and commissioned in April 1985, comprised two ship locks, one silt-flushing sluice, and a man-made navigation channel. A total of 2.7 million cubic metres of material were excavated to house the machine hall and two million cubic metres of concrete were poured. Phase 2, the Dajiang (Grand Channel) Project, was carried out between 1982 and May 1986. It comprised erecting a 989.4-metre-long section of the dam, Lock No 1, a power station and a 166.8-metre-long silt-flushing sluice. The sluice, containing nine openings with a discharge capacity of 20,000 cubic metres per second, is designed to continually flush the navigation channel and ship lock as well as dissipate flood discharges. The Erjiang (Second Channel) Project consisted of a 17-outlet flood-discharge sluice with a discharge capacity of 3,900 cubic metres per second and a seven-unit power station with a generating capacity of 4,900 Megawatts (MW). Excavated material amounted to 68.4 million cubic metres, and 6.3 million cubic metres of concrete was poured.

Fifty-five million cubic metres of rock and earth were removed to form Gezhouba's foundations. The finished dam is 2,606.5 metres long, 70 metres high, and composed of 11.3 million cubic metres of concrete—sufficient material to build a road from Guangzhou to Beijing. In addition, 77,200 tons of steel structures and equipment were used. After the main channel was closed off on 4 January 1981, the original water level was raised by 20 metres to 62 metres above sea level. The resulting reservoir covers one million square kilometres and contains 1.58 billion cubic metres of water. During the dry season, and prior to the construction of the Three Gorges Dam upstream, the reservoir extended 110 kilometres upstream to Shangguan Ferry. During the wet season, it extended a further 70 kilometres to Fengjie. Maximum controlled water level variation is 18.6 metres.

Seasonal flood discharges (water volumes) of the Yangzi River pose a constant threat to the safety of both the dam and the inhabitants of the Yangzi valley. The average discharge of the river at Yichang is 14,300 cubic metres per second, although the flow can vary considerably. The lowest water flows of about 2,770 cubic metres per second were recorded in 1937 and 1979. In contrast, the largest water flows were recorded in 1788 and 1870, 86,000 cubic metres per second and 110,000 cubic metres per second, respectively. Consequently, the dam includes a 27-bay spillway that can discharge 110,000 cubic metres of water a second, which is equivalent to the discharge of the 1870 flood. On 19 July 1981, the dam was tested during construction by a flood of 72,000 cubic metres a second. Two silt screening sluices and two silt prevention dykes were incorporated in the dam to allow sediment flushing, which will prevent, or at least reduce, siltation in the lower section of the reservoir behind the dam.

Power generation at Gezhouba began in June 1981. The Dajiang Power Station has an installed generating capacity of 14,700 MW from 21 sets of 700 MW turbine generators, all of which were manufactured in China. Electricity is primarily provided to Hubei, Henan, Hunan and Jiangxi provinces. The Dajiang 500 KV substation, with six-incoming and six-outgoing 500 kilovolt DC transmission lines, supplies electricity to east China, including Shanghai.

Gezhouba has three ship locks, first open to navigation in June 1981. Two large locks at each end of the dam, and another smaller lock at the northern end. The two larger locks are 280 metres long, 34 metres wide, and five metres deep; they have a 20-metre rise and can accommodate ships of 12,000 to 16,000 tons. The electrically-controlled lock gates are 34 metres high by 19.7 metres wide and weigh 600 tons. Following their closure, electrically-controlled water valves can fill the 280,000-cubic-metre chambers in 15 minutes. The small lock is 120 metres long, 18 metres wide, and 3.5 metres deep, accommodating 3,000 ton ships. The dam's crest is crossed by a bridge, which can be raised by 18 metres to allow ships to pass.

ENVIRONMENTAL BENEFITS OF THE DAMS

Tangible benefits derived from the Three Gorges Project, mostly in the middle and lower reaches of the river, include: protection of about 1.53 million hectares of farmland on the Jianghan Plain and in the Dongting Lake area from floods originating from upstream, along with the lives and livelihoods of the 15 million residents of those regions; Silt deposition in Dongting Lake will be reduced; Dry season flow rates can be artificially increased in the lower reaches, improving water quality by flushing the channel, and providing a reserve for the planned South To North Water Transfer Scheme; reduction of national coal consumption by up to 50 million tons a year, which in turn would eliminate the emission of 10 million tons of carbon dioxide, two million tons of sulphur dioxide, 370,000 tons of nitrous oxide, and 10,000 tons of carbon monoxide, as well as reducing the discharges of related waste water and of solids such as fly ash.

Yangzi Dams

JIANGHAN PLAINS

From Yichang the Yangzi enters the Middle Basin, flowing through Hubei, Jiangxi and Anhui provinces to Ma'anshan, on the border of Jiangsu Province, before entering its final Coastal Delta section. The river, widening abruptly from the narrow confines of Xiling Gorge, and with a pent-up force out of the Gezhou Dam, rolls through broad floodplains, fed by tributaries and lakes that used to be prone to serious floodind during heavy summer rains.

Networks of dykes and embankments—obscuring the view across the low-lying landscape—stretch the length of the river. Here the channel can be as wide as one-and-a-half to two kilometres (0.9 to 1.2 miles), and could cause widespread flooding during normal rainy seasons. In abnormal summer deluges the many lakes in the area, joining forces with the Yangzi and its tributaries, would inundate the land, forming vast expanses of water. It is anticipated that, with the construction of the Three Gorges Dam, these disastrous floods will soon become a thing of the past.

Up to the Sui Dynasty (581–618) the middle reaches were sparsely inhabited, but from the Tang Dynasty (618–907) onwards, waves of people migrated from the north, fleeing from civil wars, famines, heavy taxation and harassment by marauding Tibetans and Turks. With the sharp rise in population, dyke construction became more intense. However it was not until the Ming and Qing dynasties (1368–1644 and 1644–1911) that treasury funds were allocated to the construction of dykes—mainly along the north bank of the Yangzi—which were built as high as 10 to 16 metres (32.8 to 52.5 feet) in places. Once built, the burden of maintenance fell to local landowners and peasants, and upkeep was often neglected.

The meandering course of the silt-laden river is subject to severe silting so that the channel requires constant dredging. The wash of large boats criss-crossing the channel can erode the bank, triggering embankment failures. The rich alluvial Jianghan Plain, between the north bank of the Yangzi and the Han River, is a cotton- and grain-growing area, which was very vulnerable to flooding. In 1952 the Jingjiang Flood Diversion Project commenced. Flood prevention measures included the strengthening of the 180-kilometre (112-mile) stretch of dyke along the Yangzi's northern bank (in the Shashi region), and the construction of flood-intake sluices, regulating dams and retention basins on the south side to contain the waters. On the Han River, the Danjiangkou Water Conservancy Project and dam draw the floodwaters from this tributary to irrigate the more arid regions of northwest Hubei. The Shashi retention basin, covering an area of 920 square kilometres (355 square miles), took 300,000 workers some 75 days to construct in 1954.

A view of Gezhou Dam at Yichang. Construction began on 26 December 1970 and was completed 19 years later in October 1989. [Huang Zhengping]

Above Dongting Lake, the Yangzi forms the border between the provinces of Hubei and Hunan. The lake itself is the second largest in China. Fed by four rivers and emptying its waters into the Yangzi, the lake abounds in aquatic products. from Dongting Lake the river turns northeastwards, across plains dotted with numerous lakes, towards Wuhan, the largest city along its middle reaches. Here it is joined by the 1,532-kilometre (952-mile) long Han River, which lends its name to Hanyang and Hankou, the north bank districts of the sprawling Wuhan metropolis.

During the dry winters, low water levels exposed sandbars and pose serious hazards to boats. The navigation channel of Wuhan can be as shallow as two metres (6.5 feet).

Freshwater fish abound—silver and big-head carp, Yangzi Sturgeon (*see* page 177) and Wuchang fish, to name a few. Also native to the Yangzi is a white dolphin, *baiji*, which will probably be the first cetacean brough to extinction by man. Perhaps a few dozen are left, their habitat degraded by pollution and invaded by injurious boat propellors. Attempts by conservation groups to revive the species has met with little success. However, the extremely rare Yangzi alligator still survives in the middle to lower reaches. The world's smallest alligator, it is a protected species and a research centre in Anhui Province is trying to ensure its survival.

Having crossed the entire width of Hubei Province, the river enters Jiangxi, forming its border with Anhui. Immediately below the city of Jiujiang and the cherished, beautiful mountain of Lushan, it is joined by the fresh blue waters of Poyang Lake, the largest lake in China. From here on, the Yangzi enters the lower reaches.

A fleet of junks under full sail makes its way across the Jianghan Plain, circa 1979. These magnificent craft now no longer ply the river. [Bill Hurst]

YICHANG

Situated at the eastern mouth of the Three Gorges, Yichang is the administrative centre of nine surrounding counties. The population is engaged in light industry, chemical and steel production. Construction of the Gezhou Dam helped Yichang to grow from a small town of 30,000 into an urban centre exceeding 1 million. The Three Gorges Dam is only 44 kilometres (27 miles) upstream via a new highway cut through steep mountains. The Yichang waterfront is bordered by levees and lined with docks busy with barges and passenger vessels. The new Yiling Bridge crosses the Yangzi to the south shore over a charming riverside park.

HISTORY OF YICHANG

History records that, as early as 278 BCE, the town was razed to the ground in a battle between the armies of Chu and Qin. In the Three Kingdoms Period (*see* pages 179, 182) 50,000 Wu troops set fire to the encampments of the Shu army, utterly routing Liu Bei, who retreated upriver to Baidi Cheng.

Yichang became a Treaty Port in April 1877, in accordance with the Chefoo (Yantai) Convention of 1876 signed with Britain, and continued to be the furthest inland Treaty Port for many years, as large merchant and passenger vessels were not then able to navigate the gorges upsteam to Chongqing. Here, cargo was unloaded from the larger boats, plying the stretch of river between Yichang and Wuhan, and reloaded onto smaller ones running between Yichang and Chongqing.

An American traveller in 1921 described the port as 'crowded, incessantly busy, a perfect maelstrom of sampans, junks, lighters with cargo, steamers and gunboats.' Eventually, technology enabled the larger ships to continue the journey upstream and Chongqing itself became a Treaty Port in 1891.

The English trader Archibald Little, noting his expenses for a night's stay in Yichang, showed how far four English pennies went in the late l9th-Century town, and incidentally his solicitude for his servant:

Supper for self and coolie, 4 bowls of rice at 10 cash (copper cash),
'fixings' of cabbage and bean curd free 40
Use of straw-plaited mattress for ditto, 2 at 10 20
Breakfast, same as supper..40
Supper and breakfast for 'Nigger', my dog 20
Pair of straw sandals for coolie (his old ones being worn out)............12
Total 132 copper cash, or, in English money, 4d 132

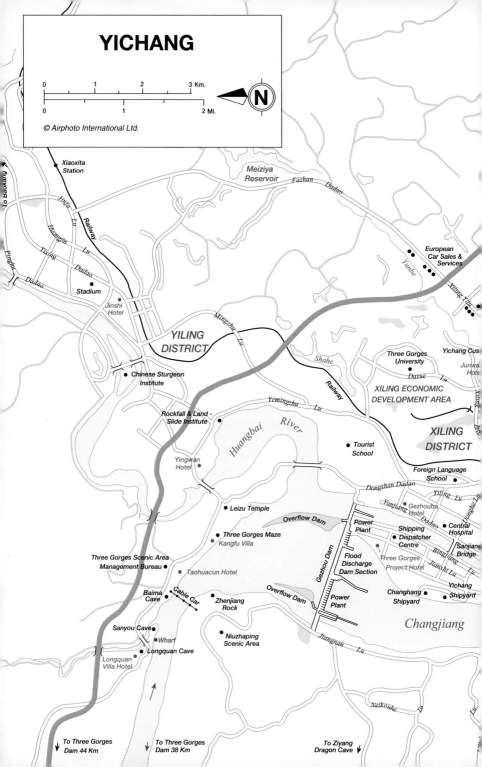

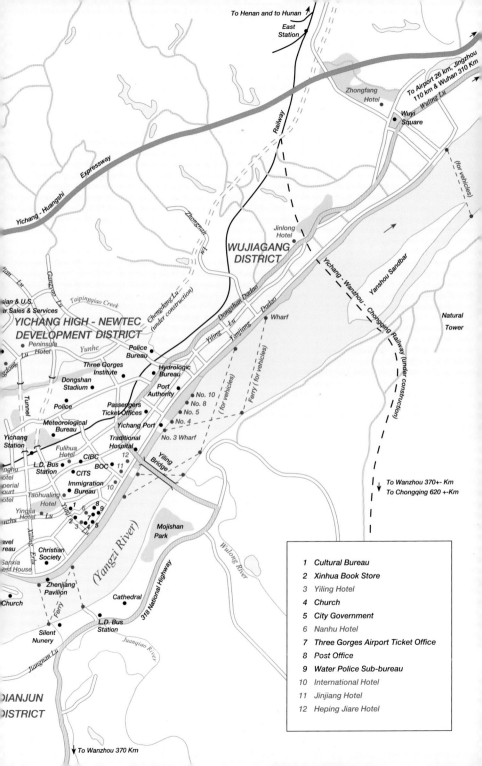

Yichang Municipality covers more than 21,000 square-kilometres (13,050 square-miles), divided into five counties, three county-level cities and five city districts. [Huang Zhengping]

During the warlord years of the early part of the last century, Yichang's revenue was greatly boosted by taxes imposed by its Opium Suppression Bureau on boats carrying homegrown opium from Yunnan and Guizhou Provinces.

During the war with Japan, the gorges above Yichang again acted as a barrier. When Wuhan fell to the Japanese in 1938, Yichang became the centre for transporting essential personnel, machinery, libraries and museum collections up the Yangzi to Chongqing. After the Battle of Yichang in 1940 the Japanese capture of Yichang marked their furthest westward advance. The Japanese also used Yichang as a staging area for bombing raids over Chongqing.

WHAT TO SEE IN YICHANG

The streets of the old town centre are lined with trees. Though the city wall was pulled down in 1929, the street names still indicate where it once stood (Eastern Ring Road, Southern Ring Road and so on). The main market is located just off Jiefang Lu. Along the waterfront, a few old foreign buildings from the Treaty Port days can still be seen, but most are now gone, replaced by modern styles. One remnant of the past is the Zhenjiang 'Protect the River' pavilion, once part of a large temple, now a tea house and disco.

THREE TRAVELLERS' CAVE

Apart from the Gezhou Dam, tourists may also visit the Three Travellers' Cave, 10 kilometres (6.2 miles) northwest of the city. In 819, three Tang Dynasty poets, Bai Zhuyi, his brother Bai Xingjian and Yuan Zhen, travelled to Yichang to make an excursion to this site. While enjoying the spectacular scenery, they inscribed some poems on the cave walls. They were then dubbed the 'First Three Travellers'. In the Song Dynasty (960–1279) the famous literary family of Su—the father and two sons—on their way to the capital to take the imperial examinations, visited the cave and added their poems. All three passed the imperial examinations at the same time. People call these gentlemen the 'Second Three Travellers'. Through the ages, other visiting literati and officials have left their contributions on the cave walls.

A small spring trickles through the rock near the entrance; local superstition maintains that if women wash their hands in its pure water it will improve their culinary skills. The hill above the cave presents a fine view of the entrance to Xiling Gorge: The Zixi Pavilion contains a memorial stone to the 11th-Century philosopher Xiu Ouyang, who lived in Yichang for three years. Nearby is a drum platform and fire watch station, said to be the site where Zhang Fei, a general of the third-Century Kingdom of Shu, beat his battle drums. A large statue of Zhang Fei stands at the site, depicting him looking to the east for enemies approaching up the Yangzi.

Statue of Zhang Fei on the site where he is said to have beaten his battle drum near Three Travellers Cave overlooking Nanjin Pass at the entrance to Xiling Gorge. [Kevin Bishop]

A cable car crosses the Yangzi near Three Travellers Cave hill, offering an aerial view of Nanjin Pass. The Tao Yuan docks just downstream from Nanjin Pass are the terminus for many cruise vessels.

Visitors are sometimes taken on a short excursion along a mountain road offering stunning views of Xiling Gorge, and passing several peaks, including Filial Mountain and Camel Mountain. The road continues over a natural stone bridge, which was originally—so legend has it—a fairy's silken sash, thrown down to help her mortal husband ascend to heaven with her. The stone gateway and its steep stone steps delineate the ancient land route crossed by travellers to western Hubei and Sichuan.

Below Yichang lies the bluff known as Tiger's Teeth Gorge that, for travellers sailing upriver, is the first glimpse of the impressive sights to come.

A preserved specimen of the giant Chinese sturgeon (Acipenser sinensis) *on display at the Yichang Sturgeon Research Centre. The lifecycle of these magnificent creatures, which can grow up to 500 kilograms (1,102 pounds) and traditionally spawn 3,000 kilometres (1,864 miles) upstream in the upper Yangtze, has been disrupted by the construction of dams on the river. [Kevin Bishop]*

YICHANG STURGEON RESEARCH CENTRE

A visit to the Sturgeon Research Centre, established in Yichang in 1982, is recommended. It was set up to protect the giant Chinese sturgeon (*Acipenser sinensis*) whose breeding cycle was threatened by the construction of the Gezhou Dam. Previously this fish, which grows up to 500 kilograms (1,102 pounds) in the East China Sea, would return to the upper Yangzi to spawn, swimming almost 3,000 kilometres (1,864 miles) inland to Yibin—coincidentally, the limit of safe navigation on the river, 370 kilometres (230 miles) upstream from Chongqing. In order to ensure the survival of this prehistoric species the Research Centre nets about 20 mature fish each autumn to breed artificially. It is hoped that the fish, which is now a protected species, will eventually adapt to breeding in the river below the dam. The Centre raises the young fish in tanks until they are six months old, and then releases them into the river to begin their long journey to the sea.

These enormous fish live up to 60 to 70 years, and grow on average to between three to four metres long, but have been known to reach five metres. The males take about nine years to reach maturity, and the females 14 years, after which they breed every four or five years. Because the fish feed only in the ocean, they will gorge themselves before setting off up the Yangzi to breed. They will eat nothing during the one year it takes them to complete their mission and return to the sea. Each female is capable of producing around 25 kilograms (55 pounds) of eggs.

As well as preserved specimens of fish at various stages of their life cycle, the Research Centre also keeps three or four large live specimens in a swimming tank so that visitors can appreciate the size of these magnificent creatures. These fish have to be carefully hand-fed as they are reluctant to eat in freshwater and cannot be kept in captivity for very long.

Although concentrating their work on the Chinese sturgeon, the Research Centre also breeds the smaller Yangzi sturgeon, a species that grows up to 200 kilograms (441 pounds), as well as studying and breeding species from overseas. Live specimens of a variety of these other species can be observed in display tanks.

The third species of sturgeon native to the Yangzi, the white sturgeon, is thought to be extinct. A more aggressive species than the other two, it proved too difficult to breed artificially, and there have been no reports of any being caught on the river in recent years.

Jianghan Plains

A FLOOD OF ARTEFACTS

In June 2003, the gargantuan, 600-kilometre-long reservoir behind the Three Gorges Dam at Sandouping was filled to a height of 135 metres (443 feet) above sea level. Some 1,208 sites of historical and archaeological importance along the Yangzi River were inundated.

When the dam's construction was approved by China's National People's Congress in 1992, the area's archaeology had not been considered. However, a UNESCO report a year later identified key sites and made various recommendations. The government appointed Yu Weichao, then director of the Chinese History Museum, as director of the Planning Group for Cultural Relic Protection of the Three Gorges Reservoir and Dam Construction. As a result, local museums have been greatly enriched and Chinese archaeology has advanced both technically and financially.

Salvage archaeology and cultural heritage preservation carried out between 1997 and 2003, from a global or national point of view, were unprecedented in terms of style of execution, scale, and time. Not only was the work arduously complicated and revolutionary in pursuing China's new 'market economy' style of management, but it applied, for the first time, scientific technology and analysis (for example, DNA testing, satellite photography, CAD computer software) never used before in these areas.

Government funds of 339 million yuan (US$38 million) were allocated, and 110 different teams across China, involving some 7,000 people, offered various levels and types of aid, such as architectural relocation and repair, underwater calligraphy preservation, archaeological excavation, cultural relic protection, as well as scientific and material value analysis.

Jingzhou Museum has artefacts from regions across China, such as this Terracotta phallus from Dengjiawan, Tianmen. [Jingzhou City (Shashi) and Museum]

Significant site findings were increasingly publicised outside China by scholars such as Elizabeth Childs-Johnson. By 2000, the archaeological community inside and outside China secured better funding enabling an expanded team of archaeologists to work on 120 of the most important sites. Despite the introduction of high-tech equipment, in archaeological terms there was hardly time to scratch the surface before reservoir levels obscured the sites forever. More than 6,000 significant artefacts unearthed represent only a tantalising hint of the rich potential of the region.

The archaeological findings have established the Three Gorges area as a main meeting place between East and West in ancient China. Excavations unearthed material that contributed a significantly revised picture of the region's early human cultures, and have marked it as having been one of the most culturally important places in China.

By Kevin Bishop, based on the research of Elizabeth Childs-Johnson

Special Topic

During the Han Dynasty, flax and hemp were used to make clothes including socks and shoes. Jingzhou Museum features a number of exhibits from the region, including Chu and Han culture from the Jianghan Plain, galleries of ancient Chinese lacquers and wooden artefacts as well as an extensive exhibit of Western Han Dynasty items salvaged from Tomb No. 168 at Fenguangshan. From that tomb came these shoes, measuring 29 centimetres (11.4 inches) long. Signs of wear indicate they were not just decorative items for interment. [Jingzhou City (Shashi) and Museum]

JINGZHOU

Jingzhou, situated on the north bank of the Yangzi, was previously the most famous city of Jiangling. The town has now been somewhat absorbed by the sprawling growth of Shashi, although it is still surrounded by its 16-kilometres (10-miles) long and nine-metres (29.5-feet) high city wall. Jingzhou is reached from Shashi, the surrounding city now referred to as Shajin.

Jingzhou was the capital of Jing, one of the nine great regions into which Emperor Yu, founder of the Xia Dynasty (2200–1800 BCE), divided China. From Jingzhou the emperor received as tribute exotic gifts of gold, ivory, cinnabar, silver and feathers. In the Spring and Autumn Period (722–481 BCE) the city was the capital of the Kingdom of Chu. Its walls, according to tradition, were first built in the Third Century by Guan Yu, a hero of the Three Kingdoms Era. Guan Yu was renowned for his strength, height and valour. A thousand years after his death he was deified as the god of war, and his fierce red-faced image appears in many Chinese temples throughout Asia. Stories of his exploits and battles over the city are vividly told in the novel *Romance of the Three Kingdoms*.

The earthen city wall of Jingzhou, built by Emperor Li of the Western Zhou Dynasty, eventually became this stolid brickwork structure measuring one metre (three feet) thick, nine metres (29.5 feet) tall and 11,281 metres (37,011 feet) in circumference [Jingzhou City (Shashi) and Museum]

WHAT TO SEE IN JINGZHOU

Because Jingzhou was the capital of 20 kingdoms during both the Spring and Autumn and Warring States periods, it is not surprising that valuable artefacts have been unearthed from the many tombs on Phoenix Hill. These relics, in particular an important collection of lacquerware, 2,000-year-old silk garments, and woven fabrics are exhibited in the fine Jingzhou Museum, which is well worth a visit. The museum, covering an area of 30,000 square metres (322,900 square feet), is located within Jingzhou's Walled Town. It was established in 1954. Early on, it became renowned as an important research centre, and its archaeologists continue to uphold its stature.

Among the museum's more memorable displays is an almost perfectly preserved male 'wet mummy'. A Han Dynasty official named *Sui* is encased in a glass vessel filled with an herbal fluid. Not a sight for the squeamish, but his remains do leave a lasting impression on museum visitors.

SHASHI

Shashi is noted for its cotton mills, which are supplied with raw cotton from the rich Jianghan Plain on which it stands. Shashi's workforce is principally employed in its many light-industrial enterprises—machinery, durable consumer goods, printing, dyeing and textiles. The city sits some 10 metres (33 feet) below the tops of the protecting levees. An old saying goes, 'Look down to see your path, look up to see ships sail by.'

Historically, the city was the port for the ancient city of Jiangling and a distribution centre for produce from surrounding towns and Dongting Lake. Goods, including cotton, beans, grain and aquatic products, were trans-shipped mostly to Wuhan. In the Tang Dynasty (618–907) Shashi already enjoyed a reputation as a prosperous city, but its peak was reached during the years of the Taiping Rebellion, in the mid-19th Century. After the rebels captured Nanjing in 1853, river trade on the Yangzi between Shashi and Shanghai more or less came to a standstill. Consequently, Shashi became vital to the distribution of products coming downriver from Sichuan.

The Sino-Japanese Treaty of 1895 opened the city to foreign trade; Japanese engaged in the cotton-seed trade formed the majority of the resident foreigners, though this community was never large.

One story relates how the army of Communist General He Long captured Swedish missionaries here in 1931. The women were released following negotiations with the Swedish Consul General, but the release of a doctor was delayed until a ransom was paid. The ransom demanded was: four-dozen Parker fountain pens, four-dozen watches and 60 or 70 cases of medical drugs!

West of the city, the seven-storey Wanshoubao Pagoda, built in the Ming Dynasty (1368–1644), stands directly on the waterfront. Bas-relief figures of Buddha, set into niches, and inscriptions by the donors adorn its brick facade. A temple once adjoined it.

Below Shashi, the river winds tortuously towards Dongting Lake for about 320 kilometres (199 miles). Villages dot the south bank of the river and water buffalo graze in the paddy fields. The north bank is commonly too high for a view of the surrounding country.

DONGTING LAKE

The beautiful Dongting Lake is rich in fairy tales and legends. On its eastern shore stands the graceful three-storey Yueyang Tower in Yueyang City, one of the Three Great Towers south of the Yangzi (the other two being Yellow Crane Tower in Wuchang, and Prince Teng Pavilion in Nanchang). From its terraces, and from pleasure boats on the lake, many famous Chinese poets have been moved to verse.

The lake embraces distant hills and devours the Yangzi, its mighty
* waves rolling endlessly.*
From morning glow to evening light, the views change a thousand,
* ten thousand times.*
On top of the tower the mind relaxes, the heart delights.
All honours and disgrace are forgotten.
What pleasure, what joy to sit here and drink in the breeze.

                                        Fan Zhongyan (989–1052)

Said to have been constructed on the site of a reviewing platform for navy manoeuvres on the lake during the Third Century, the first tower was erected in 716. The present golden-tiled, square tower dates from 1985, but it has been rebuilt in the Song-dynasty style at great expense.

Legend has it that the tower was saved from collapse by the supernatural powers of Lu Dongbin, a Daoist (Taoist) Immortal, who also got drunk here three times. These occasions are remembered in the form of the Thrice Drunken Pavilion, which flanks the tower.

An excursion can be made across the lake to Junshan Island, 15 kilometres (9 miles) away. Some 4,000 years ago, Emperor Shun, on an inspection tour, died at Mount Jiuyi on the south bank of the lake. Two of his devoted concubines, hurrying to his side, became stranded on Junshan Island. The story goes that in their distress, their copious tears blotted the local bamboo, henceforth known as the Spotted Bamboo of Junshan. They drowned themselves in the lake, and their graves remain. In 219 BCE, Emperor Qin Shihuangdi, also on a tour of Dongting Lake, was delayed at Junshan Island by a sudden storm. When he consulted his geomancer to enquire whether spirits were impeding his progress, he was told about the concubines' graves. In a fury he ordered the burning of the island and had five stone seals placed there, forbidding its name to be used or anyone to visit it.

Luxury goods from Guangzhou—from pearls to kingfisher feathers—reached the ancient capitals by way of the Xiang River, through Dongting Lake, down the Yangzi River to Yangzhou and then on up the Grand Canal.

On the 100-hectare (250-acre) island, Junshan Silver Needle Tea is grown, so highly prized that it was once presented as a tribute to the Imperial Court. The fine spindle tea leaves have the curious quality of sinking, floating, then sinking again in the brew.

Once China's largest freshwater lake, Dongting Lake now ranks second, due to sandbars and silt accumulation from the four rivers that feed it. As a result of flood prevention schemes—6,100 irrigation and drainage channels and 15,000 sluices—the surrounding land has become productive all year round and the lake acts as a retention reservoir for summer flood waters. The 3,000-square-kilometre (1,158-square-mile) lake abounds in fish.

THREE KINGDOMS' RED CLIFF

Standing above the flat bank appears a prominent rock eminence that is dotted with pavilions and interlocked with paths. This is the site of the great Battle of the Red Cliff between the huge forces of Cao Cao of Wei and the combined, lesser armies of Shu and Wu in 208 CE. Cao Cao had consolidated the power of the Kingdom of Wei in the north and sought to extend it to the Yangzi. His troops, all from the northern plains, were not accustomed to naval warfare. Nevertheless, he took his army of 200,000 men and launched an attack on the Kingdom of Shu, whose king, Liu Bei, called upon the King of Wu for assistance.

In urgent need of 100,000 arrows to repel the invaders, Zhuge Liang (adviser to Liu Bei) devised a brilliant stratagem. Twenty naval junks, beating war drums, but stacked high with only bundles of straw shrouded in black cloth, feigned an advance on the Wei encampment on a dark, foggy night. The Wei commanders responded by discharging their arrows at the indistinct hulks as they approached. By dawn, each junk bristled with thousands of arrows, more than enough for the army's requirements.

(Following page) *A fisherman works his net in the waters of Honghu, a lake not far from the stretch of the Yangzi bearing the famous battle site,* Chi Bi *or Red Cliff.* [Wong How Man]

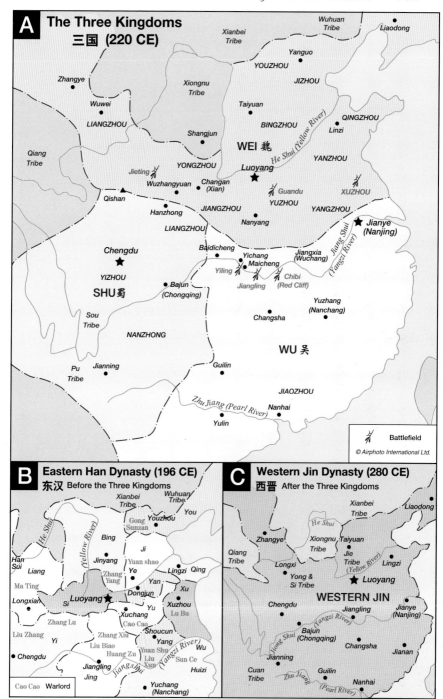

A The Three Kingdoms 三国 (220 CE)

Wuhuan Tribe
Liaodong
Xianbei Tribe
Yanguo
YOUZHOU
JIZHOU
Zhangye
Xiongnu Tribe
Taiyuan
BINGZHOU
QINGZHOU
Wuwei
Linzi
LIANGZHOU
Shangjun
WEI 魏
He Shui (Yellow River)
YANZHOU
Qiang Tribe
YONGZHOU
Jieting
Wuzhangyuan
Changan (Xian)
Luoyang
Guandu
YUZHOU
XUZHOU
YANGZHOU
Qishan
Hanzhong
JIANGZHOU
Nanyang
Jianye (Nanjing)
LIANGZHOU
Baidicheng
Jiang Shui (Yangzi River)
Chengdu
Yichang
Maicheng
Jiangxia (Wuchang)
YIZHOU
Yiling
Chibi (Red Cliff)
Jiangling
SHU 蜀
Bajun (Chongqing)
Yuzhang (Nanchang)
Sou Tribe
Changsha
NANZHONG
WU 吴
Pu Tribe
Jianning
Guilin
JIAOZHOU
Zhu Jiang (Pearl River)
Nanhai
Yulin

⚔ Battlefield
© Airphoto International Ltd.

B Eastern Han Dynasty (196 CE)
东汉 Before the Three Kingdoms

Xianbei Tribe
Wuhuan Tribe
Gong Sunzan
Youzhou
You
He Shui
Yellow River
Bing
Ji
Han Sui
Liang
Jinyang
Yuan shao
Ye
Lingzi
Qing
Ma Ting
Zhang Yang
Yan
Longxian
Si
Luoyang
Dongjun
Xu
Xuzhou
Yu
Xuchang
Lu Bu
Zhang Lu
Cao Cao
Shoucun
Yi
Zhang Xiu
Yang
Wu
Liu Zhang
Liu Biao
Yuan Shu
Sun Ce
Chengdu
Huang Zu
Liu Xun
Huizi
Jiangling
Jing
Jiang Shui (Yangzi River)
Yuchang (Nanchang)

Cao Cao Warlord

C Western Jin Dynasty (280 CE)
西晋 After the Three Kingdoms

Xianbei Tribe
Liaodong
Zhangye
Xiongnu Tribe
Taiyuan
He Shui
Jie Tribe
Lingzi
Qiang Tribe
Longxi
Yong & Si Tribe
(Yellow River)
Luoyang
Chengdu
WESTERN JIN
Jiangling
Jianye (Nanjing)
Jiang Shui (Yangzi River)
Bajun (Chongqing)
Changsha
Jianan
Jianning
Cuan Tribe
Guilin
Zhu Jiang (Pearl River)
Nanhai

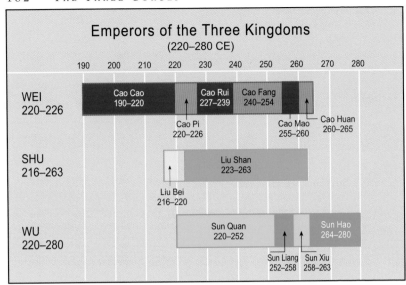

Emperors of the Three Kingdoms (220–280 CE)

MAIN AND FAMOUS EVENTS OF THE THREE KINGDOMS

Year (CE)	Events & Descriptions
25	**Eastern Han Dynasty:** Liu Xiu creates and unifies the Eastern Han Dynasty.
184	**Yellow Turban Rebellion and Three Blood Brothers:** In the late Eastern Han Dynasty the peasants revolt, but are stifled. Liu Bei, Guan Yu and Zhang Fei vow to be blood brothers and to fight for peace.
196	**Separatist Warlord Regimes:** By the end of the Eastern Han dynasty, fighting between the many warlords is rampant and the country is fragmented (*see* Eastern Han Dynasty map, 196 CE). By offering Han Emperor Xiandi "protection", Cao Cao takes effective control of the state and other nobles.
199	**Wu Kingdom's Foundation:** Sun Ce defeats Liu Xun and Huang Zui, laying the foundation for his son Sun Quan to establish the Kingdom of Wu.
200 Jan	**Xuzhou Battle:** Cao Cao defeats Liu Bei, who then goes to Yuan Shao seeking shelter, while Guan Yu surrenders to Cao Cao, who entreats Guan Yu to join him. Though Guan Yu refuses the offer, he is spared and permitted to return home.
200 Apr	**Guandu Battle:** Cao Cao's 10,000 soldiers defeat Yuan Shao's 100,000, thus laying the foundation to unify North China later as the Wei Kingdom.
201	**Three Visits to the Thatched Cottage:** Seeking advice, Liu Bei visits the sage Zhuge Liang, who finally grants council on the third visit. Zhuge subsequently becomes Liu's premier strategist.
208	**Red Cliff Battle:** Lui Bei's army, lead by Zhou Yu, joins Sun Quan's Wu army; under the pretense of surrendering, they use a favourable wind to burn Cao Cao's fleet of ships and win the battle at Red Cliff.

209 **Favour Requited at Hulukou:** While fleeing from his defeat at Red Cliff, Cao Cao encounters Guan Yu, who spares Cao Cao, letting him pass safely.

211–218 **Extension of Shu Territory:** Liu Bei wins several battles and occupies the Yizhou area in 211 CE, Chengdu in 214 CE and Hanzhong in 218 CE.

219 Aug **Three Kingdom Era Begins:** Liu Bei proclaims himself emperor and his territory (Western China) the State of Shu, with its capital in Chengdu.

219 Dec **Guan Yu's Demise:** The Wu army defeats Guan Yu at the Battle of Jiangling, he retreats to the city Maicheng. After being captured by general Lu Mung and refusing to betray Liu Bei, Guan Yu's head is presented sans corpse to Sun Quan.

220 Jan **Hua Tuo's Maltreatment:** Cao Cao, suffering severe headaches, summons the famous surgeon Hua Tuo to cure him. Hua proposes brain surgery, but Cao Cao suspects it is a plot to murder him and imprisons Hua, who rots to death there.

220 Feb **Cao Cao's Death:** Cao Cao dies in pain. His son Cao Pi deposes Emperor Xiandi, takes the throne, renames his territory as Wei and makes its capital Luoyang.

221 Jun **Zhang Fei's Murder:** Two officers in Zhang Fei's command murder the tyrant the night before he is to go to Jiangzhou (Chongqing) to join forces with Liu Bei. The two traitors then bring Zhang's head to Sun Quan and surrender themselves.

222 **Yiling Battle and Liu Bei's Death:** Sun Quan's army surrounds the Shu army for six months before the Shu succumb. Sun Quan proclaims himself Emperor, his state Wu and makes Jianye (Nanjing) his capital. Liu Bei withdraws from Zigui to Baidicheng where he dies the next year.

225 **Capture and Release Sevenfold:** On the long march to southern Lushui (Fin Shajiang), Zhuge Liang uses psychological attacks to force the surrender of the leader of the Man minority tribe, Menghuo, who professes his deep admiration of his Shu captors' tactics.

228 **Battle of Jieting and Zhuge's Harp:** Ignoring Zhuge Liang's instructions, Ma Chow loses the Jieting battle. Sima Yi leads 150,000 Wei soldiers to Xicheng and an awaiting Zhuge Liang, who only has 2,500 soldiers. With the city gates wide open and Zhuge playing his harp calmly on top of the city wall, Sima suspects entrapment and withdraws his army failing to see through Zhuge's bluff.

234 **Wuzhangyuan and Zhuge Liang's death:** Surrounded by the Wei Army at Wuzhangyuan on his fifth attack northward, Zhuge Liang falls ill and dies.

263 **Wei Destroys Shu Kingdom:** The Wei attack the Shu on Chengdu Plain, Cao Huan's general Deng Ai forces the son of Liu Bei, Emperor Liu Shan, to surrender. The Shu Kingdom is completely destroyed.

265 **Wei Kingdom *Coup d'etat*:** Wei minister Sima Yan seizes the throne and declares the start of the Jin Dynasty (now known as the Western Jin Dynasty).

280 **Western Jin Destroys Wu Kingdom:** Western Jin General Wang Jun attacks Jianye (Nanjing); Wu Emperor Sun Hao surrenders to Western Jin Emperor Sima Yan. Wu Kingdom is completely destroyed thus ending the Three Kingdom Era. However, the unified Western Jin dynasty (*see* Western Jin Dynasty Map, 280 CE) disintigrates after Sima Yan's death 10 years later.

THE STORY OF THE THREE KINGDOMS

by Madeleine Lynn

If one wishes to understand China, one must have some familiarity with the history of the Three Kingdoms and with the lore that surrounds it. Above all this is true on the middle and upper Yangtse where it seems every bend in the river leads to another site associated with this epoch and to the stories that have grown around it like the layers of a pearl around its grain of historical fact. If the events seem complicated and the stage crowded with unfamiliar actors, that too is part of China's reality. One might as well seek to know the Greeks without the Trojan War or the English without Shakespeare.

Lyman P Van Slyke, *Yangtse: Nature, History and the River,* 1988.

By 150 CE the Han dynasty (206 BCE–220 CE) was already rotting from within, the result of a series of weak emperors. The uprising of peasant rebels known as the Yellow Turbans (184 CE) gave three strong warlords (Cao Cao, Liu Bei and Sun Quan) the opportunity to amass their own independent armies. They gradually set up rival territories within the Empire and fought it out for the control of China. The history of their struggle formed the basis for the 14th-century popular novel *The Romance of the Three Kingdoms,* a compilation of fact and fiction taken from the repertoires of 12 centuries of storytellers. It is a rambling saga of heroism and treachery, of larger-than-life heroes and villains against the backdrop of the dying dynasty. Tales from this era are also the subject of many Chinese operas.

The three kingdoms were:

The Kingdom of Wei: North China, comprising the Yellow River basin; the base of the Qin and Han dynasties. Its ruler was Cao Cao, Duke of Wei, characterized in the novel as the archetypal Chinese villain, a brilliant but ruthless general. 'Speak of Cao Cao and he is there' is the Chinese equivalent of 'Talk of the devil'.

The Kingdom of Shu: the area that is now called Sichuan. It was established by Liu Bei, pretender to the throne by virtue of being a distant relation of the Han emperor. Although a rather weak and insignificant personality himself, his royal blood attracted gifted followers, the most famous of whom are Zhuge Liang and Liu's two sworn blood-brothers Zhang Fei and Guan Yu.

Zhuge Liang was Liu's premier strategist and has been held up as an example of military genius ever since. There are numerous stories of how he defeated Cao Cao's larger armies by guile and bravado rather than strength. For instance, there was the time he was staying in an unprotected city when Cao Cao's army arrived unexpectedly. As the troops approached, they saw that the city gate was wide open and that Zhuge Liang, accompanied only by one young servant boy, was perched on top of the city wall calmly playing the harp. Convinced that they were about to walk into an ambush, the enemy withdrew.

Guan Yu was so revered for his loyalty that he was gradually turned into a god. Given the honorary title Guan Gong, and also known as Guan Di, God of War, Justice and Righteousness, until recently nearly every large town in China had a temple dedicated to him. His statue can be recognized by its distinctive red face, signifying bravery and goodness.

The Kingdom of Wu: The rich and fertile lower Yangzi region, as far as the sea. This was controlled by the treacherous Sun Quan, whose family was the most influential in the region. Between Shu and Wu was the middle Yangzi basin, a no-man's land of marshes and lakes. From here one could threaten either Shu or Wu and it was here that some of the most crucial battles took place. On the run from Cao Cao's army, Liu Bei took refuge in this area and Zhuge Liang persuaded Sun Quan, the ruler of Wu, to ally with them against the powerful Cao Cao. Although their combined forces were still far less than Cao Cao's, together they routed him in the critical battle of Red Cliff, at a site upriver from modern Wuhan.

Now it was Cao Cao's turn to flee for his life. Although Guan Yu actually cornered him and could have killed him he let him go, as Cao Cao had done the same for him in an earlier encounter.

But the alliance between Liu Bei and Sun Quan did not last long. Sun Quan tried to persuade Guan Yu to betray Liu Bei and join him. When Guan Yu refused, Sun had him beheaded and sent his head to Cao Cao, hoping for an alliance with him. The grief-stricken Liu Bei ignored Zhuge Liang's advice and launched a disastrous campaign against Sun. Before the fight even began, his other sworn brother Zhang Fei was murdered by two fellow officers who planned to surrender to Sun. Liu was ignominiously defeated and retreated to Baidi Cheng, where he died a few years later.

Cao Cao also died without achieving his ambitions. Although his son succeeded in conquering the other two Kingdoms, it was a short-lived triumph, as he was toppled in a *coup d'état*. So none of the three realized their dream of ruling over the whole of China.

In another ruse, Cao Cao was persuaded by a spy in his camp to secure all his boats together before a forthcoming attack, so that his soldiers would feel as if they were on firm ground. The armies of Wu and Shu sent Huang Kei to feign surrender. His fleet's ships were laden with firewood doused in oil and as they approached Cao Cao's floatilla, Huang's men set fire to their own boats before abandoning ship. Timed with a favourable easterly wind, the great conflagration drifted into Cao Cao's fleet setting it ablaze. The defeated Cao Cao then fled northwards.

Red Cliff is said to have been scorched forever red by the flames of this day-long battle. In a victory celebration, General Zhou Yu of Wu, flourishing his writing brush, jubilantly inscribed the gigantic characters 'Red Cliff' (Chi Bi) on the cliff face, which can be seen to this day.

Pavilions on the hill commemorate specific incidents in the battle, and there is an exhibition of Three Kingdoms Period weapons found in the area that exceeds 2,000 pieces. The story of the battle is known to all Chinese, making the site a very popular tourist spot. Numerous vessels dock here, enabling visitors to explore the site and its museum, which displays dioramas of the historic scenes.

HAN RIVER

The Han River, which at 1,532 kilometres (952 miles) long is the Yangzi's longest tributary, rises in the Qingling Mountains of Shaanxi Province. In 1488 it changed course, separating the city of Hanyang from the then fishing village of Hankou. Though dykes now line much of its lower course, this stretch has a history of frequent flooding. In 1876, the British consular officer August R Margary travelled all the way from Shanghai up the Yangzi and onwards to the Burmese border, only to be murdered by tribesmen as he crossed back into China. He wrote of Hankou:

This year they have had no inundation, but it is of almost annual occurrence. Even at Hankow the foreign settlement is frequently submerged. The river rises six feet above the level of the fine stone bund they have made there, and quietly takes possession of all the lower rooms in the noble-looking mansions which the merchants occupy. All their dining-room furniture has to be removed above. Boats become the only means of locomotion, and ladies can be seen canoeing in and out of their houses, and over the bund where they are wont to promenade at other times.

Flooding occurred 11 times between 1931 and 1949; in 1931 and 1935 boats sailed down the streets of Wuhan. Though much has since been done to control the Han's waters, such as constructing retention basins, dykes, levees, hydro-electric dams and other methods, the floods of historical proportion in 1981 and 1989 are a humbling reminder that the danger of flooding is still very real.

However, the topography that lends itself to flooding, has some benefits in the form of a convenient water transportation network. Numerous waterways and canals connecting with the Han's lower course enabled junks to travel between Shashi and Wuhan almost directly across the plain, as opposed to the more circuitous route via the Yangzi.

The Han will also play a part in the South to North Water Transfer Scheme (*see* page 14). Water drawn from its upper reaches will probably cause a 21 to 36 per cent reduction flow through its middle and lower reaches, suggests the Central University of Science and Technology. While this may help solve Beijing and Tianjin's water shortages, siphoning the Han may adversely affect the downstream communities. Water supplies needed for drinking, industry and agriculture use, and waste management will be reduced. Slower flow and lower volume may concentrate pollutants in the Han, upsetting the ecological balance of the surrounding marshlands.

Jianghan Plains

Residents of Wuhan are ferried by boat along the street outside the post office during the 1931 flood. [John Warner]

WUHAN

At the centre of the Long River's course to the sea, and on the main rail line between north and south China, sprawls the tripartite city of Wuhan. Wuhan is set in the vast Jianghan Plain, a region that is more water than land. Levees protect the city from the seasonal ravages of the Yangzi. Wuhan serves as the capital of Hubei Province. It comprises three formerly separate cities, now districts of Wuhan— Wuchang, Hankou and Hanyang.

On the north bank lies Hankou, the commercial centre and port complex, now gleaming with a new skyline sprouting along its broad avenues. Hankou has always been the most developed of the three cities, ever since Treaty Port days. It is still the business and shopping heart of the city, and contains the sites of former foreign concessions and the waterfront Bund. The passenger ship terminal in Hankou is shaped like a cartoon image of a ship, and it is from here that cruise ships bound for the Three Gorges and Chongqing depart.

A Wuhan travel magazine once asked the city's famous wordsmiths to paint a mental picture of their hometown. Few had much to say. Chi Li, a popular novelist, complained that Wuhan "has no feature of its own". Fang Fang, author of several books on old Wuhan, bemoaned the "troublesome climate", concluding that Wuhan is "not a pleasant place to live".

But as the old Chinese expression goes: it's the onlooker who often sees things most clearly. There's a lot more to Wuhan than these locals suggest.

While most people know Wuhan as merely a transit point for travellers plying the Yangzi, or as a perch from which to witness China's summer floods, in recent years the city has taken on a new look. The local government has dusted off old historical sites, while a new generation of entrepreneurial Wuhanese is opening modish restaurants, bars, teahouses, coffee shops and shopping centres.

The former British Customs House, with its clock tower now topped with a red star, remains on the waterfront street, Yanjiang Dadao. Its prominence is today eclipsed by mirrored nightclubs. New hotels line the waterfront where clipper ships once loaded tea. The jumbled old neighbourhoods and alleyways where foreign sailors once entered at their own risk have been torn down for grandiose shopping malls. Some of the graceful European-style buildings of the early Twentieth Century still exist, with many renovated, particularly in the area opposite the passenger terminal.

Across the southward-flowing Han River is Hanyang, known for the Turtle Hill (*Gui Shan*) overlooking the Wuhan Changjiang Daqiao (Wuhan Yangzi Bridge), the Qing Chuan Pavilion with its superb river views and the Guiyuan Si, an active Buddhist temple. Upriver in Hanyang are vast steel plants and factories.

Jiqing Lu is popular for dining in the evenings. Restaurants serve local specialities while diners are entertained by licensed street musicians playing both modern and traditional instruments. (See page 216) [Kevin Bishop]

On the south bank of the Yangzi are the administrative and educational campuses of Wuchang, the seat of the Hubei Provincial Government and Wuhan University. The Yellow Crane Tower (*Huang He Lou*), the famous symbol of Wuhan, rises above the Great River at Wuchang near the southern end of the bridge. The Wuhan Changjiang Erqiao (Bridge) links Hankou with Wuchang downriver. The calm reaches of Wuchang's East Lake (*Dong Hu*), with its bonsai gardens and excellent museums, are the best antidote to the smoggy hubbub of the downtown districts.

Wuchang was the site of the 1911 uprising that led to the overthrow of the Qing Dynasty. Mao Zedong enjoyed staying in this city and had his own villa on the shore of the Dong Hu.

The Tian He International Airport is immediately north of the city and directly connected to it by an expressway. As the city economy continues to grow, much of the old city has been lost to redevelopment and, as in much of China, the new construction lacks the social web of the old neighbourhoods, though many of the traditional fragrances remain, especially by the riverside markets.

HISTORY OF WUHAN

The area on which Wuhan stands was settled in the First Century; in the Third Century it was part of the Kingdom of Wu. Wuchang is the oldest of the three cities. By the Yuan Dynasty (1279–1368) it was the capital of the region and was enclosed by a city wall until the end of the 19th Century.

Hanyang was founded in the Sui Dynasty (581–618) and remained a small walled city until a farsighted official of the Qing dynasty (1644–1911), Zhang Zhidong, established factories and an arsenal there in the 1890s.

Hankou was only a fishing village until the 19th Century. It is, however, the city of Hankou that is best known to foreigners because, after it was declared a Treaty Port in 1861, it became a main centre of the tea trade and the focal point of the annual China Tea Races.

There were five Foreign Concessions—British, Russian, French, German and Japanese—situated side by side along the north shore of the Yangzi. Ocean-going steamers from New York, Odessa and London anchored at their docks. Until the

Wuhan's Customs House, a British-built, Renaissance-style building with a distinctive clock tower, was renovated in 2000 as part of the Jianghan Lu Pedestrianisation Scheme. Several other histori-cal buildings, dating from the time Wuhan was known as Hankow and was a Treaty Port, have also been preserved along the riverside. Many are currently occupied by banks. [Bartlett]

This revolutionary monument stands before the Hankou Riqing International Firm Building, which was built in 1913 and originally used by the Riqing Shipping Company. [Bartlett]

foreign import of opium ceased in the first decade of last century, opium-laden ships sailed up the river as far as Hankou.

Life in the foreign concessions was similar to that in Shanghai. Horse-racing was popular, with Hankou boasting two racecourses, one for Chinese and one for foreigners, on the sites of present-day Jiefang Park and Zhongshan Park respectively. There was even a golf course, while the Recreation Club was considered by many to be the best in China at that time. There is now a new horse racing course open on the north side of the city, *en route* to the airport.

In the 1911 Revolution, much of Hankou was burnt to the ground during clashes between revolutionaries and Imperial Troops.

During the Sino-Japanese War, after the fall of the then capital, Nanjing, to the Japanese in 1937, the Guomindang government made Wuhan its capital for a year, before moving to Chongqing. In the 1938 assault on Wuhan, casualty figures were in the tens of thousands.

The Communist Party was very active in Wuhan before 1949, organizing railway strikes and peasant training programmes. It was here that Chairman Mao, at the age of 73, took his famous 15-kilometre swim in the Yangzi in 1966, heralding the coming Cultural Revolution.

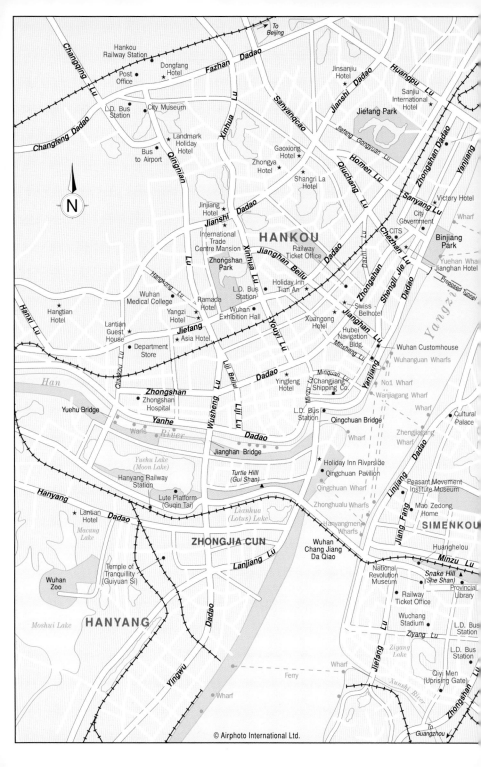

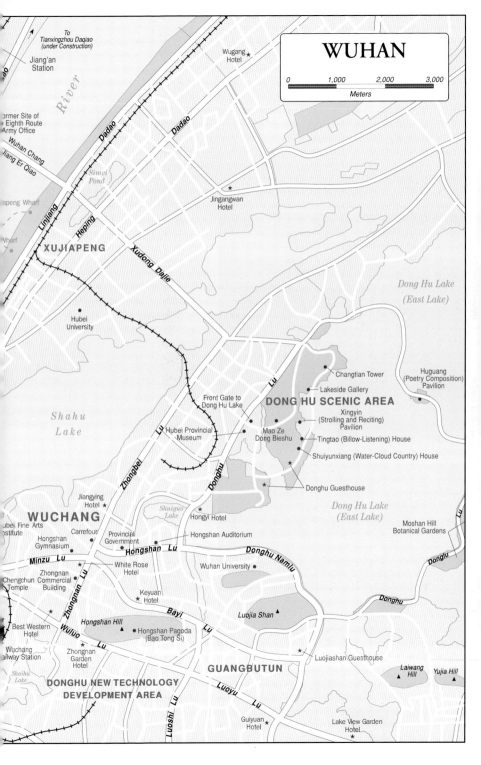

WUHAN ECONOMY

The Yangzi River port of Wuhan will become increasingly significant to the 21st Century in a big way. Left behind by the economic boom that transformed China's coastal areas in the 1980s and 1990s, China's oldest largest and inland industrial commercial centre is striving to restore its historical position as a strategic trading hub.

The three cities of Wuhan—Hankou, Hanyang and Wuchang—have always benefited from being located at the confluence of the Yangzi and Han Rivers.

Effectively, they are right in the heart of China. The area has been commercially important since ancient times, due to the Han being one of the few rivers in China that flows from north to south.

In the 19th Century, the British established a concession here, opening the city to European trade. Other Western powers and Japan followed Britain, which was a boon for the city's economic development, making Wuhan one of the most important trade hubs for the Western powers in China.

The economy slowed down after 1949, under four decades of central planning, and Wuhan slipped further behind as coastal areas experienced runaway economic growth beginning in the 1980s. But today, the city is in the midst of an economic revival.

Morgan Stanley economist Andy Xie wrote that Wuhan has the potential to become "the next Shanghai," arguing that the city could boom in the next few years. Hong Kong-based Xie says that if

The new face of Wuhan is presented in the architecture of the numerous highrises that have sprung up. [Bartlett]

Shanghai becomes too expensive, Wuhan could be an important alternative for foreign investors looking for a new place to invest their capital. Citroen, Budweiser, Philips, Coca Cola and NEC are all here already.

Wuhan has a number of advantages. Firstly, it has 35 higher education institutions, ranking third in science and education behind Beijing and Shanghai. This means that investors can select from a pool of well-trained workers and technicians. Secondly, its industrial base has become more relevant to the current stage of the country's development. Wuhan's industry is diverse, and is especially strong in iron and steel (Wuhan Iron & Steel Co is China's second largest steel producer), automobile manufacturing, shipbuilding, machinery, scientific instruments, textiles, chemicals, and food processing.

Thirdly, Wuhan is just 15 hours from Shanghai by road, and the additional cost of shipping from here is negligible. Finally, Wuhan is the largest inland rail transport hub and telecommunications centre in inland China. Dubbed the "crossroads of nine provinces," Wuhan serves as a gateway to many of the country's interior provinces. It has a network of national and provincial highways linking it to eight provinces and 195 cities. Wuhan is China's largest inland river port, open year round, with a network of waterways connecting it to 14 provinces.

Another advantage is that the city has performed an excellent job of improving living standards here. Property prices are much lower than Shanghai for both mass market and luxury housing, which means lower costs for investors.

In short, Xie says his "gut feeling" is that Wuhan is "up to global competition." If Wuhan succeeds, it will have implications that transcend the city itself. An economic revival could help reduce the growing disparity between the less dynamic inland provinces and the thriving coastal areas, helping to boost the economies of other inland areas.

WHAT TO SEE IN WUHAN

When planning an itinerary, bear in mind that Wuhan is extensive. It requires plenty of time to travel from place to place, more than one might imagine when initially looking at a map, especially with the increase in traffic that seems to blight all big cities in China today.

HANKOU DISTRICT

Hankou is the main commercial district of Wuhan. The old foreign concessions lined the embankment for three kilometres (1.8 miles), and this area is still interesting to stroll around. Many of the buildings display architecture from the colonial era, and some bear plaques that detail their history. The old Customs House with its clock tower is a distinctive landmark. During the stifling summer months, the waterfront promenade is a popular place for locals to take an evening

WUHAN OLD HANZHENG STREET 老汉正街

by Paul Mooney

There's almost a Taoist logic to the flow of people and traffic on Hankou's bustling Old Hanzheng Street. Shoppers compete for limited space with pushcarts piled high with bananas and motorcycles weighed down with boxes. Shirtless "stickmen" balance more than 100 shirts on the two ends of their shoulder poles as they bounce down the street in harmony with the up and down movement of their heavy loads, gliding past porters hauling heavy loads with nothing more than their bare hands. The crowd suddenly opens as a porter or vehicle winds its way down the street shouting "Rang! Rang!", Chinese for "Make way!" And just as suddenly, these deliverymen disappear as they are swallowed by the crowd. In between all of this are peddlers displaying their goods on plastic sheets on the street—or even an odd folding bed—and hawkers preparing Chinese snacks on makeshift stoves. Amidst this, two blind fortunetellers tap their way down the middle of the street with canes, advertising their service by clanging a metal finger clapper. Amazingly, they make their way through this sea of activity without bumping into anyone or anything.

For close to 500 years—beginning in the Ming Dynasty—Hanzheng Street has been supplying the province, and much of central China, with a wide variety consumer goods and daily necessities. As early as the 16th Century, Hanzheng Street, situated where the Yangzi and Han Rivers converge, was the main street in Hankou. In fact, it is reputed to be one of the biggest wholesale markets in China, and is said to be the oldest one, with Wuhanese referring to it as "the first street under heaven." This is also home to some of the city's laozihao, or famous old brand names. The old Ye Kaitai Drug Store was born here as was the Su Hengtai Umbrella Shop, which specializes in oiled-paper umbrellas.

Business crawled to a halt in 1949 following liberation, but the market street was allowed to resume operations with China's opening up in 1979, when about a dozen intrepid getihu, or small entrepreneurs, began peddling goods here again. Today, the area boasts some 12,000 vendors operating in the area. Rural shopkeepers still come here today to buy goods to sell back in their villages. It's particularly crowded during Chinese New Year, when people flock here to buy decorations, food and other goods for the holiday.

Just about any product one can think of can be found here, and there appears to be no rhyme or reason to what's available: tablecloths, belts, grass mats, t-shirts, toys, bras, Laughing Buddhas, sunglasses, Chinese art, plastic slippers, plants, mahjong sets, bags, and pottery. The list goes on and on. And there's more than what you see on the street. Venture down one of the lanes between shops and you'll find yourself in a maze of countless tiny stands and snack shops that seems to go on forever.

One local Wuhan travel magazine boasted about the market's reputation for customer service, describing a merchant who tied an ox in front of his shop to prove his sweaters were the real thing. This point is also driven home by a series of life-size bronze statues that can be found along the street. One shows a blind merchant and children, symbolizing that neither the old nor the young will be cheated here. A statue of a clerk measuring material at a cloth shop signifies that no miscalculations will be made.

In recent years, the street has spawned its own urban myths. Wuhanese revel in the telling of rags-to-riches tales on this street, gushing about how the money almost effortlessly rolls into the pockets of local entrepreneurs, "as easily as a child finding his way home."

Hanzheng Street is also a good place to sample snacks from all over China. A Henanese has turned a used oil drum into a coal-fired oven on wheels, slapping his dough onto the sides of the drum to bake. Another person sells tangyuan, sweet dumplings made of sticky rice and stuffed with sweet red bean paste or black sesame paste. And there is one seller who never has to shout out the name of his delicacy—the pungent scent of *chou doufu* (tofu), or stinky beancurd, can be smelled blocks away.

Special Topic

stroll in the hope of a cooling breeze blowing from the river. Whenever there is a wind, kite flying is a favourite pastime in Wuhan. Many visitors to Hankou's Bund prefer it to that of Shanghai.

The stretch of Jianghan Lu from behind the Customs House to Jianghan Dadao is the main shopping street. Much of it is pedestrianised and is lined with beautiful turn-of-the-century European buildings housing shops and boutiques selling international brand names. Keep an eye open for the handful of beautiful, slightly larger-than-life, bronze sculptures along this street, particularly towards the embankment. These depict aspects of life in old Wuhan. A couple of men playing Chinese chess, for example, attract the attention of passers-by, who pause to discuss the various merits of the next moves.

In the evenings, nearby Jiqing Lu is transformed into a lively, brightly-lit outdoor food street. Restaurants fill the area with tables and chairs and serve local specialties to diners while they are entertained by licensed street musicians.

WUHAN MUSEUM

The Wuhan Museum relates the history of the city from ancient times to today. The museum has three floors and nine exhibition halls, displaying cultural relics such as pottery, porcelain and paintings. Located at 3 Qingnian Lu, it should not be confused with its larger sibling, the Hubei Provincial Museum.

OLD HANZHENG STREET

For close to 500 years, old Hanzheng Street has been supplying the Province, and much of central China, with a wide variety of consumer goods and daily necessities. Today, the area boasts some 12,000 vendors, and just about any product can be found here. (*See* page 196)

HANYANG DISTRICT
TEMPLE OF TRANQUILLITY (*GUIYUAN SI*)

This fine Zen Buddhist temple on Cuiwei Henglu, where monks from the surrounding provinces gathered to study the scriptures, is more than 300 years old. The striking architectural complex includes Drum and Bell Towers, temple halls, the Luohan Hall and the Lotus Pond. The Luohan Hall contains 500 life-sized gold-painted wooden statues of Buddhist luohan, or monk-saints. No two faces are the same, and the statues have a wide variety of poses, with many holding symbolic objects in their hands. It is said the two sculptors employed on this task took nine years to complete them. The main hall has a statue of Sakyamuni Buddha that was carved from a single block of white jade—a gift from Burma in 1935. The scripture collection includes the rare 7,000-volume Longcan Sutra. The temple offers a vegetarian restaurant for visitors.

QING CHUAN PAVILION (*QING CHUAN GE*)

The original pavilion was a 16th-Century Ming Dynasty structure in honour of Lord Yu, who was famous for fighting floods. The current pavilion is a 1983 reconstruction. The top floor of the pavilon offers a fine view of the Yangzi River and the Yellow Crane Tower, situated on the opposite bank. There is a pleasant walkway beneath the pavilioon alongside the river.

LUTE PLATFORM (*GUQIN TAI*)

Opposite Turtle Hill (*Gui Shan*), which overlooks the Han River, is the Hanyang Workers' Cultural Palace Gardens, encompassing the charming Lute Platform, a small complex of courtyards, pavilions and gardens enclosed by a tiled wall. It was built in commemoration of two musicians, Yu Baiya and Zhong Ziqi, who lived 2,000 years ago. While visiting Hanyang, Yu played his lute but only Zhong understood and appreciated his performance. They became firm friends and arranged to meet again at the same time the following year. Yu returned only to find that his friend had died. At Zhong's grave, Yu played a farewell song and, vowing never again to use the instrument, broke it to pieces. This story has left an expression *zhi yin*, 'or knows sound', which is used to describe a very close friend who can understand your thoughts and emotions without needing an explanation.

The Lute Platform is now a haven for Chinese opera lovers (mostly men) who gather on Sunday mornings to sip tea and listen to the performers. In the gardens, *wushu* and *taijiquan* (martial arts and exercise) classes are held. Paintings by local artists are exhibited and sold in the main hall. Nearby is a Qing memorial stone dedicated to the lute player.

WUCHANG DISTRICT

YELLOW CRANE TOWER (*HUANG HE LOU*)

On Snake Hill (She Shan) is the site of the ancient Yellow Crane Tower (Huanghe Lou), widely celebrated by Chinese poets throughout the ages. Cranes are one of the traditional Chinese symbols of long life. The legend concerns a Daoist (Taoist) sage who flew away on a yellow crane to become an Immortal. The tower has been rebuilt many times. It has five levels covered with yellow tiles and supported by red columns. Being more than 50 metres (165 feet) high, the top level offers a wonderful view of the entire Wuhan area. Beside the new Yellow Crane Tower (completed in 1986) is a white stupa that dates from the Yuan Dynasty (1279–1368). A giant 'Peace Bell', 10 metres (33 feet) high, was added to the park behind the tower in 2000.

Wuhan's Yellow Crane Tower (Huang He Lou) has been celebrated by many Chinese poets. A climb to the top, at more than 50 metres (164 feet) high, offers a superb view of the city. [Kevin Bishop]

Jianghan Plains

HUBEI PROVINCIAL MUSEUM (*HUBEI BOWUGUAN*)

Off Donghu Lu, facing East Lake, this excellent museum has a rich collection of more than 200,000 artefacts excavated in the Province. A visit is highly recommended. Of special interest is a display of finds from the tomb of Marquis Yi of Zeng from the Warring States Period (480–221 BCE), which was discovered when soldiers of the People's Liberation Army stumbled across the tomb while building a radar site. The coffin was found floating in water, which apparently saved the contents within. Among them is a set of 64 bronze chime bells, which are reputedly still splendidly sonorous after some 2,400 years of being buried (*see* pages 206–7). Replicas of these bells have been cast, and concerts of ancient music are given by a special chime-bells orchestra under the auspices of the Hubei Provincial Museum and the Art Institute of Wuhan.

The bells and other bronze items, such as the bronze sword of Gou Jian, King of Yue, Spring and Autumn Period (770–476 BCE), reflect the mastery of bronze working that was attained just prior to the advent of the iron age.

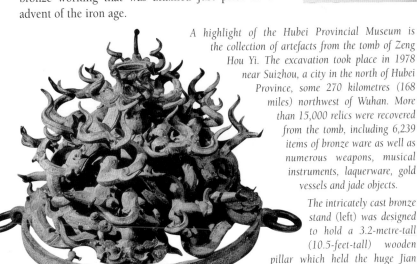

A highlight of the Hubei Provincial Museum is the collection of artefacts from the tomb of Zeng Hou Yi. The excavation took place in 1978 near Suizhou, a city in the north of Hubei Province, some 270 kilometres (168 miles) northwest of Wuhan. More than 15,000 relics were recovered from the tomb, including 6,239 items of bronze ware as well as numerous weapons, musical instruments, laquerware, gold vessels and jade objects.

The intricately cast bronze stand (left) was designed to hold a 3.2-metre-tall (10.5-feet-tall) wooden pillar which held the huge Jian drum, a reconstruction of that is shown (above). [Hubei Provincial Museum]

A reproduction of a beautifully decorated horse's helmet. The original, in lacquered leather, was found preserved in perfect condition within Marquis Hou Yi's resting place. The black lacquer was applied both inside and outside. Several pieces of armour and thousands of weapons were unearthed from the tomb. [Hubei Provincial Museum]

The most significant discovery in Zeng Hou Yi's tomb is this set of bronze chime bells, 65 in all, that hang in three tiers from a wooden and bronze stand (below). In the centre of the lower rack hangs the magnificent Bo bell (left). The 31 characters inscribed on its side explain its origin. When the king of the State of Chu heard of Zeng Hou Yi's death in 433 BCE, he had the bell specially made for interment in the tomb. [Hubei Provincial Museum]

Jianghan Plains

A pair of large bronze hu, or wine vessels, on a stand. A total of 117 well-preserved ritual bronze vessels were found in the tomb of Zeng Hou Yi, many of which are on display in the Hubei Provincial Museum, including the two excellent examples shown above. [Hubei Provincial Museum]

Exquisite bronze Zun (wine vessel) and Pan (plate). The Pan is 57.6 centimetres (22.6 inches) in diameter and 24 centimetres (9.4 inches) high. The Zun is 33.1 centimetres (13 inches) high. The vessel was made using a variety of techniques including whole founding, separate casting and welding. The hollowed-out ornaments were cast using the lost-wax method. One of the earliest examples of this technique discovered in China. [Hubei Provincial Museum]

Bronze Jian and Fou (square inner container), decorated with hollowed-out or relief sculpture and dragons. The vessel, which is 63.3 centimetres (25 inches) high, was constructed as a wine cooler. Ice could be packed into the Jian that would cool the wine contained in the Fou. [Hubei Provincial Museum]

TEN THINGS TO DO IN WUHAN   By Paul Mooney

Walk along the new Riverside Promenade (汉口江滩), which at 9.8km is 8 times longer than the bund in Shanghai. Have a drink at one of the kiosks, take in an occasional performance, let the children romp in the playground, or just sit on the grass or on a bench and enjoy the river view with boats chugging up and down the Yangtze. In the early morning, watch Chinese practice taiji, martial arts, and ballroom dancing.

Fly a kite on the beach below the Riverside Promenade (江滩). Vendors on the beach sell a wide variety of colourful kites.

Jump in East Lake (东湖沙滩), sun bathe along the lakeshore beach, or go fishing along the shores of the lake.

Watch Chinese at play beneath the Changjiang Bridge (长江大桥), northwest of the Yellow Crane Tower. Each afternoon beginning at 2pm, observe elderly opera lovers performing Hubei's popular Chu opera on a makeshift park stage to the accompaniment of a Chinese band. Or watch neighbourhood grannies doing a traditional drum dance. Walk past hawkers peddling traditional medicines on the street, fortune tellers shaking their bamboo joss sticks on to the ground, people playing mahjong and cards, curbside masseuses pounding on backs, and dentists bent over open-mouthed patients sitting in folding chairs. Or enjoy professional and amateur singers belting out pop songs on the pavement backed up by a full Chinese band—a member of the band passes a basket after each performance.

See Wuhan's colourful local opera, or Hanju (汉剧), which has a history dating back more than 400 years to the Ming Dynasty. Hanju is said to have been the forerunner of Peking opera, which did not appear until 200 years later. Performances of Wuhan Opera are staged every Friday and Saturday at the People's Theatre (人民剧场) in Hankou at 1:30 p.m. Chu opera (楚剧) can be seen on Saturdays and Sundays at 1:30 at the Peace Theatre (和平剧场).

Stroll along the 1,210 metre-long Jianghan Road pedestrian street (江汉路，步行街), lined with small shops, department stores, crafts shops, Chinese and Western restaurants, coffee shops, and cinemas. View the beautiful turn-of-the-century European architecture along this broad street.

Ride on the 888 metre-long Jianghan cable car across the Han River, which links the tourist section of Hanyang with the commercial section of Hankou.

Take in Wuhan's night views with a water tour of the harbour (江城水上游). The Wuhan Ferry Tour takes 90 minutes. Beverages and Chinese snacks are free on the boat. Boats leave from the Yuehan Port (粤汉码头) on Yanjiang Dadao (沿江大道), opposite Chezhan Lu (车站路), every evening at 8pm. Tickets cost 50 yuan. Tel: (027) 8278 2992 .

Stroll through Tanhualin (昙华林), an old street in Wuchang where one can still see traces of the history of old Wuhan. View Christian churches built in the 1800s by missionaries from Sweden, England and the United States; the former house of Xiong Shili, an anti-Qing revolutionary; and the foundation of the old Wuchang city wall.

Take a walk along the pleasant tree-shaded Shuiguohu Road (水果湖路). Wander through the snack market on the first floor of the Food Market (水果湖路菜市场一楼的南北风味小吃) at No. 89 (水果湖路89号), where dozens of stalls offer snacks from Wuhan and all around China. These include pigs' ears, duck necks, duck heads, chicken claws, noodles, lotus roots, meat pies, and no less than 28 kinds of pickled vegetables. There is a wide variety of snacks including sesame cakes, green- and red-bean buns, candied haws, fried wonton skins, and fried twisted dough sticks. At the end of the street is European Street (欧式一条街), lined with interesting European architecture, which contains hotels, restaurants and coffee shops.

Special Topic

HEADQUARTERS OF THE 1911 REVOLUTION (HONG LOU)

Known as the Red House, this building was the headquarters of the 1911 Revolution against the Manchu Qing Dynasty, led by Dr Sun Yat-sen. On the 10 October, 1911, Hubei revolutionaries prematurely started the Wuchang Uprising when a bomb exploded ahead of schedule. The next day the Hubei Military Government of the Republic of China established its office here, declaring an end to Manchu rule. Today, the building houses historical relics and a large collection of historical photographs. Unfortunately, there are few English captions. A statue of Dr Sun stands at the front of the museum, which is located at the foot of Sheshan on Wuluo Lu, near the approach to the Yangzi River Bridge.

EAST LAKE (DONG HU)

A large scenic area, in the eastern suburbs of Wuchang, is centred on East Lake. Established in 1949, this enormous park covers 73 square kilometres (28 square miles) of lake shore. The lake itself is six times the size of West Lake (Xi Hu) in Hangzhou. The park is full of natural beauty, containing over 372 plant varieties, as well as more than 80 species of birds and fish. Around its shores are numerous pavilions, museums and halls, including a memorial to Qu Yuan, the Third Century

A cormorant fisherman with two of his birds, a timeless image. [Tom Nebbia]

BCE poet (see page 134), and a monument (*Jiu Nudun*) to nine heroines who died fighting the Manchu troops during the Taiping Rebellion in the 19th Century. A low causeway leads to Moshan Hill and the botanical gardens, with uninterrupted views across the city and the beautiful countryside.

BAOTONG SI

Located on the slopes of Hong Shan, Baotong Zen Temple, built between 420–479, is the oldest temple in Wuhan. The temple was ruined and rebuilt several times on this site. The current structure was completed in 1909. It features a Grand Hall, Meditation Hall and Abbots Hall. There are two gargantuan iron bells here, almost 900 years old, dating back to the Southern Song Dynasty. It is located inside Hongshan Park.

CHANGCHUN TAOIST TEMPLE (*CHANGCHUN GUAN*)

The largest and best-preserved Taoist temple in Wuhan, and one of the 10 holy places of Taoism in China. The temple consists of numerous corridors and stone staircases with grand eaves and arches. Originaly built in the early Yuan Dynasty (1271–1368), Changchun Temple was built in memory of Qiu Changchu, the founder of the Quanzhen sect of Taoism. Decorating the halls are life-size carvings and niches. Most of the religious relics were destroyed during the Cultural Revolution. Now restored, the temple now displays a wide range of Taoist cultural relics. It is located in the Dadongmen area, near the intersection of Zhongshan Lu and Wuluo Lu.

WUHAN UNIVERSITY (*WUHAN DAXUE*)

Founded in 1913, it is still considered one of the best universities in the country. The campus displays many examples of pre-1949 Chinese architecture. It is located at the foot of Luojia Shan near East Lake.

ZHONGSHAN WARSHIP
BAISHAZHOU, WUCHANG

Originally built for the Qing government by the Japanese in 1910, the Yongfeng Warship was later used by the Nationalist navy, and named after Dr Sun Yat-sen. The ship was destroyed in a Japanese bombing attack in 1938. In 1997, workers successfully salvaged the Zhongshan from the Yangzi River. The ship has been refurbished and is now a museum.

Jianghan Plains

HUBU LANE

By Paul Mooney

It's a little after 8am, but Hubu Lane is already bustling with activity. As you enter the narrow alley you find yourself sandwiched between the more than 100 small eateries that line both sides of the street, the "kitchens" extending right out on to the street. Steam rises from stacks of bamboo steamers, woks, and huge pots of soup, the cooks appearing and disappearing from behind a haze of smoke. Although some Chinese say it's impolite to eat on the street, people walk the narrow alley unabashedly shoveling food into their mouths, many still in their pajamas. Some even bring their own enamel bowls along. One guy slurps a bowl of wonton while straddling his bicycle. "No time to sit down," says another man walking as he downs a bowl of noodles. "I've got to get to work."

It's unlikely that there is any place that can match Wuhan when it comes to what for most people is the least important meal of the day. The Wuhanese take breakfast so seriously that they have even coined their own name for this daily rite—guozao (过早). And the best place to sample the breakfast that made Wuhan famous is Hubu Lane, a small alley tucked away in a corner of Wuchang. Sample some of the foods here and you'll understand why the Wuhan breakfast is such an institution.

Reganmian (热干面), or hot dry noodles, is the most popular dish in the lane. Fang Fang, a local writer, says that just the thought of this dish can bring tears to the eyes of Wuhanese who are far from home. A variety of things can be added to the noodles: sesame oil, finely chopped garlic, diced radish, vinegar, white pepper, mustard tuber, ginger, scallion and chili. The key ingredient is sesame paste, or tahini sauce.

Another favorite is doupi (三鲜豆皮), said to date back 140 years. Doupi is a thin fried pancake made from the pressed liquid of mung beans and rice. The skin is then filled with minced meat, dried shrimp or dried mushroom, bamboo shoots, and dried beancurd. As a man flips the huge pancake over in his large wok, a small crowd has already gathered to watch. "It's Chinese pizza," he says without looking up, and the crowd laughs. He slices the two-and-a-half foot circle into small rectangles with a large plate and throws the pieces into a wok behind him, where a fellow worker scoops them into small plastic bows. In less than a minute, the pie is sold out. The dish became nationally known in 1958 when Chairman Mao tried it at Laotongcheng, a famous old Wuhan restaurant.

Mianwo (面窝), another bestseller, is made of glutinous rice, soybean, sesame, ginger and scallion. A donut-shaped ladle is used, with french-fry shaped pieces of sticky rice placed in the circular part. The ladle is then filled with a batter and dipped into hot oil until it turns a golden brown. Nearby another small shop is preparing fresh fish soup (鲜鱼汤). The owner says her family has been in the business for 130 years, although they just moved to this street in 2004 from Hankou. The soup, which is simmering in a huge pot, has a thin milky consistency. Nearby, a woman bends over a large wooden bucket ladling out slivers of shiny white douhuanao (豆化脑), a soft gelatin-like beancurd dish with sugar sprinkled sugar on top. Many of the steamed items are placed in bamboo steamers on a bed of pine needles (松针). "The pine needles give the food a special flavor," says a cook who has a mobile phone earplug stuck in one ear.

There are also popular foods from around China. Niuroubing (牛肉饼), a flat piece of dough sprinkled with small pieces of beef and bits of red pepper, baked inside a small coal-fired drum, comes from Nanjing. Roujiamo (肉夹馍), minced pork served in a bun, is a Shaanxi favorite. There are also stuffed buns from Yangzhou, hand-pulled noodles from Lanzhou, and shaomai from Guangdong.

A couple sits in a restaurant eating intently. They're not from the neighborhood, but say they frequently travel across town to have breakfast here. "If something is really good, it doesn't matter where it is," the man says between bites. "Even if it's in an alley, people will come."

WHERE TO EAT IN WUHAN

As a crossroads for nine provinces, Hubei has been influenced by other regions of China. Consequently, its cuisine is varied and interesting. The Province is noted for its freshwater fish dishes, including bream, Mandarin fish, shrimp, crab, turtle, eel and clams. The remarkable fact about restaurants in Wuhan is that the food is excellent and the cost is very reasonable, even in the most expensive-looking restaurants. Popular local dishes include: steamed Wuchang fish (武昌鱼), or bream, sparerib and lotus root soup (排骨藕汤), doupi (豆皮), pancakes stuffed with pork, meat, and either mushrooms or shrimp, and hot-dry noodles (热干面). Wuhan's fine dishes would not be as well known were it not for Chairman Mao Zedong, who had an affinity for the city. Both Wuchang Yu and doupi became nationally known after the Chairman's visits to the city in the 1950s. Hubei beers are a great complement to the local dishes.

Chutianlu Dashi Jiudian 楚天卢大师酒店

387 Fazhan Dadao Avenue, Hankou, Tel: (86-27) 8260 8337

Xiaolanjing Zajiting Liaosuodian 小蓝鲸杂技厅连锁店

Taipei Lu Teyihao, Hankou. Tel: (86-27) 8580 0777

Sanwuchun 三五醇

338 Zhongshan Street, Wuchang District. Tel: (86-27) 8884 3535
武昌中山路 338 号

5 Xinhua Xialu, Hankou. Tel: (86-27) 8577 4678
汉口新华下路 5 号

69-71 Huangxiao Helu, Jiang'an District. Tel: (86-27) 8261 3535
江岸区黄孝河路 69-71 号

Sanwuchun is a large and bright restaurant with a huge main dining hall that looks more like a grand European ballroom than a restaurant. Try chives and pork steamed in pearly rice balls (韭菜元子), stir-fried bean curd, cooked with green and black beans, and red peppers (豆米炒豆丁), mushroom soup (野菌汤), and boiled dumplings (北方水饺). For dessert sample red bean cake, actually cake with a layer of what appears to be ice cream (冰红豆糕).

Xie Xiansheng Canting

Yanyangtian Hotel, Pengliuyang Street

Cucha Tanfan 粗茶谈饭

Cucha Tanfan has an old Wuhan flavour to it, with black and white photographs of the city hanging on the walls. Popular dishes here include: tea-smoked duck (樟茶鸭), bean curd balls (小磨豆腐元子), fish head casserole (开胃鱼头王), shredded pork with bamboo shoots (南笋肉丝), and flat bread stuffed with meat (肉夹馍).

117 Jianghan Beilu. Tel: (86-27) 8574 9226
汉口江汉北路 117 号

143 Aomen Lu. Tel: (86-27) 8242 0217
汉口澳门路 143 路

616 Wuchang Minzhu Lu. Tel: (86-27) 5070 1819
武昌民主路 616 号

78 Hanyang Dadao. Tel: (86-27) 8477 8325
汉阳大道 78 号

Hujin Jiulou 湖锦酒楼

5 Xinhua Xialu Te, Hankou. Tel: (86-27) 8579 8088
汉口江汉区新华下路 5 号特

105 Bayi Lu, Wuchang District. Tel: (86-27) 8727 8811
武昌八一路 105 号

6-8 Sanyang Lu, Hankou, Tel: (86-27) 82711668
汉口三阳路 6-8 号

Hujin Jiulou, also known for its Hubei cuisine, is another of Wuhan's grand restaurants, with high ceilings, a huge dining area, and a second-floor balcony. Order drunken shrimp (醉虾), fish balls (江城鱼丸), braised Mandarin with scallion (葱烧桂鱼), mushroom cooked with bamboo shoots (花姑烩芦笋), west Hunan style streaky pork (湘西土肥肉), range chicken soup (土鸡烫), and bean curd cooked with crab egg (蟹黄豆腐).

Chu Lao Song 楚老宋

138 Yanjiang Road, Hankou. (86-27) 82857778
汉口沿江大道 138 号

This restaurant, which specialises in Wuhan dishes, is a favourite with locals. Specialities include frozen bean curd fried with vegetables (冻豆腐炒青菜), pumpkin broiled with chilli (青椒烧南瓜), fried eggs with chilli paste (酱椒炒土鸡蛋) and stewed taro with beef (柳汁香芋煲).

Kanglong Taizi Jiuxuan 亢龙太子酒轩

With its modernistic look, this is one of the most trendy restaurants in Wuhan, but it is still quite cheap. Popular dishes here are taizi "prince" duck (湖北太子片皮鸭), beef casserole (肥牛锅仔), roast suckling pig (烤乳), roasted crispy pigeon (脆皮乳鸽), quail wrapped in tinfoil (锡纸包鹌鹑) and shrimp with egg yolks (蛋黄炒虾).

1 Hongshan Sports Stadium, Xinkai Building, Wuchang
武昌洪山广场体育馆路 1 号新凯大厦
Tel: (86-27) 8732 0588

735 Jianshe Dadao. Tel: (86-27) 8579 8288
建设大道 735 号

226 Yanjiang Dadao, Hankou. Tel: (86-27) 8271 3338
汉口沿江大道 226 号

Yunjizhai Vegetarian Restaurant 云集斋素菜馆
Inside Guiyuan Temple; Tel: (86-27) 8484 2673
This vegetarian restaurant, located on the grounds of the Guiyuan Temple, serves a wide variety of meatless dishes, many prepared to look and taste like the real thing. Five-spiced beef (五香牛肉) has the exact texture and colour of this meat dish; turned-over streaky pork (百花菜扣肉) even came with a strip of "fatty pork" on each piece; vegetarian goose (素斋鹅), three fresh vegetables (三鲜娃娃菜), red-cooked mushrooms (吉祥红珊瑚), and tasty vegetarian steamed buns (素包子).

Zen Garden 六合宴
228 Yanjiang Dadao.
汉口沿江大道 228 号
Tel: (86-27) 8271 7777

If you need a change from Hubei cuisine, try this beautiful restaurant that serves fine Huaiyang dishes from cities downriver from Wuhan. Liuhe spare ribs (六合大排), twice-cooked pork (盐菜回锅肉), corn with egg yolk (蛋黄玉米), pan-fried beancurd (香煎老豆腐), stir-fried shrimp with chives (韭菜炒河虾), beef tenderloin in black pepper (铁板黑椒牛柳), steamed pumpkin with Chinese yam (南瓜蒸山药), sweet peas and diced ham (火丁甜豆), and West Lake duck casserole (西湖煲老鸦).

Changdi Street Night Market
200 metres down the street opposite Qiaokou Park
桥口公园对面的路口入内 200 米

This snack street offers a wide variety of local favourites: steamed dumplings filled with minced meat (水货汤包), fried beef dumplings (锅贴牛肉饺), red oil turnip soup (红油萝卜汤), and water chestnut paste (菱仁糊).

Jingwu duck neck (精武鸭脖子 / 精武鸭颈)
Served at a number of stalls along Jingwu Road (精武路) near Xinhua Road(新华路)

Dozen of small stalls along Jingwu Street specialise in this dish. Ducks are stewed in a soup made with dozens of Chinese herbs. Locals say the meat of the spicy duck neck is especially tasty, albeit tough, and they say the bones are even tastier, especially with beer. Jingwu duck neck shot to national prominence in 2002 after it was introduced in a TV drama based on a novel by the well-known writer Chi Li, a native of Wuhan. Restaurants around the country now serve this dish, and people are said to fly here from all over China, just to buy some to take back home

WUHAN NIGHTLIFE

Numerous bars, restaurants and cafes have opened along the Hankou Riverfront (沿江大道). If you are visiting Wuchang's Shuiguohu Lu (武昌水果湖路), try any of the many coffee shops housed in old buildings on "European Street."

York Tea Room 约克茶馆
162 Yanjiang Dadao
汉口沿江大道 162 号
(86-27) 8279 1110

This is much more of a bar than a tea room. The outdoor bar and seating area is the perfect place to watch Wuhan pass by. This friendly bar is a favourite with expatriate working and studying in Wuhan.

God's Music Bar 神曲艺术酒吧
25 Chezhan Lu (off Yanjiang Dadao)
汉口车站路 25 号
(86-27) 8280 5939

Known as the Church of the Blessed Mother (圣母堂) before it was converted into a bar, this former church is hidden inside a gate on Chezhan Lu, just north of Yanjiang Dadao.The front now covered by a façade that disguises what is inside. This is a beautiful example of church architecture, dating back at least seven decades. Unfortunately, the owner, allegedly an interior designer, has ruined the interior. Still a worthwhile place to have a drink, if only to look at the nave and its tri-domed ceiling. The bar is at the entrance, and the altar has been replaced by the karaoke stage. Visit the second floor choir loft. Live music is played later in the evening.

Victoria Coffee House 维多利亚咖啡馆
171 Yanjiang Dadao
汉口沿江大道 171 号
(86-27) 8282 2110

This pleasant coffee shop is in the former Banque De L'Indo-Chine, a grand European structure built in 1917. The inside has an old world flavour. Choose a table beside the window, or if the weather is pleasant, enjoy the large outdoor seating area.

JIQING STREET

By Paul Mooney

We arrive at Jiqing Street 吉庆街 just as the night is beginning. The dozen or so restaurants that line this street have already put their tables and chairs out onto the street under yellow sheets of plastic. The touts are out in force, using their bodies to direct our flow into their establishments. The food is good enough here, but the real pull is the some 300 licensed performers who work the street, roaming from table to table, restaurant to restaurant, in search of an audience.

I've never seen anything like it. Guitarists, banjo players, accordionists, erhu players opera and rock singers, comedians, shoeshine and flower girls and cigarette sellers crowd the street, their instruments and voices straining to compete with one another. It's like having dinner while the New York Philharmonic spends an entire evening tuning up their respective instruments.

As we sit down, one guy does a small jiggle between the tables singing an aria from a local opera. We then hear the strains of a three-piece traditional ensemble playing a classical piece of Chinese music before suddenly switching to a popular Mozart piece. I ask one of the musicians what he does during the day and he says he recently retired from the People's Liberation Army. His female colleague says she recently "xia ganged," a euphemism for being laid off. Like the other performers, they are here every night until 2 or 3am.

Meanwhile, at the table next to us a husband and wife team dressed in bright silk Chinese outfits perform a Chinese opera duet. The wife sings as she goes through intricate operatic motions, fingers, hands, and body shifting constantly in conjunction with the music. While she's doing this, her husband, whose head is shaved barring a small tuft of hair at the top of his forehead, looking like a comic book character, plays a Chinese instrument. A minute later, they switch roles and he does a series operatic flips in the narrow space between the dining tables.

Many of the performers here take their work quite seriously, presenting promotional materials about themselves as a sort of clincher. A man, who specializes in female roles in the regional Henan opera, displays a picture of himself dressed in a colorful female opera costume, complete with make-up. "I'm the Mei Lanfang of Henan," he boasts, referring to the legendarydan, or female, performer in Peking Opera.

The Caihong Meimei, aka the Rainbow Sisters, have been performing here since they were 14, or for five years, making them the youngest artists on the street. They display a laminated copy of a newspaper article that was written about them. They say they've also been featured on CCTV. Like the other performers here, they carry a list of the songs they perform. I choose a syrupy old Theresa Deng ballad. The four teenage girls, wearing identical pink jackets and head bandanas, begin to sing in Chinese, "You ask how much I love you ... my love is as big as the moon."

Another teenage group pleads with us. "Hao ma? Hao ma?" begging in the pouty voices Chinese girls use with their fathers or boyfriends. "Just one song, please?" We are firm, and when they walk away one looks over her shoulder and says, "I hate you! You're such a cheapskate." I feign a look of pain and they break into laughter. I call them back to sing.

I spot a woman at least 6 feet tall with shimmering blond hair hanging to her waist and am surprised to find a Western performer at our restaurant. But when she turns around I notice she's actually Chinese. She flirts with me, saying, "Hey handsome, want to hear a song?" I decline and she immediately spins and walks away.

At the table in front of us we see a tall thin man wearing sunglasses. He has the diners laughing loudly as he goes through a comic monologue, using his mobile phone as a pretend microphone. I can't understand what he's saying, but I also can't help cracking up when he puts a hand towel on his head and begins to walk in a slow motion, overly exaggerated manner.

The highlight of the evening is when the flamboyant Lasi makes his grand entrance. He looks somewhat like a camp Chinese Zoro, with a black cowboy hat and a flowing cape, and a few things Zoro never dared to wear--multi-colored flashing earrings and finger rings and bright red lipstick. On his cape he proudly displays the words "Sida Tianwang Zhiyi," or "One of the Four Heavenly Kings." The other kings are Cucumber, Peacock and Laotongcheng, who has taken the name of one of Wuhan's oldest restaurants —no one seems to know why. Lasi dances as he plays his stringed instrument, rings and earrings flashing different colors in the night, cape swinging behind him. His dining table audience laps up his performance.

My friend points out the mustached Peacock sitting at another table, singing in a loud raspy voice. Unfortunately, the other two kings have not appeared yet, and it's time for us to leave. I now have an excuse to go back.

A dinner costs about 100 yuan for two-to-four people and the average performance costs 10 yuan per song. Three red roses go for 10 yuan and a portrait costs 30 yuan.

FACTS FOR THE TRAVELLER

VISAS

If you are travelling independently, either as a tourist or business visitor, you must obtain a visa before entry into China. Applications should be made through Chinese Embassies or Consular Offices in your country. If you are entering through Hong Kong, visas are easily obtained from various travel agencies, including CITS, CTS and the Foreign Ministry of the People's Republic of China. Visa applications can be processed on the same day in Hong Kong, though if you can wait two or three days the cost is considerably reduced. One to three month tourist visas (L visas) are readily available as well as business visas (F visas). These can be issued for up to one year, including multiple entries. Just one passport photograph and a completed application form are necessary. Generally business visas issued overseas will require an official letter from the host organisation in China, whereas in Hong Kong this regulation can be waived. Tourist visas can normally be extended in Beijing or Shanghai for a maximum period of one month, on no more than two successive occasions.

Tourists entering China as part of a group may have a document listing members details on a single group visa prepared by their tour operator and handled by the tour leader or allotted group member. These are valid for the duration of the tour only and the whole group must enter and leave China together. However, some companies ask that you obtain your own visa to give greater flexibility to group participants who may add optional tours to the beginning or end of standard tour itineraries. This also obviates any difficulties in amending the group visa that would result in a group member being unable to complete the tour.

Border formalities are generally painless and efficient. Those on individual visas receive entry and exit stamps and must complete entry and departure forms. Those on group visas do not receive passport stamps and are not required to complete entry or departure forms. Health declaration forms are issued on the journey to China and should be handed over upon arrival. Importantly, your passport should be valid for at least six months after your departure from China.

CUSTOMS

The ordinary visitor is required to complete a customs declaration form. Visitors must declare currency exceeding Rmb20,000 and foreign currency exceeding the equivalent of US$5,000 being taken into China. A litre-and-a-half of alcohol over 12 per cent proof, 400 cigarettes (or 100 cigars), unlimited film and medicines for personal use may be taken in free of duty. The carriage of fresh food produce into China is prohibited by health and quarantine regulations. When buying antiques one must remember that only items made after the reign of the Jiaqing Emperor (1820) may legally be exported and all must bear a red wax seal affixed by the Bureau of Cultural Relics. Receipts for major purchases such as legitimate antiques and gold products should be retained in case inspection is required on departure.

AIR TICKETING AND TAXES

China's air ticket market has an element of competition, but is not fully subject to market conditions. Occasionally, government directives will decrease or increase the amount of discount that can be offered on tickets. Price wars break out quickly in times of relative deregulation. A 20 per cent discount off the listed fare is possible. Departure taxes are incorporated into the cost of your air ticket.

Tickets purchased in China are generally not subject to the restrictions of those bought outside the country. Although buying a ticket at the airport generally means paying full fare, airfares in China do not increase or decrease based upon advanced purchase. They are far more flexible than the non-refundable, non-changeable tickets that are now the norm of international air travel.

Safety on Chinese airlines has improved dramatically during the past 20 years, and China's air fleet is now one of the newest in the world. You are more likely to be on a new Airbus or Boeing aircraft when flying with a Chinese airline than with a US-based carrier. Although service still lags behind some Asian competitors, such as Singapore Airlines and Dragonair, Chinese airlines are often a low-cost alternative flying the same routes as their foreign counterparts. Air China should not be confused with Taiwan-based China Airlines, which has a questionable safety record.

GETTING THERE

Chongqing, one of the municipalities directly answerable to Beijing, is the most popular starting point for downriver Yangzi cruises. Most upstream cruises now originate in Yichang, though some still commence from Wuhan. Boat departures are normally early morning affairs, so spending the night at your departure point is *de rigueur*. The journey through the Three Gorges from Chongqing to Yichang and on downstream to Wuhan takes three days, while the upriver journey, from Yichang to Chongqing, takes four days. Following the completion of the *San Xia Ba* (Three Gorges Dam), as the portion of the river between the dam and Chongqing has become lake-like, upstream speeds have increased, and downstream ones slowed slightly. Night navigation has become possible in formerly dangerous reaches, though cruise operators are usually careful to schedule their sailings to make sure you pass through the Three Gorges in daylight hours.

GETTING TO CHONGQING

BY AIR

Chongqing's international airport also handles domestic flights from all of China's larger cities. An increasing number of open-skies agreements with other nations makes travel from Asia, Australia, Europe and North America much easier than in the past, with Beijing or Shanghai the most-favoured entry points. For those travellers including Hong Kong in their itinerary, note that it is usually cheaper to fly from Shenzhen, Guangzhou or Zhuhai than to fly directly from Hong Kong.

BY RAIL

The rapid expansion and modernisation of the Chinese railway network has yet to make much difference to services to Chongqing. Trains south and west to Kunming, or south and east to Guangzhou pass on a single track line. This is a miracle of engineering through spectacular mountain scenery and remote and impoverished areas. From Beijing's West Station it is a double overnight journey, and from Guangzhou about 11 hours. A link to Lhasa has sheduled service every other day.

BY ROAD

With China's rapidly expanding network of highways, travel by road must seriously be considered as an alternative to air and rail. In the past, even relatively short road journeys could take many hours of uncomfortable travel, whereas they are now more likely to take less than half that time in a modern air-conditioned vehicle.

GETTING TO YICHANG

BY AIR

Yichang has almost daily air services from large cities, including Beijing, Changsha, Chengdu, Chongqing, Guangzhou, Huangshan, Kunming, Nanjing, Qingdao, Shanghai, Shenzhen, Xi'an and Zhengzhou.

BY RAIL

There are direct trains from various cities, including Wuhan, Xi'an and Beijing, but many services require a change at the nearby junction of Yaqueling. From Wuhan comfortable express buses are more convenient.

GETTING TO WUHAN

BY AIR

There are scheduled services direct from Hong Kong: China Southern offers daily flights between the two cities while evening flights to Wuhan via Dragonair are every Sunday, Wednesday and Friday as well as an afternoon flight every Thursday. There are domestic flights from all the main cities of China.

BY RAIL

Wuhan is on a fast north–south route between Hong Kong's Kowloon Station and Beijing West Railway Station, with comfortable expresses leaving Hong Kong on alternate days. However, you may not use the Kowloon service when coming south from Beijing, but there are excellent overnight expresses with sleeping cars. They depart Beijing in the evening and arrive in Wuhan in time for breakfast at either Hangkou station on the Yangzi's north bank or Wuchang station on the river's south bank. Direct trains may also be taken from Chengdu, Xi'an, Tianjin, and Guilin.

CLIMATE

The three large cities along the Yangzi River—Chongqing, Wuhan and Nanjing—are known traditionally as the 'three furnaces of China'. Between April and September, the temperature in the Yangzi River valley reaches 36°C (97°F) and above. Spring and autumn are therefore the best seasons for cruising the river. However, with the tall mountains surrounding the gorges through which the river threads its path, precipitation is very high and the peaks are often shrouded in cloud and mist. Summer rains are torrential. The winters are short, cold and crisp. Late-summer travel will coincide with the high-water periods, when the river rises swiftly, almost perceptibly.

CHONGQING

AVERAGE TEMPERATURES

	Jan	Feb	Mar	Apr	May	Jun	Jul	Aug	Sep	Oct	Nov	Dec
°C	7	10	14.5	19.5	23	25.5	29	30	25	19	14	10.5
°F	44.6	50	58.1	67.1	73.4	77.9	84.2	86	77	66.2	57.2	50.9

AVERAGE RAINFALL

	Jan	Feb	Mar	Apr	May	Jun	Jul	Aug	Sep	Oct	Nov	Dec
mm	15	20	38	99	142	180	142	122	150	112	48	20
in	0.6	0.8	1.5	3.9	5.6	7.1	5.6	4.8	5.9	4.4	1.9	0.8

WUHAN

AVERAGE TEMPERATURES

	Jan	Feb	Mar	Apr	May	Jun	Jul	Aug	Sep	Oct	Nov	Dec
°C	2.7	5.2	10	16.2	21.1	26.1	29.1	28.4	23.9	17.6	11.4	5.5
°F	36.8	41.3	50	61.1	69.9	79.8	84.3	83.1	75	63.6	52.5	41.9

AVERAGE RAINFALL

	Jan	Feb	Mar	Apr	May	Jun	Jul	Aug	Sep	Oct	Nov	Dec
mm	152	152	203	279	305	381	254	203	178	178	152	127
in	6	6	8	11	12	15	10	8	7	7	6	5

CLOTHING

Light summer clothing is all that is required between April and September, with a woollen cardigan or warm jacket for the cool evenings on board. To combat the summer mugginess, travellers should wear cotton rather than synthetic fibres. The Yangzi River towns are very informal indeed; wear comfortable everyday clothes when you visit them. Steep steps from the jetties to the towns require good walking shoes, and since many streets turn to mud within minutes of a heavy rainfall, you may need an extra pair. Umbrellas can be bought cheaply almost anywhere. On board the more deluxe ships, many women like to carry a smart outfit, and the men a jacket and tie, to dress a little more formally for the last night of the cruise.

Warm clothes are essential for the river journeys during seasons other than summer. The boats can be draughty and the wind piercing. However, clothing is one of the best bargains in China, with excellent down or quilted jackets available in many of the big towns and cities, though not always in the largest Western sizes. Bring a pair of light hiking boots as the terrain can be hilly, rocky and muddy.

MONEY
CHINESE CURRENCY
Chinese currency is called Renminbi (meaning 'people's currency'), which is abbreviated to Rmb. It is denominated in yuan, referred to as *kuai* in everyday speech. The yuan is divided into 10 jiao (colloquially called *mao*). Each jiao is divided into 10 fen. There are large notes for 100, 50, 5, 2 and 1 yuan, small notes for 5, 2, and 1 jiao, and coins and notes for 5, 2, 1 fen and 1 yuan.

FOREIGN CURRENCY, TRAVELLER'S CHEQUES AND CREDIT CARDS
There is a limit to the amount of foreign currency you can take into China, US$5,000 or its equivalent. Traveller's cheques are changed at a slightly better rate than cash. All major European, American and Japanese traveller's cheques are accepted by the Bank of China. International credit cards may be used to draw cash at larger branches (1,200 yuan minimum, four per cent commission) and for payment in international hotels. ATMs are widely available in major Chinese cities, and they accept Western bank cards.

TIPPING
The accepted standard for tipping in the West is rapidly becoming the norm in modern China. While it is not normally practised in local establishments, tipping would certainly be expected by local guides, drivers and waiters in places frequented by foreigners.

BARGAINING

With the exception of stores with marked prices, always bargain in markets and shops. Even state-run stores will often give discounts on expensive items like carpets intended for tourists. Bargaining in China can be good-humoured or it can be infuriating; it is a game won by technique and strategy, not by anger or threats. Thus, it should be leisurely and friendly, and not be seen as a one-way process at all, since the Chinese enjoy it. Finally, it is bad manners to continue to bargain after a deal has been struck.

COMMUNICATIONS

China's post-office system is rather slow, but reliable. Every post office counter has a pot of glue, as low-denomination stamps do not have glue on the back. International Direct Dialling is available everywhere, and even by satellite phone from the more luxurious cruise vessels (although at great cost). Long-distance calls within China are often clearer than local ones, and even fairly modest hotels have business centres with fax and (slow) Internet connections.

LOCAL TIME

Amazingly for a country measuring 3,220 kilometres (2,001 miles) from east to west, most of China operates from one time zone eight hours ahead of GMT and 13 hours ahead of EST. From Urumqi to Kashgar, local people work to a 'local time', which is two hours behind Beijing. This time difference is 'unofficial', but determines transport timetables and other services in the region.

PACKING CHECKLIST

As well as carrying along any prescription medicines you may need, it is a good idea to pack a supply of common cold and stomach trouble remedies. Taking a basic first-aid kit including antiseptic cream and plasters is a good idea. Pack insect repellent—though insect pests are not of any great concern in the city centres. You should also pack anti-diarrhoea tablets and painkillers—although aspirin is widely available. It is wise to carry sunscreen outside of the winter months. While it is not necessary to pack toilet-paper these days, it is advisable to take some with you when going out sightseeing, as public toilets do not provide it. Bring plenty of film and batteries for your camera. Although film is widely available, you may not always be able to find the type you want. Be aware it may have been sitting on the shelf in the hot sun long after its "best before" date. Comfortable, non-slip shoes are a must.

If you wear glasses then bring a spare pair as well as your prescription. Soft contact lens solutions are widely available, but RGP and hard lens solutions are not.

A fairly comprehensive range of complimentary toiletries can be found in all good hotels, including soap, shampoo, tooth paste, shower caps and often a lot more. Moisturizer is usually provided, but you are advised to carry your own preferred brand. Wet wipes may be useful as well.

HEALTH

For visits to China's main cities there are no mandatory vaccination requirements. In recent years the US Consulate in Hong Kong has recommended innoculations against hepatitis A and B, Japanese encephalitis, tetanus, polio, cholera and malaria for travellers to China. Still, you should consult your doctor regarding precautions and the desirability of having an immunoglobulin vaccination before departure. If you are travelling on to more remote parts of China in the summer months then give more consideration to health matters.

It is highly advisable to pay attention to your daily water intake. Bottled water is widely available and provided in hotel rooms, but mineral is preferable to distilled. Ice cubes and ice-creams are generally safe to consume—but caution should be exercised in the summer months and when eating outside well-established hotels and restaurants. Mild stomach upsets are not uncommon. You should take some basic precautions—always peel fruit and avoid seafood in local restaurants during the summer months.

The discomforts caused by cigarette smoke have often been remarked on by foreign visitors. Though the government has banned smoking in many public places, a 'No Smoking' sign does not ensure compliance. Smoking is not permitted on tour buses, Chinese international and domestic flights, nor on most, if not all, sections of trains. Smoking is also prohibited at most tourist sites.

The most common ailments contracted by visitors to China are respiratory tract infections and the common cold. Safeguard yourself as much as possible by regulating your room temperature and maintaining your body temperature as best you can.

On arrival you will notice that heat-detectors will greet you at the airport to test your temperature. Many other strict safeguards have also been put in place to protect public health. The past incidence of SARS should not obscure the fact that China is a very safe place to visit, but of course you should keep up with the latest health advice in general. For the latest travel advice, not only on health but on visa requirements and other important matters, see Australia's www.smartraveller.gov.au, the UK Foreign Office's www.fco.gov.uk/travel or the US State Department's http://travel.state.gov/china.html.

For the treatment of minor ailments, many of the better hotels have a clinic or a doctor on call. For consultations and prescriptions, payment is made on the spot and most major credit cards are accepted. It is highly recommended that all visitors have adequate travel insurance coverage.

CHRONOLOGY OF PERIODS IN CHINESE HISTORY

NEOLITHIC	7000–2600 BCE
FIVE LEGENDARY RULERS	2600–2070 BCE
XIA	2070–1600 BCE
SHANG	1600–1027 BCE
WESTERN ZHOU	1027–771 BCE
EASTERN ZHOU	770–256 BCE
SPRING AND AUTUMN	770–476 BCE
WARRING STATES	475–221 BCE
QIN	221–206 BCE
WESTERN (XI) HAN	206 BCE–25 CE
EASTERN (DONG) HAN	25–220
THREE KINGDOMS	220–280
WESTERN JIN	265–316
EASTERN JIN (INCLUDING SIXTEEN KINGDOMS)	317–439
NORTHERN AND SOUTHERN DYNASTIES	420–589
SUI	581–618
TANG	618–907
FIVE DYNASTIES	907–960
LIAO (KHITAN)	916–1125
NORTHERN SONG	960–1127
SOUTHERN SONG	1127–1279
JIN (JURCHEN)	1115–1234
XIXIA (TANGUT)	1038–1227
YUAN (MONGOL)	1279–1368
MING	1368–1644
QING (MANCHU)	1644–1911
REPUBLIC OF CHINA	1911–1949
PEOPLE'S REPUBLIC OF CHINA	1949–

A small note about the above chronology: Every effort has been made to make it as accurate and complete as possible. However, it would be impossible to give the full chronology in one page as smaller periods overlap with significant ones as the struggle for power and unification continues through time. For example, the Xin period (9–24 CE) is not noted here due to its small size, short span and having relatively little influence. The Qin era which preceded it, though also brief, had a great influence having achieved great unity and accomplishments such as establishing The Great Wall.

A BRIEF GUIDE TO THE CHINESE LANGUAGE

Mandarin (*Putonghua* or common speech), designated as the official Chinese language by the Guomindang government in 1912, is historically a dialect of the Beijing area. The Beijing dialect is one of five main dialect groups—another one being Wu that is spoken in the Shanghai region. The differences between the Shanghai and Beijing dialects can be compared to the differences between the English and French languages.

Regardless of the differences in the spoken language it is consoling to find that the written script is uniform throughout China. The only quandary presented is that over 50,000 characters are entered in the largest dictionary. In practice, however, educated people ordinarily use just 4,000 to 5,000 characters. The mammoth 900,000 character *Selected Works of Chairman Mao* is based on a glossary of just over 3,000 different characters.

Each character is a syllable, many of which can stand alone as words. In fact words with one or two syllables account for more than nine out of 10 of those found in the Chinese language. Characters based on pictures formed the basis for the development of the Chinese script. For instance the character for a person (人) is based on a side view of a human being, the character for big or large (大) resembles a man standing legs apart and arms widespread, whilst the character for a tree (木) depicts a tree with roots and branches. Whilst there are only a few hundred such pictographic characters there are many more which build upon them, though an association or indication to form other words. For example, one person behind another person (从) means to come from or follow and one person above two others (众) means a crowd.

The Chinese government introduced the pinyin system in 1958 allowing an approach to the spoken language through the 26 characters of the Roman alphabet and its associated numerals. Around the same time, the written script was 'simplified' with many characters being rewritten in a less complicated arrangement so as to make them easier to learn. The pinyin system enables foreigners to achieve a reasonable level of spoken Chinese without any knowledge of the characters. This approach is also used in primary education as an aid to basic character recognition.

You will encounter pinyin on road signs, some maps and store fronts and in the Western media. You will initially meet with some difficulty in pronouncing Romanized Chinese words, despite the fact that most sounds correspond to usual pronunciation of the letters in English. The exceptions are:

Initials

   c   is like the *ts* in 'i*ts*'

   q   is like the *ch* in '*ch*eese'

   x   has no English equivalent, and can best be described as a hissing consonant that lies somewhere between *sh* and *s*. The sound was rendered as *hs* under an earlier transcription system.

   z   is like the *ds* in 'fa*ds*'

   zh is unaspirated, and sounds like the *j* in 'jug'.

Finals

   a   sounds like '*ah*'

   e   is pronounced as in 'h*er*'

   i   is pronounced as in 'sk*i*' (written as *yi* when not preceded by an initial consonant). However, in *ci, chi, ri, shi, zi* and *zhi*, the sound represented by the final is quite different and is similar to the *ir* in 's*ir*' but without much stressing of the *r* sound

   o   sounds like the *aw* in 'l*aw*'

   u   sounds like the *oo* in '*oo*ze'

   ü   is pronounced as the German *ü* (written as *yu* when not preceded by an initial consonant). The last two finals are usually written simply as *e* and *u*.

Finals in Combination

When two or more finals are combined, such as in *hao, jiao* and *liu*, each letter retains its sound value as indicated in the list above, but note the following:

   ai   is like the *ie* in 't*ie*'

   ei   is like the *ay* in 'b*ay*'

   ian is like the *ien* in 'V*ien*na'

   ie   similar to '*ear*'

   ou   is like the *o* in 'c*o*de'

uai sounds like '*why*'

uan is like the *uan* in 'ig*uan*a' (except when proceeded by *j, q, x* and *y*; in these cases a *u* following any of these four consonants is in fact *ü* and *uan* is similar to *uen*.)

   ue   is like the *ue* in 'd*ue*t'

   ui   sounds like '*way*'

Tones

A Chinese syllable consists of not only an initial and a final or finals, but also as tone or pitch of the voice when the words are spoken. In *Pinyin* the four basic tones are marked ¯, ´, and `. These marks are almost never shown in printed form except in language text.

HOTELS

The list below is by no means exhaustive, but focuses on five- and four-star properties.

CHONGQING (CODE: 23)

Chongqing Marriott Hotel, 77 Qing Nian Lu, Yu Zhong District
Tel: 6388-8888; Fax: 6388-8777; www.marriott.com/property/propertypage/ckgon

Harbour Plaza Chongqing, Wuyi Road, Yu Zhong District
Tel: 6370-0888; Fax: 6370-0778; toll free (within China only) 800-889-9988
www.harbour-plaza.com/hpcq

Hilton Chongqing, 139 Zhongshan San Road, Yu Zhong District
Tel: 8903-9999; Fax: 8903-8600; www.hilton.com

Yongchuan Min Hao Hotel
The address for this new Jin Jiang Group property was not available at the time of publishing; for more information, browse www.jinjianghotel.com

Chongqing Guesthouse, 235 Minsheng Lu, Yu Zhong District
Tel: 6384-5888; Fax: 6383-0643

Chongqing Taiji Hotel, 16 Tiyu Road (S), Fuling District
Tel: 7288-8888; Fax: 7222-4555; www.jinjianghotel.com

Hoi Tak Hotel, 318 Nanping Road.
Tel: 6283-8888; Fax: 6280-5747; www.hoitakhotel.com

Holiday Inn Yangtze Chongqing, 15 Nanping Bei Lu
Tel: 6280-3380, toll-free from US 1-800 HOLIDAY; Fax: 6280-0884
www.holiday-inn.com

Huang Jia Grand Hotel, 85 Zhongshan Road, Qixinggang, Yu Zhong District
Tel: 6352-8888; Fax: 6352-9999; www.yuangjiahotel.com

InterContinental Chongqing Hotel, 101 Minzu Road, Yu Zhong District
Tel: 8906-6888; Fax: 89066; www.ichotelsgroup.com

Wanyou Conifer Hotel, 77 Changjiang 2nd Road, Daping
Tel: 6871-8888; Fax: 6871-3333; www.wanyouhotel.com

YICHANG (CODE: 717)

Guo Bin Garden Hotel 国宾花园酒店
46 Shenzhen Road, Development Zone. Tel: 633-1111
Innca Hotel 宜昌盈嘉酒店 12 Pearl Road. Tel: 673-6666
Peach Blossom Hotel (Taohualing Binguan) 宜昌桃花岭饭店
29 Yunji Lu. Tel: 643-6666; Fax: 623-8888
Peninsula Hotel, Yichang 宜昌半岛酒店

25 Shen Zhen Road, Dongshan Development Zone. Tel: 634-5666
Three Gorges Project Hotel, Yichang 宜昌三陕工程大酒店
Ba He Kou, Three Gorges. Tel: 661-3666
Yichang International Hotel (Yichang Guo Ji Da Jiudian) 宜昌国际大酒店
127 Yanjiang Road. Tel: 622-2888; Fax: 622-8186

Wuhan (Code: 27)
Best Western Mayflowers Hotel 最佳西方五月花大酒店
385 Wuluo Road, Wuchang. Tel: 6887-1588; www.bestwestern.com
East Lake Hotel 东湖大厦
231 Yaojialing, Wuchang. Tel: 6781-3999
Haiyi Jin Jiang Hotel 武汉海怡锦江大酒店
1 Hongshan Road, Wuhan. Tel: 8712-6666; Fax: 8712-6868
Holiday Inn Riverside 武汉晴川假日酒店
88 Ximachang Street, Hanyang. Tel: 8471-6688; www.china.basshotels.com
Holiday Inn Tian An Wuhan 武汉天安假日酒店
868 Jiefang Dadao Avenue, Hankou. Tel: 8578-7968
Howard Johnson Pearl Plaza Wuhan, 102 Dongting Street, Hankou
Tel: 5223-3388; Fax: 5223-3388; Email: sales.wuhan@hojoplaza.com
Huameida Tianlu Jiudian 华美达天禄酒店
5 Qingnian Street, Hankou. Tel: 8363-0888
Jianghan Hotel 江汉饭店
245 Shengli Street, Hankou. Tel: 6882-5888
Jin Jiang International Hotel 锦江国际饭店
The address for this new Jin Jiang Group property was not available at the time of
publishing; for more information, browse www.jinjianghotel.com
Lake View Garden Hotel 115 Luoyu Road, Wuchang. Tel: 8778-2888
Novotel Xinhua Wuhan 武汉新华诺富特大饭店
558 Jianshe Dadao Avenue, Hankou. Tel: 8555-1188; www.accorhotels-asia.com
Oriental Hotel Wuhan 东方大酒店
Hankou Railway Station Square, Hankou. Tel: 8588-8668; www.orientaltravel.com
Shangri-La Hotel 香格里拉大饭店
700 Jianshe Dadao Avenue, Hankou. Tel: 8580-6868; www.shangri-la.com
Super 8 Hotel
96 Donghu Street, Wuchang. Tel: 5070-5388
Yangtze Hotel 武汉长江大酒店
113 Jiefang Dadao, Hankou. Tel: 8363-2828

SELECTED TOUR OPERATORS

There are many companies offering complete tour packages to the Three Gorges, however the following tour operators, listed in alphabetical order, are some of those with which we have had personal experience.

Abercrombie and Kent International, Inc
UK: Abercrombie & Kent Travel, Sloane Square House, Holbein Place, London SW1W 8NS. Tel (0207) 730-9600; fax (0207) 730-9376

Hong Kong: 19th Floor, Tesbury Centre, 28 Queen's Road East, Wanchai Tel (852) 2865-7818; fax (852) 2866-0556i

USA: 1520 Kensington Road, Suite 212, Oak Brook, Chicago, Il 60523-2156 Tel (630) 954-2944, toll-free (800) 554-7016; fax (630) 954-3324 www.abercrombiekent.com

Bales Worldwide Holidays
Bales House, Junction Road, Dorking, Surrey, RH4 3HL, England Sales (0870) 752-0780; fax 01306 740048 Email: tailormade@balesworldwide.com; www.balesworldwide.com

Cox & Kings Travel Ltd
4/F, Gordon House, 10 Greencoat Place, London, SWIP 1PH, England Tel (0207) 873-5000; fax (0207) 630-6038. www.coxandkings.co.uk

Explore Worldwide Ltd
1 Frederick Street, Aldershot, Hants, GU11 1LQ, England Tel (0125) 276-0000; fax (0125) 276-0001. www.exploreworldwide.com

Helen Wong's Tours
Australia: Level 17 Town Hall House, 456 Kent St, Sydney, NSW 2000 Tel (02) 9267-7833; fax (02) 9267-7717; Reservations 1300-788-328 Email hwtaus@helenwongstours.com

China: 7 Jianguomennei Avenue, Beijing 100005 Tel (010) 6518-8168; fax (010) 6518-8169. Email hwtpek@helenwongstours.com www.helenwongstours.com

Maupintour, LLC
2688 South Rainbow Blvd. , Las Vegas, NV 89146-5196, USA. Tel 800-255-4266; fax 702-260-3787. Email info@maupintour.com www.maupintour.com

Mountain Travel Sobek
1266 66th Street, Emeryville, CA 94608, USA.
Tel 888-687-6235; fax 510-594-6001. www.mtsobek.com

Pacific Delight
3 Park Avenue, 38th Floor, New York, NY 10016-5902, USA.
Tel (212) 818-1781; toll-free 1-800-221-7179. www.pacificdelighttours.com

Page & Moy Ltd
56 Burleys Way, Leicester, LE1 9GZ, England.
Tel (0116) 250-7336; fax 0-8700-1062-11; Bookings: 0-8700-1062-12.
www.go-nowtravel.com

Peregrine Adventures
258 Lonsdale Street, Melbourne 3000, Australia.
Tel (03) 9663-8611; fax (03) 9663-8618. www.peregrineadventures.com

Regent Holidays
15 John Street, Bristol, BS1 2HR, England.
Tel (0117) 921-1711; fax (0117) 925-4866. www.regent-holidays.co.uk

Saga Holidays Ltd
The Saga Building, Enbrook Park, Sandgate, Folkestone, Kent CT20 3SE, England.
Tel (0800) 504-555, from overseas (44) 01303 771-111. www.saga.co.uk

Steppes East Ltd
51 Castle Street, Cirencester GL7 5ET, England.
Tel 01285 651010; fax 01285 885888. www.steppeseast.co.uk

Sundowners
Suite 15, 600 Lonsdale Street, Melbourne 3000, Australia.
Tel (03) 9670 5300; fax.(03) 9672 5311. www.sundownerstravel.com

Tauck World Discovery
10 Norden Place, Norwalk, CT 06855, USA, PO Box 5020
Tel 1-800-788-7885. Email info@tauck.com; www.tauck.com

Travelsphere Ltd
Compass House, Rockingham Road, Market Harborough, Leicestershire, LE16
7QD, England. Tel 01858 468400; fax 01858 434323. www.travelsphere.co.uk

Voyages Jules Verne
21 Dorset Square, London NW1 6QG, England.
Tel (0207) 616-1000; fax (0207) 723-8629. www.vjv.co.uk

SELECTED CRUISE-VESSEL OPERATORS

The most luxurious way of seeing the Three Gorges is to book a passage on one of the cruise vessels that cater mainly to foreign tour groups. The most favoured journey is downstream between Chongqing and Yichang with some venturing as far as Wuhan, or upstream from Yichang to Chongqing.

Several cruise vessel operators offer longer trips, some as long as nine nights, sailing from Shanghai to Chongqing, for instance. The cruise season is primarily from the beginning of April, peaking in September and October, with a few operators offering sailings throughout the year. Fitted out with private bathrooms for each cabin, air-conditioning, observation decks, gift shops and bars, these ships offer arranged excursions on shore and other entertainments during the cruise.

Bookings for all Yangzi cruises should be made well in advance, particularly for peak tourist season. Although most people take these cruises as part of a group tour, it is also possible to buy individual tickets for the cruise only. The following cruise operators are companies which we have ourselves worked closely with.

China Regal Cruises
Nantong Lihui International Shipping Co Ltd, 6/F Changhang Building, 133 Yan Jiang Avenue, Wuhan, 430014, China.
Tel (027) 8276-3387; fax (027) 8284-9921. www.regalchinacruises.net

Orient Royal Cruiser Ltd
China: (Head Office) 316 Xinhua Road, Suite E, Liang You Building, Hankou, Wuhan, 430012. Tel (027) 8576-9988, 8577-2220; fax (027) 8576-6688.

USA: 43 Conforti Avenue, Unit 72, West Orange, New Jersey 07052.
Tel: (888) 543-8088, (888) 664-4888; fax (888) 287-8188.

Hong Kong: ORC (Asia) Ltd, Room 1318, Two Pacific Place, 88 Queensway.
Tel (852) 2824-9022; fax (852) 2824-9092.
www.orientroyalcruise.com; www.orientcruisetravel.com

Victoria Cruises Inc
USA: 57–08 39th Ave, Woodside, NY 11377.
Tel (212) 818-1698; fax (212) 818-9889

China: 3/F, 3 Xin Hua Road, Chongqing, 400011.
Tel (023) 6380 4512; fax (023) 6381 4474. www.victoriacruises.com

WEIGHTS AND MEASURES CONVERSIONS

LENGTH	MULTIPLY BY
Inches to centimetres	2.54
Centimetres to inches	0.39
Inches to millimetres	25.40
Millimetres to inches	0.04
Feet to metres	0.31
Metres to feet	3.28
Yards to metres	0.91
Metres to yards	1.09
Miles to kilometres	1.61
Kilometres to miles	0.62

AREA	
Square inches to square centimetres	6.45
Square centimetres to square inches	0.15
Square feet to square metres	0.09
Square metres to square feet	10.76
Square yards to square metres	0.84
Square metres to square yards	1.20
Square miles to square kilometres	2.59
Square kilometres to square miles	0.39
Acres to hectares	0.40
Hectares to acres	2.47

VOLUME	
Cubic inches to cubic centimetres	16.39
Cubic centimetres to cubic inches	0.06
Cubic feet to cubic metres	0.03
Cubic metres to cubic feet	35.32
Cubic yards to cubic metres	0.76
Cubic metres to cubic yards	1.31
Cubic inches to litres	0.02
Litres to cubic inches	61.03
Gallons to litres	4.55
Litres to gallons	0.22
US gallons to litres	3.79
Litres to US gallons	0.26
Fluid ounces to millilitres	30.77
Millilitres to fluid ounces	0.03

TEMPERATURE	
°C	°F
-30	-22
-20	-4
-10	14
0	32
5	41
10	50
15	59
20	68
25	77
30	86
35	95
40	104
45	113
50	122
55	131
60	140
65	149
70	158
75	167
80	176
85	185
90	194
95	203
100	212

WEIGHT	
Ounces to grams	28.35
Grams to ounces	0.04
Pounds to kilograms	0.45
Kilograms to pounds	2.21
Long tons to metric tons	1.02
Metric tons to long tons	0.98
Short tons to metric tons	0.91
Metric tons to short tons	1.10

USEFUL WEBSITES

The Web provides an invaluable resource for learning more about China—whether you are an interested spectator, a serious student, a potential investor, resident, or a past or prospective traveler. Sites come and go all the time so we cannot guarantee that all these sites will be up and running when you hit the button.

GENERAL

www.embassiesinchina.com: Embassy and consulate addresses throughout China.
www.healthinchina.com: Medical advice and contacts for travellers.
www.fmprc.gov.cn/eng: Official foreign-policy information and news.
www.CTGPC.com: Official site of the China Three Gorges Project Corporation.
www.sichuan.gov.cn: Official site of the Sichuan Provincial Government.
www.hebei-window.com/index.php: Official site of the Hebei Provincial Government (limited English content).
www.uk.cn: The official British website representing Britain in China.
www.irn.org: International Rivers Network examines the relationships between rivers, dams and their communities.
www.chinesepod.com: Learn Mandarin through podcasts.

TRAVEL SITES

www.cnta.com: The domain of the China National Tourism Authority, with basic information on practicalities, hotels, restaurants, shopping, attractions and festivals.
www.cnto.org: The official site of the China National Tourism Office—based in the US.
www.c-trip.com: Chinese site, also in English, useful for finding hotels.
www.odysseypublications.com: Information on an array of Odyssey Books & Guides.

NEWS SITES

www.chinadaily.com.cn: Online version of China's only English daily national newspaper. Features national and business news, as well as weather and sport.
www.china.org.cn/english: Authorized state portal with daily updates of general and business news. Contains topical features and a travel guide section.
www.cnd.org: Topical news and an extensive historical archive, from 1644 to the present, with an extensive photo library covering most places you are likely to visit.
http://english.peopledaily.com.cn/home.shtml: English version of the main Communist Party daily with official news, topical features and city weather.
http://www.einnews.com/china/: Part of the European Internet News global network. Extensive general and business news, with links to travel-related sites.
www.sinolinx.com: A collection of China-related headlines culled from the Net.
www.xinhua.org: News from China's official news agency.

BUSINESS-RELATED SITES

www.ccpit.org: Trade and associated matters from the China Council for the Promotion of International Trade.

www.chinallaws.com: Useful information on doing business with legal perspectives. (site becomes—www.1488.com)

www.chinabiz.org: Comprehensive online daily full of business oriented news, with numerous links to news and entertainment sites.

www.chinabusiness-press.com: Government-approved China business magazine, with links to numerous Chinese companies.

www.chinaonline.com: Business-focused US news site.

www.chinapages.com: Up-to-date news and information on Chinese companies.

www.english.mofcom.gov.cn/: Ministry of Commerce business information.

www.sinofile.net: Multi-sector business news based on a wide range of Chinese press reports—and special business features.

www.sinonews.com: Highlights news on business and investment opportunities.

www.sinosource.com: Offers a China business directory.

www.stats.gov.cn/english: Official statistics from the National Bureau of Statistics on all aspects of the economy and society.

BEIJING

www.ebeijing.gov.cn: The Beijing Municipal Government's introduction to the city.

http://en.beijing2008.com: The official website for the 2008 Olympics.

english.bjta.gov.cn: Domain of the Beijing Tourism Administration and the Beijing Tourism Industry Bureau featuring nation-wide travel news, shopping guides and bizarre travel tips.

www.cbw.com/btm: The government monthly travel journal—*Beijing This Month.*

www.crienglish.com: Beijing-based China Radio International provides recorded news, features and music as well as a text magazine regarding 8 modern China.

www.TheBeijingGuide.com: A well-designed site, steeped in cultural delights, with traditional music, 360° vistas, videos and more including practical information.

SHANGHAI

www.english.eastday.com: News from The Shanghai Daily newspaper.

www.english.pudong.gov.cn: News and information from the Pudong government.

www.gingergriffin.com: Sketches of old Shanghai and historical tours of the city.

www.shanghai.gov.cn: Practical information from the Shanghai Municipal Government.

www.shanghai-star.com.cn: News from The Shanghai Star paper.

www.tourinfo.sh.cn: Site of the Shanghai Tourist Information and Service Centre.

www.expo2010china.com: The 2010 Shanghai World Expo news site.

CHONGQING

www.cq.gov.cn: The official website of the Chongqing Municipal Government.

YICHANG

www.yichang.gov.cn: The official website of the Yichang Municipal Government.

WUHAN

http://english.wh.gov.cn: The Wuhan Municipal Government's official website.

www.wuhantour.gov.cn: The Wuhan Tourism Administration's official website.

Note: Some of these sites may not be accessible in China, so it is best to check these sites before you arrive in the country.

AIRLINES

Most good hotels have travel agents on their premises or can direct you to one near by, prices will vary depending upon the season and even the time of day. Below is a list of websites, in alphabetical order, for the main Chinese airlines and a selection of offshore airlines serving China.

Aeroflot: www.aeroflot.com
Air China: www.airchina.com.cn
Air France: www.airfrance.com
Air India: www.airindia.com
American Airlines: www.aa.com
British Airways: www.britishairways.com
Cathay Pacific: www.cathaypacific.com
China Eastern Airlines: www.ce-air.com
China Northwest Airlines: www.cnwa.com
China Southern Airlines: www.cs-air.com
China Southwest Airlines: www. cswa.com
China Xinjiang Airlines: www.cxa.web.ur.ru
Dragon Air: www.dragonair.com
Lufthansa: www.lufthansa.de
Northwest Airlines: www.nwa.com
Qantas: www.qantas.com.au
Singapore Airlines: www.singaporeair.com
Thai Airways International: www.thaiairways.com
United Airlines: www.united.com
Virgin Atlantic Airways: www.virgin-atlantic.com

BIBLIOGRAPHY & RECOMMENDED READING

GENERAL BACKGROUND & HISTORY

Bergere, Marie-Claire, *Sun Yat-sen* (Stanford: Stanford University Press, 1998)

Capon, Joanna, *Guide to Museums in China* (Hong Kong: Orientations Magazinef Limited, Text Copyright © 2002 Joanna Capon)

Crow, Carl, *Handbook for China* (Oxford University Press, Hong Kong 1984, facsimile of 4th edition, originally published by Kelly and Walsh Limited, Shanghai, 1933)

Earl, Lawrence, *Yangtse Incident: the Story of HMS Amethyst* (New York: Knopf, 1951)

Eastman, Lloyd E, et al, *The Nationalist Era in China, 1927–1949* (New York: Cambridge University Press, 1991)

Elder, Chris ed, *China's Treaty Ports* (Hong Kong: Oxford University Press, 1999)

Epstein, Israel, *Woman in World History: Soong Ching Ling (Madame Sun Yat-sen)* (Beijing: New World Press, 1995, Second Edition)

Han Zongshan ed, *Landslides and Rockfalls of Yangtze Gorges* (State Commission of Science and Technology, PRC & Ministry of Geology and Mineral Resources, PRC, 1988)

Johnston, Tess & Erh, Deke, *Frenchtown Shanghai: Western Architecture in Shanghai's Old French Concession* (Shanghai: Old China Hand Press, 2000)

Lan Peijin ed, *The Three Gorges of the Yangtze River* (Foreign Languages Press, Beijing, 1997)

Levathes, Louise, *When China Ruled the Seas...1405–1433* (New York: Oxford University Press, 1996)

Li Xianyao & Luo Zhewan, Translated by Avery, Martha, *China's Museums: Cultural China Series* (Beijing: China Intercontinental Press, 2004)

Lou, Rongmin ed, *The Bund: History and Vicissitudes* (Shanghai: Shanghai Pictorial Publishing House, 1998)

Luo Zhewen & Shen Peng (compilers), *Through the Moon Gate: A Guide to China's Historic Monuments* (Oxford University Press, Hong Kong, 1986)

Murphy, Rhoades, *Treaty Ports and China's Modernization* (Ann Arbor: University of Michigan, 1970)

Perry, Hamilton Darby, *The Panay Incident: Prelude to Pearl Harbor* (New York: Macmillan, 1969)

Phillips, C E Lucas, *Escape of the Amethyst* (New York: Coward-McCann, 1958)

Rowe, William T, *Hankow: Commerce and Society in a Chinese City, 1796–1889* (Stanford: Stanford University Press, 1984)

238 The Three Gorges

Salisbury, Harrison E, *The Long March* (New York: Harper & Row, 1985)

Schiffrin, Harold Z, *Sun Yat-sen: Reluctant Revolutionary* (Boston: Little Brown, 1980)

Spence, Jonathan D, *God's Chinese Son* (New York & London: W W Norton & Co, 1996)

Stone, Albert H, & Reed, J Hammond, editors, *Historic Lushan, The Kuling Mountains* (Hankow: Arthington Press/Religious Tract Society, 1921)

Tretiakov, Sergiei M, *Chinese Testament: The Autobiography of Tan Shi-Hua As Told to S Tretiakov* (Westport CT, Hyperion Press, 1976)

Van Slyke, Lyman P, *Yangtse: Nature, History and the River* (Reading, Massachusetts: Addison-Wesley Publishing Company Inc, 1988)

White, Theodore H, & Jacoby, Annalee, *Thunder Out of China* (New York: W Sloane Associates, 1946; reprinted with new introduction by Harrison E Salisbury, Da Capo Press, 1980)

Wills, John E, *Mountain of Fame: Portraits in Chinese History* (Princeton: Princeton University Press, 1994)

Wu, Wo-yao, *Vignettes from the Late Chi'ing: Bizarre Happenings Eyewitnessed Over Two Decades* (Hong Kong: Chinese University of Hong Kong, 1975)

Xu, Silin, *Yue Fei: Glory and Tragedy of China's Greatest War Hero* (Singapore: Asiapac, 1995)

Yang Xin, *The Source of the Yangtze: A Photographic Account of the Landscape, Ecology and Humanity in the Headwaters of the Yangtze River* (Greenriver Book Series, WWF/Friends of the Earth (Hong Kong), 2000)

Zhao Songqiao, *Physical Geography of China* (Science Press, Beijing & John Wiley & Sons, 1986)

Travel and Exploration

Baber, Colborne E, *Travels and Researches in Western China* (London: John Murray, 1882; Taipei: Ch'eng Wen Publishing Co, 1971)

Baker, Barbara ed, *Shanghai: Electric and Lurid City* (Hong Kong: Oxford University Press, 1998, Anthology)

Bangs, Richard & Kallen, Christian, *Riding the Dragon's Back: The Race to Raft the Upper Yangtze* (New York: Atheneum, 1989)

Beaton, Cecil, *China Diary & Album* (London: Batsford, 1945; Hong Kong: Oxford University Press & John Nicholson Ltd, 1991)

Bell, Dick, *To the Source of the Yangtse* (London: Hodder & Stoughton, 1991)

Bird, Isabella, *The Yangtze Valley and Beyond* (London: John Murray, 1899; Virago Press, 1985)

Bonavia, Judy & Hayman, Richard, *Yangzi: Yangtze River and the Three Gorges, from Source to Sea* 7th Ed (Hong Kong: Odyssey Books & Guides, 2004)

Cooper, Thomas Thornville, *Travels of a Pioneer of Commerce in Pigtail and Petticoats: or, an Overland Journey from China towards India* (London: John Murray, 1871)

Cox E H M, *Plant-hunting in China* (London: William Collins Sons & Co Ltd, 1945; Reprinted with introduction by Oxford University Press, Hong Kong, 1986)

Danielson, Eric N, *The Three Gorges and the Upper Yangzi* (Times Editions–Marshall Cavendish, 2005)

Farndale, Nigel, *Last Action Hero of the British Empire Cdr John Kerans 1915–1985* (Short Books, 2001)

Gellhorn, Martha, *Travels with Myself and Another* (London: Eland Publishing Ltd, 2002)

Gill, William, *The River of Golden Sand: The Narrative of a Journey through China and Eastern Tibet to Burmah* (London: John Murray, 1880; Farnborough, UK: Gregg International Publishers Ltd, 1969)

Hayman, Richard Perry, *Three Gorges of the Yangzi: Grand Canyons of China* (Close-up Guides, Odyssey Publications, Hong Kong, 2000)

Hessler, Peter, *River Town: Two Years on the Yangtze* (HarperCollins, 2001); *Oracle Bones: A Journey Between China's Past and Present* (HarperCollins, 2006)

Hobart, Alice Tisdale, *Within the Walls of Nanking* (New York: MacMillan Co, 1927)

Little, Archibald, *Through the Yangtse Gorges* (London: Sampson, Low, Marston & Co, 1898; Taipei: Ch'eng Wen Publishing Co, 1972)

McKenna, Richard, *The Sand Pebbles* (Annapolis: Naval Institute Press, 2000)

Meister, Cari, *The Yangtze* (Edina: Abdo, 2000)

Palmer, Martin, *Travel Through Sacred China: Guide to the Soul and Spiritual Heritage of China* (Royal House, 1996)

Pan, Lynn, *Old Shanghai, Gangsters in Paradise* (Reprinted by Cultured Lotus, Singapore, 2000)

Payne, Robert, *Chinese Diaries: 1941–1946* (New York, Weybright and Talley, 1970)

Percival, William, *The Land of the Dragon: My Boating and Shooting Excursions to the Gorges of the Upper Yangtse* (Hurst & Blackett Ltd, 1889)

Pollard, Michael, *The Yangtze* (New York: Benchmark, 1998)

Sergeant, Harriet, *Shanghai* (London: John Murray, 1991)

St John, Jeffrey, *Voices from the Yangtze: Recollections of America's Maritime Frontier in China* (Napa: Western Maritime Press, 1993)

Theroux, Paul, *Riding the Iron Rooster: By Train through China* (London: Hamish Hamilton, 1988)

Theroux, Paul, *Sailing Through China* (Boston: Houghton Mifflin Co, 1984)

Thubron, Colin, *Behind the Wall: A Journey through China* (London: Heinemann, 1987)

Till, Barry & Swart, Paula, *In Search of Old Nanking* (Hong Kong: H K S H Joint Publishing Company, 1982)

Wasserstein, Bernard, *Secret War in Shanghai* (London: Profile Books, 1998)

Wilson E H, *A Naturalist in Western China: With Vasculum, Camera and Gun* (London: Methuen & Co, 1913; Cadogan Books, 1986)

Winchester, Simon, *The River at the Centre of the World: A Journey Up the Yangtze and Back in Chinese Time* (London: Viking Press, 1997)

Wong, How Man, *Exploring the Yangtse, China's Longest River* (Hong Kong: Odyssey Productions Ltd, 1989)

Yatsko, Pamela, *New Shanghai: The Rocky Rebirth of China's Legendary City* (New York: John Wiley & Sons, 2001)

Zhao Guilin, ed, *The Great Karst Funnel and Valley* (Beijing: China Intercontinental Press, 2001, compiled by Beijing Jingzin Cultural Development Co Ltd)

LITERATURE, AUTOBIOGRAPHY

Espey, John J, *Tales Out of School: More Delightful, Humorous Stories of a Boyhood in China* (New York: Knopf, 1947)

Han, Suyin, *Destination Chungking* (London: Jonathan Cape, 1942; Panther Books, 1973)

Hersey, John, *A Single Pebble* (New York: Alfred A Knopf Inc, 1956; Vintage Books Edition, Random House Inc, 1989)

Li Po & Tu Fu, Selected & translated with introduction and notes by Arthur Cooper (Harmondsworth: Penguin Books, 1973)

Luo, Guangzhong, *Romance of the Three Kingdoms* (Tokyo: Charles E Tuttle Co Inc, 1973). The classic 14th-century novel about the three Warring States along the Yangzi. *Excerpts from Three Classical Novels* (Panda Books, Beijing 1981) contains an excerpt from the novel entitled, *The Battle of the Red Cliff*, that vividly describes this event at a site just above Wuhan.

Lynn, Madeleine, *Yangzi River: The Wildest, Wickedest River on Earth* (Hong Kong: Oxford University Press, 1997). An anthology selection spanning 13 centuries, offers a literary history of China's longest river, including classical poetry and Victorian memoirs.

Waley, Arthur, *The Poetry and Career of Li Po* (George Allen & Unwin, 1989)

Wu, Ching-tzu, translated by Yang Hsien-yi and Gladys Yang, *The Scholars* (Beijing: Foreign Languages Press, 1973)

Xu, Xuanzhong, *100 Tang and Song Ci Poems* (Hong Kong: Commercial Press, 1986)

Index

Compiled by Don Brech. Records Management International Limited Hong Kong

Note for Users:

The order of index entries is word-by-word.

Both the main text and the text of captions to photographs have been indexed. Page references to these entries are in normal typeface.

Photographs have also been indexed and page references for these entries are in bold type.

Where the same subject appears in both text and a photograph on the same page, two entries for that page number are given, one for the text, and the other for the photograph, viz: Ciqikou, 63, **63**

A very special thanks is extended to the fine photographers and our good friends in Yichang, Wuhan, Chongqing, New York and elsewhere who have contributed to this guide by providing access to their photographs and precious information on the Three Gorges area, particulary:
    Lu Jin, Yin Chun, Huang Zhengping, Lesley Yu, Sharp Sun, Mao Zhigui, Katy Pi, the staff at the Hubei Provincial Museum, the staff at Jingzhou City CITS (Shashi) and Museum, at NGA/NASA, at China Yangtze Three Gorges Project Development Corporation, the Imperial War Museum, as well as Maximus Li Kai Man, Carl Crow, Ian Howard, John Hatt, Rose Baring, Barnaby Rogerson.
    To those helpful comrades who may have been inadvertently overlooked, please speak up so that the next edition of this guide may sing your praises.